Crafts in the World Market

SUNY Series in the Anthropology of Work
June Nash, editor

Crafts in the World Market

*The Impact of Global Exchange
on Middle American Artisans*

Edited by
June Nash

State University of New York Press

Cover photo by Sharon Dean

Published by
State University of New York Press, Albany

For information, address State University of New York
Press, State University Plaza, Albany, N.Y., 12246

Production by Dana Foote
Marketing by Dana E. Yanulavich

Library of Congress Cataloging in Publication Data

Crafts in the world market : the impact of global exchange on Middle
    American artisans / edited by June Nash.
        p.   cm. — (SUNY series in the anthropology of work)
    Includes bibliographical references and index.
    ISBN 0–7914–1061–7 (HC : acid-free). — ISBN 0–7914–1062–5 (PB :
acid-free)
    1. Indians of Mexico—Industries.   2. Indians of Central America—
Guatemala—Industries.   3. Indians of Mexico—Economic conditions.
4. Indians of Central America—Guatemala—Economic conditions.
5. Handicraft industries—Mexico.   6. Handicraft industries—
Guatemala.   7. Export marketing—Mexico.   8. Export marketing—
Guatemala.   I. Nash, June C., 1927–   .   II. Series.
F1219.3.I5C74   1993
338.4′77455′0972—dc20   91–21308
                                                                        CIP

10 9 8 7 6 5 4 3 2 1

Contents

Figures and Tables

Figures

Pen and ink illustrations preceding chapters 2–9 are by Christine Eber.

Preface

The inspiration for this anthology and the conference and exhibition that led to it is the reflective view engendered in this quincentennial celebration since the arrival of Christopher Colombus to what was to be called the Americas. In the past centenary celebrations of this event, people addressed the achievements of the Europeans who dared to sail into the unknown waters to find new trade routes and markets. This year scholars are focusing on the achievements of the people and cultures of the western continent that were so abruptly thrust into the world orbit. Nothing demonstrates their achievements as effectively as the textiles and pottery that are made with the same techniques and designs in many cases as those produced five hundred years ago.

The New York Council for the Arts funded the exhibition of indigenous textiles and pottery and conference that accompanied it at the Graduate Center of the City University of New York. Among the participants invited to share their knowledge and insights were four Mayan artisans who have become leaders in organizing artisan cooperatives in their communities: Magdalena Arias, Juliana Lopez Shunton, Pedro Mesa Mesa, and Manuela Perez. Their performance of prehispanic arts in weaving and pottery convinced the audience drawn to the display in the lobby of the Grace building on 42nd Street of the living traditions exemplified in the clothing and containers still used in their villages.

I am grateful for the advice of Walter Morris, Jr., a MacArthur scholar and author of *The Living Maya,* and Mary Jane Lenz, curator at the Museum of the American Indian, Smithsonian Institution, in the early planning stages of the conference, and for the dedicated assistance of Sharon Dean, Director of Photo Archives at the Museum of the American

Indian, in bringing it into being. Tressa Berman, a Ph.D. candidate at the University of California in Los Angeles, suggested the market theme for displaying the objects, some of which were borrowed from the private collection of Nancy Modiano and others from the cooperative Sna Jolobil and the Instituto Nacional Indigena. She joined Sharon Dean, Mary Jane Lenz, and myself in the cataloguing and presentation of the artisan products, which were mounted in the display area by Laura Nash and Ronald Norris. Jane Schneider, Executive Director of the Program in Anthropology in the Graduate Center, gave her enthusiastic support and endorsement of the conference, participating in many of the sessions and providing many insights from her vast knowledge of textiles. We were honored to have the late Harold Prozhansky, President of the Graduate Center, open the conference with welcoming remarks to the participants. Discussants for the papers included Gerald Sider, Professor of Anthropology at Statten Island; Gobi Stromberg-Pellizzi, cultural program consultant with the Mexican Consul in New York; Ronald Waterbury, Professor at Queens College; and Brackette Williams, Professor at Hunter College now at the University of Texas; all of whom added intellectual depth and a comparative dimension to the proceedings.

June Nash
August 15, 1992

Introduction:
Traditional Arts and Changing
Markets in Middle America*

June Nash

Artisans are producing traditional craft objects for a growing world
market of travellers and, increasingly, those who shop at home through
catalogue retailers. The objects are a medium of communication between
people who live profoundly different lives but who can respond to the
symbols, textures, and forms that express distinct cultural traditions. The

*The papers were presented at a conference at the City University of New York Graduate
Center in September, 1988. The event was sponsored in part by a grant from the New York
Council for the Humanities, the Bildner Center, and the Department of Anthropology. The
success of the exhibit and conference owes much to the devoted assistance of Sharon Dean,
Mary Jane Lenz, and Tressa Behrman, who donated their time and expertise in countless
ways that ensured an attractive and significant presentation of the articles exhibited. The
Maya craftspeople, including Juliana Lopez Shunton, Manuela Perez, Magdalena Arias, and
Pedro Mesa Mesa, communicated in demonstrations of their work and in words the significance of these traditions to their people. Gerald Sider, Gobi Stromberg-Pellizzi, Ronald
Waterbury, and Brakette Williams stimulated discussions as they chaired sessions throughout the three-day conference. Laura Nash and Ron Norris assisted in both the physical and
aesthetic aspects of mounting the exhibit in the Grace Building. We appreciate the donation
of space in their main lobby by the management of the Grace Building for the two-week
showing of textiles and pottery.

flow of goods from the industrial centers of the world to the colonies in earlier centuries is now met by a reverse flow as consumers seek the exotic and unique objects of handicraft production in Third World countries. This has given birth, as Jane Schneider (1987) has pointed out, to new forms chosen and redesigned to fit the world view of the receivers. Many of the consumers want to know more about the way of life of the people who make these objects, and producers are curious about those who purchase their goods. This book is an attempt to answer some of the questions they may ask.

The articles are by anthropologists who have studied the production and marketing of crafts by indigenous people in the area known as Middle America that stretches from the central plateau of Mexico to Honduras and Costa Rica. Before the European discovery of America, these people shared a common tradition derived from the Olmec civilization that flourished in the coastal Gulf of Mexico region over three thousand years ago. The ritual calendar based on thirteen months of twenty days, and solar calendar of 365 days, the four-path way symbolized in the foliated cross, the elusive feathered serpent god Quetzalcoatl, and other beliefs symbolized in paintings, pottery, and stone carvings indicate the intercourse and trade that linked the people who created and spread this early tradition from the coastal areas to the Yucatán Peninsula, the high plateaus of the interior, and southern mountainous areas of Mexico and Guatemala. (Gossen 1986).

The crafts made by contemporary representatives of the distinct Maya, Zapotec, and Nahuatl groups preserve techniques and art traditions over a thousand years old. The textiles, pottery, and metal work whose high quality astounded the Spaniards when they arrived in Mexico persisted in many areas where they were made for daily use. The simple technology, including the backstrap loom and hand-coiled pottery with open-hearth firing, kept the cost of production so low that these goods could compete with manufactured articles introduced during the colonial and independence periods. Household production of crafts complemented the semi-subsistence small plot farming that ensured year-round employment of family members.

These surface manifestations of continuity have deep cultural roots that continually generate responses to change. In the Popul Vuh, often called the Bible of the Quiche speaking migrants into the western highlands of Guatemala, we learn that creation for the Maya was an experimental work of craftspeople, not the design of an all-powerful god. In Dennis Tedlock's translation (1985), the creation myth accounts for how the "Grandmother, Grandfather" Xpiyacoc Xmucane, with the help of

Figure 1. Pottery similar to that found in pre-conquest site in Amatenango del Valle is shown in a contemporary Chiapas artisan exhibit.

their twin sons, One Hunahpu and Seven Hunahpu, the "Maker, Modler," brought forth life on earth. Their first attempts were not successful, and so they tried again. "So then comes the building and working with earth and mud," it is related (Tedlock 1985:79). "They made a body, but it didn't look good to them. It was just separating, just crumbling, just loosening, just softening, just disintegrating, and just dissolving. Its head wouldn't turn, either. Its face was just lopsided, its face was just twisted. It couldn't look around. It talked at first, but senselessly. It was quickly dissolving in the water." The "Mason and Sculptor" put his creation aside in disgust, saying, "It can't walk and it can't multiply, so let it be merely a thought." After speaking with each other, the Bearer, begetter and Maker, Modler brought their "manikins, woodcarvings" into being, able to talk and to multiply, yet they still lacked "legs and arms, blood and lymph, sweat and fat, and their faces were dry and crusty, until the maker modeler gave them a heart."

These oral traditions are still alive in the area today, along with the crafts that inspired them. In 1964 when I was doing field work in Amatenango del Valle, a pottery-making village thirty-seven miles from the department capital of Chiapas on the Pan American Highway, I heard the same creation myth from an old man. Human beings, he told me, were made of *lum,* clay or soil. The first attempt was not well formed, just as some pots do not come out well. It had only one foot and one hand and could not stand or work. In two successive tries the mother and father of us all improved their creation, adding a heart and genitals and teaching it to make the milpa and to eat corn tortillas.

When I returned to Amatenango twenty-five years later, I wanted to check the story with that in the Popul Vuh, but the old man had died and so I talked to his daughter, now in her sixties and a master potter. She told me that after the first trial when the figure could not stand or walk, the ancestors broke it, as one would crumble a badly formed pot. On the second attempt it did not have genitals nor an anus, and so it could not multiply or eat. Again the ancestors broke their creation. On the last attempt it was well formed but could not live until the creators gave it a little corn and showed it how to plant, then how to cook and eat their food. Then the ancestors said, "Now it is good."

For these Mayan inheritors of the ancient Middle American traditions, creation is not the omniscient act of an all-powerful god as in the Christian-Judaic tradition. Like the craft process of trial and reworking, the father and mother of us all shape and reform their creation, trying it out at each stage, continually improving upon their model until it functions well. This creative process remains central to artisan production even as craft workers respond to changing markets.

Where production is still tied to the household unit and skills are transmitted from mother to daughter or father to son, there is greater continuity in traditions than in capitalized production. In the production of traditional crafts, households reproduce themselves in an ongoing tradition. Pottery in Amatenango del Valle is still produced using the coil technique and open-hearth firing, and products are similar to those excavated in the late pre-conquest site near the present center. Designs used by contemporary weavers of Tenejapa replicate those found in stelae at Yaxchilán on the Guatemala-Mexico border (Morris 1984). In producing the distinctive woven and brocaded blouses, the weavers transmit an identification of themselves and their families as indigenous people.

Continuity in social traditions is ensured in craft production. Under the tutelage of their mothers and later mothers-in-law, girls find their place within the family. As skilled potters and weavers, women have contributed to the family income in a way that has become essential for the survival of small-plot cultivation in the growing cash economy. Husbands and fathers bring in wood for firing pottery, or assist in the pasturing and sheering of sheep for wool in weaving villages. They often market the

Figure 2. Daughter in Amatenango del Valle household with three potters specializes in doves for tourists.

Figure 3. Magdalena Arias (left) *addresses women of the cooperative awaiting a delegation of the Partido Revolución Institutionalizado (PRI) in San Cristóbal de las Casas, Mexico.*

products, thereby controlling the revenues and ensuring the persistence of patriarchal peasant families. The value of continuity is stressed in prayer where ritual practitioners constantly reassure each other that they are doing things as the ancestors did, here "in the eyes of the ancestors" (Nash 1985).

While production processes have remained remarkably constant throughout the colonial period and up to the present, the commercialization and exchange of goods have changed considerably. With men increasingly forced to work as wage laborers, often on distant commercial plantations, women frequently go themselves to the towns and cities to sell their goods. Inflationary costs of raw materials and transportation add to the pressure on artisans as they try to price their products at rates that will allow them to continue in production. In an attempt to assist these women, the Mexican government has sponsored cooperatives both for the purchase of raw materials and for the sale of artisan products through the National Indian Institute (INI). Women have gained greater autonomy and a political role in leadership positions in these organiza-

Figure 4. Mother of Mexican President Salinas Gortari (center) *helps promote indigenous crafts in her visit with the cooperative led by Magdalena Arias during the presidential campaign in 1989.*

tions. This has threatened the patriarchal structure of the family as they expand their contacts throughout the region. The lengthy betrothal suits initiated by parents are now often avoided by young couples who use their own earnings to elope and set up independent households. Some women choose not to marry, supporting themselves and often their parents and younger siblings, or their own children born out of wedlock, with earnings from sale of their crafts (Collier 1990; Eber and Rosenbaum, Nash this volume).

The contributors to this volume explore the differential impact of these changes at the local level within this changing regional pattern. The experience of the Maya in Guatemala differs considerably from that of the Maya in Chiapas and Yucatán. In Guatemala the military attacks on the Indians combined with Protestant conversion discourage identification with a distinctively Indian tradition (Annis 1987; Carlsen, Verrillo and Earle, and Ehlers, this volume). The distinctive woven and brocaded products of Guatemala have found ready entry to the United States market, with tie-dyed textiles selling in department stores, in street bazaars,

*Figure 5. Children learn weaving in Ministry of Public
Education classes in Venustiano Carranza taught by indigenous weavers.*

and through catalogues such as "Pueblo to People" or "The Peruvian
Connection," but the production of clothing that identifies people as
members of a particular community is each day further reduced. By purchasing these articles, even without travelling to find them, consumers are
enjoined to enter into an adventurous expedition to the regions from
which they come. Even more, they can contribute to the work for social
justice, as the catalogue "Jubilee Crafts" announces, by buying the crafts
made by oppressed peoples.

In contrast to the strategies private commercial interests have used to
promote international markets for Guatemalan crafts, Mexican government agencies have developed a tourist market within their borders
through exhibitions in museums and competitions that cultivate existing
skills and expand the marketability of products. Although the actual
capital invested is low, government programs in Chiapas have cultivated
an awareness of the indigenous skills still practiced in contemporary villages (Nash, this volume). In Oaxaca, where the development of tourist-
oriented production of textiles and pottery was developed more than two
decades ago, the government promotes an ethnic identity related to craft
products sold in national museum outlets and bazaars sponsored by

Figure 6. Magdalena weavers sort skeins in one of Sna Jolobil cooperatives.

regional artisan institutes (Cook 1984, García Canclini 1982, Novelo 1976, Stephen this volume, Waterbury 1989). Paradoxically, as the sale of these traditional blouses and other products formerly worn by the indigenous women increases, the actual use by the artisans declines (Carlsen and Stephen, this volume; Waterbury 1989).

The relations involved in artisan production vary, in accord with Novelo's (1976) conception of the sphere of activity, from family production in the household to wage work in capitalized shops where the owner and/or members of the family continue to work on production, to shops using wage labor only. The unaccounted work of women and children in the household enables incipient entrepreneurs to amass capital to expand the operation and ultimately exploit the labor of others. The common characterization of objects called "artisan products" is the high level of manual labor and correspondingly low level of capital investment in machinery and automatic controls (Cook, this volume).

The intrinsic value of crafts to the sophisticated traveller or catalogue consumer is precisely the human labor embodied in the product and what it tells about a whole way of life. In contrast to industrial production, with the minutely subdivided tasks defined by engineers and controlled by managers remote from the work process, artisan production still links conception with execution. The traditions of the society that produces the craftspeople inhere in the form and function of the objects. The search for singularity, in itself a byproduct of a society in which most goods and services are commoditized (Kopytoff 1986), is satisfied in the acquisition of unique objects from such societies.

Yet artisans are not unaffected by the market forces that inspire much of their production. Feedback, based on sales or promotional agents, regarding the popularity of certain items or designs inevitably influences future production. This can be either positive or negative, depending on the channels of communication. An intelligent awareness of the real costs in labor time and raw materials would help avoid the debasement of crafts that often occurs with exposure to tourist markets. Quality control initiated by intermediaries can cultivate appreciation of consumer tastes and artisan skills that promote the level of production. Culturally sensitive agents in such an exchange process have often succeeded in revitalizing lost techniques such as vegetable dyes that were used before the introduction of synthetic dyes, or hand-spun yarns instead of factory-produced skeins. In this volume, Gobi Stromberg-Pellizzi shows the tenuous connection between craftsperson and consumer in her case study of Taxco silversmiths. The pressures exerted by highly competitive international markets can destroy the qualities that attracted the custom-

Figure 7. San Juan Chamula women knit while they sell products in the local market.

ers initially. She contrasts the resistance to this kind of debasement by weavers of the cooperative Sna Jolobil to the situation she found in Taxco. Inspired by Walter Morris, who did research on the designs and techniques involved in the textiles (1984), the cooperative Sna Jolobil, now directed by the son of one of the Tenejapa weavers Pedro Mesa Mesa promotes traditional techniques and designs that were in danger of being debased as these crafts were commoditized in the growing tourist market that came late to the state of Chiapas.

Even with the expansion in national and international markets, few artisans have benefited from the greater returns. Again the exception can be found in the cooperative Sna Jolobil. By opening a collector-oriented market for backstrap loom textiles, Morris was able to find a clientele willing to pay a price that took into account the hours, weeks, and even months required for producing each item.

Yet even in the protected environment of a cooperative with enlightened leadership, the women have not asserted control over the profits nor taken as active a role in decision making as the organization allows. This is a result of socialization within patriarchal structures that encourages women to assign leadership roles to men. They are also warned by incidents such as the murder of the female cooperative leader in Amatenango

Figure 8. Chamula shopkeepers sell Guatemalan textiles with their own products in street market of San Juan Chamula.

del Valle described in Nash's contribution to this volume that any assertion of autonomy will be punished.

The commercialization of artisan production bridges the contrasts in gift giving and commoditized exchange that are often posed as polar opposites (Appadurai 1986; Hart 1982). Tourism epitomizes the newly monetized yet culturally embedded encounters that characterize the value of these exchanges as the culture of the artisans is packaged along with the product. Tourists are called upon to learn about the producers, and their curiosity often exceeds the information provided in the guide books as they intrude into the sites of production. Artisans resist some of the intrusion, particularly that of photographing them as they work. But even this has become comoditized as weavers or potters demand a thousand pesos for a shot, or add the favor of posing for a shot if the tourist will buy their wares. Some towns, like San Juan Chamula, have created stalls in municipal markets where women sell their own crafts along with those made in other towns. Civic officials may even sell permits for tourists to enter the churches or take photographs in public arenas. By comoditizing the relationship with the visitors, the indigenous people have overcome

Figure 9. Brocaded huipiles of Tenejapa have just recently entered the market.

the hostility that has often resulted in assault and even the killing of intrudors in the past. But this process may indeed involve a renewed colonization as these semisubsistence farmers become ever more dependent on distant markets and the vagaries of economic cycles over which they have no control. As Geshekter (1978:70) warned, "Tourism is an extremely competitive industry and promoting it within the framework of international capitalism involves selling a country as a product."

In the dozens of indigenous communities surrounding the provincial city of San Cristóbal de Las Casas in the state of Chiapas, visitors can find the entire gamut of commercialization that Bourdieu (1977) defines as the commodity status of artisan production. Some of the items have been produced for market for centuries, such as the pottery of Amatenango del Valle. Other items, such as the brocaded *huipiles* of Tenejapa, have just moved into commoditized exchange within the memory of living weavers. A master weaver seventy years of age who spoke only Tzeltal told us about how she ventured into the city of Las Casas to sell a pair of woven trousers twenty-five years ago. She described how she was so fearful of her encounters with merchants that she sold work that involved

Figure 10. Manuela Guzman, Coordinator of Artisan Production Cooperative of Instituto Nacional Indigenesta, examines backstrap loom textiles from her native village of Oxchuk, Chiapas.

several weeks of labor for the price of a handful of fruit. Some of the textiles woven by women of her town replicate designs that can be seen in the robes of Maya figurines on stellae that are dated at a thousand years (Morris 1984). In other towns such as Aguacatenango, commoditization of the embroidery work that was utilized in making women's own blouses occurred within the last three decades. The colonial designs of realistic flowers that these women embroidered on their blouses have recently been augmented by designs introduced by dealers from the United States and Canada.

Oaxaca artisans have been involved in commodity production for several centuries. Waterbury (1989) speculates that the embroidery craft was probably introduced by Dominican friars during the colonial period. Its growth was sparked by the post-World-War-II tourist trade in the 1950s. Other more mundane crafts such as grinding stones and mats, discussed by Cook (this volume) precede the conquest. The government began to sponsor these indigenous crafts over two decades ago, promoting the ethnic identity of the producers. Building on these images, importers extoll their "2000-year-old heritage . . . as deep and fertile as the Oaxacan valley of southern Mexico where the Zapotec Indians have woven a culture from the fibers of their own strong roots dyed with influences from the Mayans, Aztecs, the colonial Spanish and more recently the modern world as it spins towards the 21st century" (cited in Stephen this volume).

Stephen goes on to show the contradictions that result from the interactions of these producers with the growing international market. Zapotec weavers protect their local traditions in opposition to the commoditized version of "Indian" culture promoted by the state. This has enabled them to retain some control over the production and distribution of their distinctive products in international trade circuits. Class distinctions noted by Cook in Oaxaca communities are further corroborated in Stephen's study, showing how these complicate the attempt to maintain autochthonous traditions. Yet relations of production are still mediated through ties of kin and *compadrazgo,* (ritual godparenthood), often providing the basis for reciprocal labor networks, used at fiestas, that define and reinforce a sense of common identity.

Stephen also shows how the state's active intervention transformed the local economy from subsistence-based activities to wage work for men and commoditization of women's crafts as far back as the 1920s. Migration in the *bracero* program to the United States allowed some men to accumulate enough capital to expand commercialization of artisan production when they returned. The completion of the Pan-American Highway stimulated the market potential of the area. At the very point in time when synthetic textiles were being adopted locally, the government promotion of artisanry for tourists encouraged the revitalization of this dying enterprise.

Contradictory trends in the development process in Oaxaca result in the producer's ethnic identities being contested as communities fight for their share of the market in international spheres. With whatever remains of traditional arts and culture, Zapotec weavers can exert greater control over the markets they enter than the Taxco silversmiths described by Gobi Stromberg-Pellizzi. The cheapening of production processes and the intense competition among silversmiths have not as yet been countered by the development of internal organization to set prices and maintain quality of artisan products. The vulnerability of the producers to a volatile market reduces many of them to the role of pieceworkers in a putting-out system that enriches the intermediaries at the expense of the producers.

The wide range of differences in production processes among the brickmakers and weavers Cook studied in Oaxaca is reflected in distinct levels of consciousness. Yet even in the smallest shops he discovered capitalist production relations. The accumulation of capital goes on in the small shops as the owners reinvest capital to further production. This can increase productivity, especially when the owner pays piece rates in order to maximize the extraction of surplus value, paving the way to increased wealth distinctions. As workers become conscious of the disproportionate gains of merchants and producers, the growing class differentiation can lead to conflict within the community.

These case studies from Oaxaca and the central plateau indicate a more advanced process of commercialization of crafts than in Chiapas where market exchange for textiles is relatively recent. In the indigenous communities of Chiapas, domestic relations of production are transformed by commoditization. Eber and Rosenbaum in this volume show the conflicts experienced by weavers of Chamula and Chenalho as they try to balance the need for cash against the negative reaction of their husbands and the wider community to their entry into the market. Both authors found that men particularly resented the women's involvement in the politics of the cooperatives. This parallels the response of men in Amatenango to women's direct access to these new political arenas.

Nash's longitudinal study of pottery in Amatenango del Valle in Chiapas reveals the impact of an intensified pottery production on the domestic economy. Commoditization of this craft in Amatenango del Valle occurred probably even before the conquest. What is novel in the present enlarged sphere of exchange is the growing contribution that women make to household economy with the cash earned by the sale of pottery, and their greater sense of autonomy within the household. Men contribute an ever-larger share of labor in pottery production because of its increasing importance, bringing in most of the wood for firing and assisting in the collection of clay, a task men never engaged in during the 1960s when I had last done field work in the town.

The persistence of small plot, semi-subsistence household production supplemented by artisan production is a cultural preference that cannot be explained in economic terms alone. Commercialization of traditional arts in San Antonio and Santiago Atitlan, Guatemala makes it possible for men to remain in their homes and avoid the arduous trips to work in coastal *fincas*. In addition, a compelling dynamic holding together an economic unit such as the household is the high level of satisfaction for men accustomed to a dominant position within the indigenous family and community. In Amatenango, the control by men of the sales of pottery enabled them to take advantage of the cash earned by women in pottery production to further their own investments in cattle, horses, and—more recently—the purchase of trucks. Yet the unequal return has already sown rebellion as women choose to live alone in the village or even escape to the city. The domestic violence documented by Eber and Rosenbaum in Chamula and Chenalhó as men try to reinforce their control over women within the domestic unit is paralled by the murder of the president of the Amatenango cooperative.

Tracy Ehlers' article delineates a new model of artisan development in the San Antonio Palopó township where weaving sales to tourists have enabled the population to abandon migratory plantation labor and improve standards of living. The direct sale of products to the U.S. market, bypassing the local and regional intermediaries who formerly dominated the market, enables the weavers to command higher prices and to hold on to more of the proceeds. Yet the production for use that formerly motivated household activity is being subverted by the very gains from expansion of commodity sales as the importation of new ideas and goods subverts the wearing of the indigenous garments.

The high stakes, both in terms of potential profits and community loss, of drawing the traditions of these Maya communities into national and even international markets, is nowhere clearer than in Guatemala. Robert Carlsen's article on textile production in Santiago Atitlán shows the international implications of craft production in this hub of tourist trade in the lake area. In the use of dyes he teaches us to read the changing world fortunes that affect Guatemalan Indian craftspeople. As World War II expanded from the European theater to Asia, the scarcity of German dyes was followed by the scarcity of silk. The military repression of the current decade is marked by a shift from cotton to cheaper acrylic yarns. The Mayans, as Carlsen succinctly states, have made the changes necessary for staying the same. Here again the production for use is in transition to production for sale in ways that respond to shrinking land and expanding markets for craft goods. Ethnic identity expressed in the continued use

of locally woven garments has both fortuitous as well as culturally con-
strained bases. It acts as an integrative mechanism preventing the centrif-
ugal tendencies that threaten cultural disintegration. By entering into the
new circuits of commoditization while drawing inspiration from the
achievements of the past, the artisans have achieved in some cases new creative syntheses.

Sol Tax captured the ingenuity of these entrepreneurial artisans
many years ago in this monograph *Penny Capitalism* (1950). He illustrated this in class with the story of a Panajacheleño weaver-entrepreneur
who had sold him and his wife Gertrude so many pieces that they had
no need or desire left, but he continued to return with offerings, each
time pegged so much lower in price that they felt forced to take advantage of the offer. Finally Sol asked the man how he could sell at a price
so much reduced from the first items he had sold. The man told him to
bring those earlier sale items out, and then he pointed out the progressive
reduction in size and complexity of design that made the lower price
possible.

Four decades later Tracy Ehlers has discovered the same eager response to ever-more-distant markets as artisans adapt their weaving talents to the production of belts, bags, and a variety of garments that have
found markets as well as imitators throughout the world. In the town of
San Antonio where she studied weaving in the 1970s, she saw the inception of a weaving cooperative started by a Peace Corp volunteer and returned to find it actively operating with several other lines in 1989.
Although the returns to the producers were low and only a few of the
entrepreneurs gained uncommon wealth, the income enabled these farmers to avoid contracting out their labor in the coastal plantations.

Duncan Earle and Erica Verrillo in their article examine two groups
of Mayas displaced by the violence against indigenous populations carried
out by the military. The authors have promoted a craft project enabling
refugees in exile camps in Chiapas to survive in an environment where
their entry into the agricultural labor force encounters the opposition
of Mexican Indians. Across the border a development project for Maya
widows, which incorporates a craft component as a by-product of sheep
and goat pastoralism introduced in 1985, ensures survival of women and
children whose husbands or fathers have been killed or who live in exile.
They find that these low-cost, grass roots development projects sensitive
to the skills of women and cultural proclivities of the population provide
an important transition away from the politics of terrorism and the economics of despair let loose by the military. Yet the low returns to women
compared with those who traffic these commodities in government and

private export enterprises perpetuate the exploitation characteristic of Ladino/Indian relations.

The relationship between art, politics, and the social system explored in all the papers is focused in the setting of museums in Flora Kaplan's paper. She elucidates the formation of national identity in Mexico through exhibits and shops that promote the sale of craft work. The validation of both authenticity and aesthetic qualities receives the final seal of approval in these circles, contributing to the rise in prices as well as the promotion of sales.

As the art forms of these indigenous cultures still possessing distinctive traditions pass into metropolitan centers of the world, the vulnerability of the creator to new pressures in this wider context is evident, yet the survival of these art forms may require entry into international circuits. In Guatemala, Mayan communities respond to dictates of the export market in finding new sources of cash to survive in the new national economy. Those who have gone into exile in Mexico have even less choice in defining their products. Nonetheless the wearing of a proper costume "puts one in the form of one's ancestors," as Carlsen notes in his article, and by maintaining their craft the producers retain an important part of

Figure 11. Lacandon woodcraft, the most recent craft introduced into museum shops, combines traditional objects— wooden bowls and spoons—with new sculptural forms and even clocks.

their identity. In Oaxaca, Zapotec artisans are subsidized by the government to commoditize their culture, yet they seek to preserve an autochthonous identity distinct from the commercialized entity. The communities of Chiapas, which entered the commercialized tourist world decades after those in Oaxaca, relive the past in each task that they undertake. In Amatenango del Valle each prayer intoned in rituals reiterates "And so we shall be able to do what our mothers did and what our fathers did here where our Holy Father sees us and our Holy Mother sees us," (Nash 1985:xv). The artisan potter or weaver may continue to be the agent, along with the museum exhibitors and collectors who make their enterprise viable, in transmitting the program of the ancestors.

Whether they will reaffirm those traditions, ensuring that the culture has not strayed from the path set down at the beginning of time by the ancestors, will depend on the nature of the relationship existing among the artisans, the intermediaries, and the consumers. The "alternative" trading organizations represented by Pueblo to People or Jubilee Crafts, and publicly or privately subsidized cooperatives, may assure a non-exploitative basis for this relationship. In this postmodern world of amalgamated cultures and the search for identity through consumerism, the strange alliance of a politically conscious consuming elite and culturally rooted producing communities may continue to generate new and beautiful forms and textures in artisan products.

REFERENCES CITED

Annis, Sheldon
    1987   *God and Production in a Guatemalan Town*. Austin: University of Austin Press.

Appadurai, Arjun
    1986   *The Social Life of Things: Commodities in Cultural Perspective*. Cambridge: Cambridge University Press.

Bourdieu, Pierre
    1977   *Outline of a Theory of Practice*. Cambridge: Cambridge University Press.

Collier, George
    1990   *Seeking Food and Seeking Money: Changing Productive Relations in a Highland Mexican Community*. United Nations Research Institute for Development. Occasional Paper.

Cook, Scott
1984   *Peasant Capitalist Industry.* Lanham, MD: University Press of America.

García Canclini, Néstor
1982   *Las culturas populares en el capitalismo.* Mexico D.F.: Editorial Nueva Imagen.

Geshekter, Charles L.
1978   International Tourism and African Underdevelopment: Some Reflections on Kenya. In Mario D. Zamora, Vinson H. Sutlive and Nathan Altshuler, eds., pp. 57–88. *Tourism and Economic Change.* Williamsburg, VA: Department of Anthropology.

Gossen, Gary
1986   *Symbol and Meaning beyond the Closed Community.* Albany: SUNY Press.

Hart, Keith
1982   "On Commoditization," in E. Goody, ed., *From Craft to Industry,* pp. 38–49. Cambridge: Cambridge University Press.

Kopytoff, Igor
1986   The Cultural Biography of Things: Commoditization as Process. In *The Social Life of Things; Commodities in Cultural Perspective,* ed. A. Appadurai, pp. 64–91. Cambridge: Cambridge University Press.

Morris, Walter F. Jr.
1984   *Mil años del tejido en Chiapas.* Instituto de la Artesanía Chiapaneca.

Nash, June
1985   *In the Eyes of the Ancestors: Belief and Behavior in a Maya Community.* Prospect Heights, IL: Waveland Press. First published in 1970, Yale University Press.

Novelo, Victoria
1976   *Artesanías y capitalismo en Mexico.* Mexico, D.F.: Editorial Nueva Imagen.

Schneider, Jane
    1987   The Anthropology of Cloth. *Annual Review of Anthropology*
    16:409–48.

Tax, Sol
    1950   *Penny Capitalism*. Washington, D.C.: Smithsonian Institute.

Tedlock, Dennis
    1985   *Popul Vuh: The Mayan Book of the Dawn of Life*. New York: Simon and Schuster, Inc.

Waterbury, Ronald
    1989   Embroidery for Tourists: A Contemporary Putting-Out System in Oaxaca, Mexico. In *Cloth and the Human Experience,* ed. A. Weiner and J. Schneider, pp. 243–271. Washington: Smithsonian Institution Press.

Drawing by Christine Eber

2

Weaving in the Fast Lane: Class, Ethnicity, and Gender in Zapotec Craft Commercialization*

Lynn Stephen

INTRODUCTION

Contemporary Mexican craft production operates in a double-edged history of consumption linked to the internationalization of capital. Blankets, shawls, and pottery which were once produced for local people to sleep under, wear, and cook in have become exotic craft goods. They are now consumed by middle-class and elite sectors of Mexico, the United States, and Europe where a desire for the "traditional" is met with the consumption of hand-produced commodities coming largely from the Third World. The same mechanization which makes industrial consumers long for "genuine" crafts also eliminates peasant consumer markets for

*Funding for field research was provided by the Inter-American Foundation, the Wenner-Gren Foundation for Anthropological Research, and the Damon Fellowship of Brandeis University. Additional research and writing time was funded by the Center for U.S.–Mexican Studies, University of California, San Diego.

hand-produced objects as they are replaced by polyester/wool blankets, nylon jackets, and water jugs—industrial articles which are more attractive because they are cheaper or are associated with modernization (García Canclini 1982:96).

As international commercial capital reaches craft-producing communities such as those in Mexico, it alters the relations of production and can produce local conflicts along class and gender lines. Within craft-producing communities, the changing dynamics of capitalist development do not always produce uniform results, even within one community. A contradiction can frequently be seen between defending a common community claim on a particular craft item on the one hand, and increased social and economic differentiation, on the other (Cook, this volume).

This contradiction is examined here in Teotitlán del Valle, Oaxaca, where textiles have been transformed from use objects to handicrafts during this century. This transformation took place slowly after the Mexican Revolution as the economic base of the community began shifting from merchant to commercial capital (See Stephen 1992; Young 1976, 1978). This transition is related to the centralization of the Mexican state, the creation of a national "Indian" identity, state development programs for craft industries, migration, the promotion of tourism, and changes in the Mexican textile industry. After briefly reviewing these topics and relating them to local-level change in Teotitlán, I shall summarize how these policies and events have produced changes within the community, particularly in class and gender relations. In may discussion I include information from several other communities to elucidate the regional context in which Teotitlán del Valle functions. This community has dominated production and marketing relations of weaving production in the Tlacolula arm of the Oaxaca Valley since the colonial period.[1]

COMMERCIAL CRAFT PRODUCTION AND ETHNICITY

Most analyses of capitalist development and the international division of labor focus primarily on industrialized commodity production of electronics, textiles, or food processing, and have recently included commercial agriculture. While Benería and Roldán's (1987) analysis of homework in Mexico City emphasizes the importance of home-based piecework in the international division of labor, craft production for export which also involves piecework is seldom included in analyses of the world economy. Yet the very presence and development of what is now a world market for crafts depends on the existence of integrated international enterprises. The international market for crafts is built on an elite consumer ideology contrasting manufactured, mass-produced, internationalized modern objects with hand-produced, authentic local crafts.

In commercialized craft production, producers can also be seen as part of an international labor force when the economies of industrial manufacture and of craft production are linked. Artisans who produce crafts for elite national and international consumption are also part of an international labor force. They are segmented on the basis of their ethnicity, their so-called traditional means of production, and their subordinate position in the international marketing process. Ultimately, the specific ethnic identity and ethnically based economic claims of producers can become divorced from what they produce—blankets, shawls, rugs, or whatever. In this process the construction of ethnicity and development of ethnically based economic claims become important issues as communities, or larger population segments, struggle to maintain control over their product. At the same time, however, just who controls claims made on specific ethnic products—and how—are critical political questions as producing communities become more strongly differentiated between producers and merchants, particularly under conditions of commercial capitalism.

In discussions of capitalist development, ethnicity and class relations are often viewed as exclusive of one another. As pointed out by many contemporary students of class and culture (Sider 1986; Bourgois 1988; LiPuma and Keene-Meltzoff 1989; Roseberry 1989), ethnicity and the cultural content that specific ethnic groups claim as their own are often reduced to an epiphenomenon of material class relations or are described as completely autonomous from the relations of production with a motor all their own. An exploration of the changing cultural and economic context in which craft production takes place affords us an excellent opportunity to examine how the realities of ethnicity and class are linked through the changing lives of contemporary craft producers. The concept of ethnicity must be clarified, however, before embarking on this exploration.

Ethnicity must be understood not as an objective collection of empirical traits, but as contested terrain. It involves a particular group of people asserting a self-generated identity based on a claim to historical autonomy and perceived natural or cultural traits that are emphasized as a primary source of identity. Such traits must be recognized both internally and externally. The invocation of a specific ethnic identity or claim is usually triggered by political, economic, or social reasons in relation to one or more other social groups. Because the content of ethnic identity is flexible and changes through time according to the cultural material available to a particular group of people to work with, there is no such thing as "real" or "genuine" ethnic content. A particular group of people may create and recreate their own ethnic identity in response to dominant culture, absorbing aspects of that culture and reworking it according to their own definition—engaging in what Gramsci termed counter-hegemonic activity (Stephen 1991c).

As used by Sider (1986), Varese (1988), and others, the concept of hegemony suggests that cultural and economic patterns of expression and consumption involve a two-way dynamic in which the marginalized sectors of a national population absorb and rework material conditions, ideology, and culture imposed on them by dominant classes. When ethnicity is defined locally, at the level of community (which historically is the case in Teotitlán and other indigenous communities in southern Mexico), counter-hegemonic definitions of ethnicity can occur at the level of community, often in opposition to state-defined ethnicities or ethnic categories.[2]

ETHNICITY AND CLASS UNDER CHANGING CONDITIONS OF CAPITALISM IN TEOTITLÁN

A striking example of the dialectical construction of ethnicity comes from the people of Teotitlán del Valle, where an apparently unified local identity projected to outsiders can contrast with internal representations of that same identity, depending on the context and the relationships involved, as explained below. Two of the common elements found in local constructions of Teotiteco ethnic identity include participating in social and cultural institutions which reproduce kinship relationships, and being the first people in Oaxaca to produce wool weavings. Because of the various levels through which Teotiteco identity is manipulated, however, the common heritage of a united community of weavers bonded together by kinship ties has been used by different sectors of the population in different ways throughout history. The context of capitalist development and the transition of the economic base of the community from merchant to commercial capitalism has affected the way in which ethnic identity is constructed and ethnically based economic claims are asserted. On the ground, this involves who claims Teotiteco Zapotec identity and how, both in relation to outside merchants and consumers and internally in the relations of production.

While the more "commercial" version of their identity that Teotitecos maintain for outsiders emphasizes a united community of kin producing unique textiles and participating in an elaborate and important ceremonial life, internal representations of that same identity take on the appearance of swiss cheese, particularly in relation to more recent class relations under commercial capitalism. Riddled with contradictions, the picture painted of recent local history and identity by older men and women suggests a complex reality. According to them, while the community did have a common history of weaving production and a rich ceremonial life, it also included differences in terms of what people wore, what they ate, the kinds of houses they lived in, how many godchildren they had, how many fiestas they were able to sponsor, and what the material conditions of their lives were. On the one hand, these histories offer a strong image of community identity and emphasize the importance of how things were done by *be:n(i) lo'gets* (Teotiteco Zapotec for "people of the town"), but on the other hand they also focus on the contested realities of that history for a gendered and economically differentiated population.[3] Today Teotitecos still use the language of kinship and solidarity to manipulate each other towards specific ends. For example merchants use the language of kinship and *compadrazgo* (ritual kinship) to recruit their godchildren as pieceworkers.

As documented by Young (1976, 1978), indigenous peasant economies in the Oaxaca region are characterized by the intervention of independent merchant capital (local capital not directly tied to a larger systematic process of industrialization) from 1870 to 1930 and then commercial or circulation capital after 1930. These two types of capital (merchant and commercial) also guided economic development in Teotitlán and have resulted in changing manifestations of class relations and ethnic identity at different times in this century. Under merchant capitalism, a small group of local merchant-landowners maintained a position of economic dominance through acquiring labor and land in return for loans made to help the majority of the community fulfill their ritual obligations as sponsors of cult celebrations for local saints (*mayordomías*). This small group, which also served as *mayordomos* and supported the religious and political authority of local elders, maintained a position of economic dominance until the 1930s when mayordomía (cult celebrations of local saints) sponsorship became voluntary and the system of sponsorship began to slowly decline. In the late 1940s and 1950s when the regional economy was commoditized and indigenous Oaxacans migrated to the United States as braceros (officially contracted migrant laborers), alternative opportunities to earn cash loosened the hold of this group of merchants and produced a transitional period in the class structure of the community. As the weaving industry began to serve tourists and U.S. and European export markets, commercial capital came to dominate the community and the relations of production were characterized by direct appropriation of surplus labor by merchant/employers from producing weavers. Labor relations were no longer obliquely mediated by the ritual relations of mayordomías. In the course of these changes, the way in which ethnic identity was represented, both internally and externally, changed considerably.

ZAPOTEC WEAVING PRODUCTION AND DISTRIBUTION TO REGIONAL MARKETS UNTIL 1960

Historically the weaving complex centered around Teotitlán del Valle included the neighboring communities of Díaz Ordaz (Santo Domingo), Santa Ana del Valle, and to a limited degree Macuilxóchitl. These communities wove cotton for local consumption as well as for tribute payments before the arrival of the Spaniards (Acuña 1984:335; Barlow 1949:map). Wool was introduced to Teotitlán by the first bishop of Oaxaca sometime between 1535 and 1555 (Gay 1881). Burgoa (1934) mentions the weaving of woolen blankets and sarapes as an important economic activity in Teotitlán as well as in Santo Domingo del Valle (now Díaz Ordaz), Mitla, Tlacolula, and Macuilxóchitl. Throughout the colonial period and through independence, Teotitlán, Santa Ana, Díaz Ordaz and Macuilxóchitl continued to weave in conjunction with subsistence farming. After the Mexican Revolution the communities of Teotitlán, Santa Ana, and Díaz Ordaz continued to weave, with each specializing in a particular type of blanket to meet the needs of the indigenous regional market.[4]

Díaz Ordaz artisans produced a third-class blanket called a *pelusa,* which is a mixture of animal hair and cotton (Vargas-Barón 1968:46). This cheaper product occupied an important niche in local markets until the 1930s. Santa Ana artisans specialized in production of second-class woolen blankets with little or no design while Teotitecos wove first-class woolen blankets with complex designs. In her thesis, which traces changes in the development of the Oaxaca Valley weaving complex of Díaz Ordaz, Santa Ana, and Teotitlán, Vargas-Barón (1968) describes how the regional market for weavings expanded during the 1940s and then was replaced by a national and international market for high-quality weavings in the 1950s. As a result of this change, weaving activities have greatly declined in Díaz Ordaz while they have increased in Santa Ana and Teotitlán. As people in Díaz Ordaz abandoned weaving, they began to make technological improvements in cultivation techniques. The opposite occurred in Teotitlán and Santa Ana, where increased weaving activity displaced subsistence agriculture.

Until 1890, the network for sales distribution of blankets from Díaz Ordaz, Santa Ana, and Teotitlán extended only to the markets of Oaxaca and Tlacolula. From 1890 to 1920 this network expanded locally to include other valley markets in the area such as Ocotlán, Etla, and Miahuatlán. The years from 1920 to 1950 are marked by significant growth in the industry, particularly in relation to the production of first-class blankets. The peak in demand for pelusa blankets was from 1910 to 1930, according to Vargas-Barón (1968). In the 1930s a steady decline occurred in the number of weavers from Díaz Ordaz, with pelusa production extinguished in the late 1940s as factory-produced blankets from Puebla and Tlaxcala arrived in Oaxaca via the Pan-American Highway.

Teotitlán and Santa Ana marketed first- and second-class woolen blankets to the Sierra Júarez and to Chiapas from 1920 until 1950. The booming market of Tlacolula apparently was a center for travelling salesmen and merchants who travelled by mule. About twelve to fifteen *viajeros* (travelling merchants) from Teotitlán continued to sell in Chiapas, the Isthmus, and in the Sierra Júarez until the 1950s. See Table 1 for figures on the growth of the merchant population of Teotitlán during this century.

LOCAL CLASS RELATIONS, 1920–1940

Prior to 1931, Teotitlán was characterized by a shifting group of six to seven merchant-trader households who dominated economic relations through trade and had an indirect hold on labor through debt-peonage connected to mayordomías. Because of continued poor economic conditions during and after the Mexican Revolution, cult sponsorship of mayordomías was obligatory with future sponsors named, often against their will, by ritual elders. Unable to pay up front for their sponsorship, many men and women had to sell their land and their own and/or their children's labor to this small group of merchants in order to cover ritual expenses. The local merchants who were the beneficiaries of this system also engaged in farming, trading, and—to a limited degree—cattle ranching.

During the 1920s and 1930s, merchant capitalism provided a context in which labor relations of dominance and subordination were indirect. The exploitation of labor was mediated by local cultural forms which were controlled by local elders and were simultaneously mediums of community solidarity (see Sider 1986:34). The mayordomía system which sometimes resulted in debt-peonage and cheap land sales for merchants, also pulled large sectors of the community together in celebrations which

Table 1. Numbers of Merchants From 1868–1986 in Teotitlán del Valle

Year	Population	No. of Merchants	Census Source	No. of Merchants Cited by Informants	No. of Viajeros Cited
1868	1,899	3	Padron General de Teotitlán, 1868		
1890	2,742	3	Padron General de Teot. Archivo General del Estado, Oaxaca		
1900	2,540	16	Dir. General de Estádistica 1906:4, 44–45		18
1910	2,634	n/a	Dir. General de Estádistica 1918–1920:54		
1920	1,891	n/a	Dept. de la Estádistica Nacional 1925–1928:166–167	5–6	8–10
1927				8	16
1930	2,116	6	Dir. General de Estádistica 1936:275	10	
1932				9	
1940	2,290	28	Dir. General de Estádistica 1946: 566	6–7	
1945				15	
1948				20	
1950	2,511	19	Dir. General de Estádistica 1956:445	22	
1960	2,881	27	Dir. General de Estádistica 1963:1898	25	
1970	3,394	22	Dir. General de Estádistica 1973:406	52	
1980	3,496	53	Instituto Nac. de Estádistica, Geografia y Vivienda 1983, Vol. 1, Tomo 2: 398	80	
1986	4,500	110	Stephen: 1986 household survey, Teotitlán		

triggered reciprocal goods and labor exchanges and symbolically united all community members with the protective saints (see Stephen 1990).

The class system in Teotitlán under conditions of merchant capitalism was not characterized by direct and overt exploitation of labor by merchant-traders. The ritual authority of community elders who had already served as mayordomos sanctioned the desperate behavior of mayordomos (both men and women) who sold whatever necessary to fulfill their sponsorship obligations. While many elders apparently were poor themselves and had been victims of the same system of obligatory mayordomía, they directly supported the interests of merchants who in return gave them political support and legitimized their ritual and political authority in the civil-religious hierarchy. The indirect hold which the small group of merchant-traders had over the population began to change in the 1930s as a consequence of state intervention and the penetration of commercial capital in the community.

COMMUNITY REACTION TO THE CENTRALIZATION OF THE MEXICAN STATE

When Elías Plutarco Calles took the office of president in 1926, the weaving industry centered in Teotitlán appeared to be stabilizing. The number of merchants was on the upswing and trade was expanding into the Sierra Júarez and down to Chiapas by mule. This process was occurring quietly in the south of Mexico without much discussion of it at the national level. The government had not made a detailed census count of people or production in Oaxaca since 1910. The period of the Mexican Revolution had left national information agencies in a shambles.

In Mexico, the 1920s were marked by the centralization of the state and the creation of institutional machinery set up for government intervention in the economy (Hamilton 1982:79). By the time Calles took office, institutions such as the National Commission of Roads, the National Agrarian Commission, the National Irrigation Commission, and the Agricultural Credit Bank had already been established. Calles' tenure is remembered most clearly for its rabid anticlericalism, the Cristero Rebellion, and his interpretation of the 1917 constitution that gave legitimacy to the concept of an interventionist, centralized state (Hamilton 1982:109).

While building his political power from a fundamentally different constituency, particularly that of the working class and peasants, the following administration of Lazaro Cárdenas upheld the notion of an active interventionist state, controlling and directing the economy down to the local level. The theme of the six-year plan outlined in 1933, which was the blueprint for Cárdenas' time in office, emphasized integration. It gave the state wide leeway in directing and redirecting society, focusing on physical integration through the construction of roads and communication links as well as ideological and cultural integration through the dissemination of so-called "socialist education" (Hamilton 1982:136).

In Teotitlán, detailed questionnaires began to come to the *municipio* (county seat) during the Calles administration as the state moved to document agricultural and industrial production with an eye towards increasing production. They continued with the Cárdenas administration in the 1930s. An examination of Teotitlán community correspondence with different state offices during the 1930s reveals that municipio officials in Teotitlán reluctantly responded to inquiries regarding the doings of local government and the specifics of economic production (*Copiador de Oficios* 1930–1940).[5] The town is probably not atypical. After the revolution, many indigenous communities tried to defend what little autonomy they may have gained as a result of land redistribution and bureaucratic links to the federal government which fell apart during the revolution.[6]

In Teotitlán, instead of responding straightforwardly to official inquiries regarding their economy, municipal officials avoided reporting any details about weaving production and marketing. Officials described Teotitecos as both agriculturalists and weavers and did not include specific information on the economic activities of women and children or the quantity of textiles produced in the community. They also carefully reproduced dominant ideas regarding poor, humble Indians struggling to survive, engaging in counter-hegemonic activity to protect their own interests. Merchant activities were deemphasized and uniform poverty was projected as the norm. A response from the *presidente* of Teotitlán in 1932 to the *Jefe de Estadística Nacional* (Head of National Statistics) is representative of such letters (see Stephen 1991c for a more extensive description).

> 1. The majority of the people in this town have looms with which they make the beautiful blankets which have brought significant fame to our state of Oaxaca, but they do not have enough resources to work daily. They must also work as wage laborers and during the agricultural seasons they work as subsistence agriculturalists in order to grow grain for their own consumption.
> 2. Commerce is very dead in our community because of a lack of money. Many have stopped working and although

names can't be provided, I can say that there are no houses here which could be considered factories.[7]

3. The only people who have a regular income are those *regatones* (merchants) who resell their product in Oaxaca.

4. We estimate the total income generated from production to be about 50 pesos per month from different sized products. (Archivo Municipal de Teotitlán de Valle 1932, my translation).

This answer to official inquiries regarding the number of weavers, merchants, presence of factories, and income from farming and weaving shows the defensive posture of the community, but also indicates that local authorities were well aware of the stereotypical picture that they are reproducing for the Office of National Statistics. While guarding the exact nature of their production and only referring vaguely to a few merchants operating in Oaxaca, other correspondence from the same decade indicates that the community had an avid interest in merchant activity and in improving local infrastructure. Local merchants in the community appear to have had their interests well represented by municipal authorities in Teotitlán who covered for their small businesses.

Authorities' efforts to defend the community's economic interests is perhaps best reflected in a letter sent to President Cárdenas in 1938, in which the undersigned asked the president to intervene internationally to prevent the Japanese from fabricating imitations of their blankets. The very fact that Teotitecos were aware of the dynamics of international trade and marketing indicates the foresight with which they protected their interests. The letter also indicates a developed understanding of state constructions and claims on indigenous ethnicity as seen by the way its authors emphasize the importance of history and specific designs. The letter reads as follows:

The native citizens of Teotitlán del Valle, Tlacolula, State of Oaxaca, state for you that we have become aware of the fact that in the country of Japan they are producing Mexican articles with the intent of passing them off as Mexican. Among these articles . . . are found those from the small industry of Oaxacan blankets, adorned with designs and idols which signify the history of Mitla and Monte Albán and Zapotec and Toltec figures. We understand for certain that among other things, Japan is producing articles which imitate the Oaxacan blanket to which we dedicate ourselves as humble people working on simple home looms. This notice has caused us great alarm because at the moment we are in a precarious economic situation and it has therefore occurred to us to request that you dictate measures which will protect our small weaving industry here in Oaxaca—also international measures which will take care of this phenomenon which has come to our notice. . . . (Archivo Municipal de Teotitlán del Valle 1938). My translation.

Teotitecos clearly saw the state as necessary for protecting their interests at a national and international level, yet also resisted providing the specific information on production requested by the Office of National Statistics. Later, the community's policy of distancing itself from state offices was repeated as Teotitecos resisted becoming involved in state-run cooperatives and craft development projects which set up bureaucrats as middlemen for the marketing of crafts. By emphasizing stereotypical images of themselves as "humble people working on simple home looms" and distancing themselves from state development programs, Teotitecos came to exert a significant degree of control over the marketing and distribution of their product within Mexico. This, of course, benefitted the emerging merchant sector who were instrumental in defending local ethnic claims on the textiles. The context for the internationalization of those claims began with the second wave of Mexican migration to the United States.

TEOTITECO MIGRATION TO THE U.S.

In the 1940s, following Cárdenas' tenure in office, the initiation of the second United States Bracero program had a major impact on the textile industry centered in Teotitlán. Along with the completion of the Pan-American Highway, it facilitated the commoditization of the Oaxacan economy. Migration to the United States was also critical in redefining local class relations and strongly affected the lives of women who sustained the local economy with their labor while large numbers of men temporarily migrated.

Claiming that they were suffering a severe labor shortage during the Second World War, United States growers persuaded their government to establish a second Bracero Program with Mexico in 1942 based on the claim that their workers had abandoned them for higher paying jobs in the defense industry (Kiser and Kiser 1979:67). Word of the program didn't reach Teotitlán until 1944. That year about fifteen to twenty Teotiteco men signed up for eight-week contracts running in May, June, and July. Many did not go initially because of rumors that they would be sent off to fight the Americans' war. In July 1944, the first fifteen to twenty men who went to the United States returned safely with shoes, blue jeans, other items of clothing, and most importantly, cash. In 1945 when the recruiters returned, between 150 and 300 men left the community to be braceros.

Many Teotitecos recall 1945, 1946, and 1947 as the years when there were only women left in the community. Women recall the *braceria* of the 1940s and the continued absence of men in the 1950s as a time of great hardship. Many had no source of income while the men were gone, and were saddled with additional chores. Women reported that their husbands sent them little or nothing while they were gone, leaving them as the sole income earners for their families. While some men later returned with savings, others did not. Some women wove during this time, but also had to maintain their food processing, child care, and animal care workloads in addition to taking care of agricultural work. Many tried to earn extra cash by selling the yarn they spun, not having time to weave it themselves or not knowing how. The labor of women which sustained the community while men were gone also indirectly allowed men to begin accumulating capital and skills which were later put to use in building merchant businesses (Stephen 1991c).

While the numbers of Teotitecos who went to the United States was greatest during 1945, 1946, and 1947, a steady stream of migrants has continued. Continued migration was funded by previous migration. About 25 percent of the households in Teotitlán continued to send one or more workers to the United States on an annual basis throughout the duration of the Bracero Program (until 1964) and afterwards as undocumented workers. Recently, some have obtained permission to work under the 1986 Amnesty Law and are applying for temporary residence in the United States. Today, approximately 63 percent of the households in Teotitlán have at least one member who temporarily migrated to the United States and about half have at least one member who temporarily migrated to another part of Mexico.

The period of the Bracero Program (1942–1964) also marked the emergence of commercial capital in the community as well as in the region as a whole (Young 1978). As male migrants returned with cash, it was used to purchase goods which had previously not been used or had been locally produced. With time, cash was also used to purchase agricultural labor to take the place of male laborers who were in the United States, changing the nature of local class relations. Labor became a commodity which was directly bought and sold on the market. In Teotitlán, paying cash for agricultural labor preceded the widespread piecework relations of production found today in which labor is purchased through paying workers by the piece for individual textiles.

The experience of living and working outside of the Oaxaca region also supported the development of local commercial enterprises in other ways. Teotitecos who migrated to the United States not only brought back goods such as televisions, but ideas as well. They returned informed about life in the United States and were often inspired to try and start a business in order to improve their standard of living. The migration experience of these men has been important in the growth of commercial production and marketing of Zapotec weavings. While it has allowed some Teotitecos to build up capital to begin businesses with and kept a relatively high level of commercial control within the community, it also resulted in the exclusion of women from the commercial sphere because of their lack of experience in dealing with Americans. Women's marginalization in commercial activity has also been exacerbated by their low literacy levels and higher percentage of Zapotec monolingualism than that found among the male population (Stephen 1991c).

COMPLETION OF THE PAN-AMERICAN HIGHWAY AND THE DEVELOPMENT OF SYNTHETIC FIBERS IN MEXICO

As Teotiteco Zapotecs migrated to the United States, changes were also taking place at home which were to have an important impact on weaving production and consumption. While the indigenous consumer markets of Oaxaca and Chiapas remained fairly isolated from international industry until the late 1940s, the completion of the Pan-American Highway in 1948 paved the way for the articulation of Oaxaca with the industrial economies of Mexico and the United States. Specifically, the completion of the Pan-American Highway opened up Oaxaca as a market for the highly developed textile industries of Mexico City, Tlaxcala, and Puebla that had flourished during the 1940s. When the Pan-American Highway connected Oaxaca City and smaller towns with the larger Mexican economy, the mechanized textile industries of Tlaxcala and Puebla began to reach into a consumer market which had previously been supplied by blankets, ponchos, and shawls produced by the Zapotecs of the central valleys and other indigenous groups.

The indigenous consumer market was also influenced by the availability of cheaper synthetic fibers beginning in the 1960s used to make blankets, jackets, and shawls. The growth spurt that the cotton and wool textile industry experienced during the 1940s was cut short by 1960 as the production of polyester and other synthetics began to take hold in Mexico (Stephen 1991c). Between 1960 and 1976, national production of wool fibers declined from 3,000 metric tons per year to 1,000 metric tons. Production of synthetic fibers during the same period went from 20,000 metric tons in 1960 to 187,000 metric tons in 1976 (Mercado García 1980:138), primarily for internal consumption as part of Mexico's import-substitution policy. The growth of the polyester industry marked a decrease in the consumption of hand-loomed blankets as use objects.

Mexico's policy of promoting industrialization, including the development of polyester textile production, was not functioning in isolation. By the late 1950s, the state had also begun to preoccupy itself with tourism. While the production of synthetics produced a dramatic reduction in regional consumption of articles such as those produced in Teotitlán, government policies promoting artisanry for tourist and national consumption helped to open a new market for textiles, which were transformed from use articles to handicrafts.

"Indian" Identity, Craft Production, and the Creation of New Markets

During the 1940s, people from all over Mexico, the United States, and Europe began to arrive in Oaxaca and southern Mexico as tourists in larger numbers than ever before. The new Pan-American Highway, which passed within six kilometers of Teotitlán, made the state capital of Oaxaca infinitely more accessible to Teotitecos, and Teotitlán more accessible to tourists. It became possible to make a trip to Oaxaca in half a day, encouraging Teotitecos to hawk their wares in Oaxaca on a more regular basis. The road also began to draw tourists to Teotitlán who wanted to see for themselves how Zapotec weavings were produced.

To capture the interests of tourists, particular features of culture and material production were commoditized and packaged for sale by the federal government. The ideological package which was and is sold to tourists who come to states with high indigenous populations is based on a homogenized image of "Indian culture" and the material remains of that culture which can be visited or purchased and taken home. Of primary import in this cultural package is the Mexican "Indian."

The modern construction of "Indian" identity began in the 1920s after the Mexican Revolution. The contradictory indigenist policy of the postrevolutionary state called for mainstreaming indigenous people while letting them retain their "unique" cultural characteristics. As such, the policy fit well with two other problems the state inherited—first, the necessity for a national identity to bring together a nation fractured by diverse ethnic, linguistic, and political identities, and secondly, a way of distinguishing Mexico from its dominant northern neighbor, the United States, and bringing it into a position of prominence in Latin America. The promotion of "Indian" identity in public schools and cultural missions along with an overhaul in the municipal structure in the 1920s was supposed to provide Mexico's indigenous population with recognition and a ready link to national identity. As a national characteristic, the presence of "Indian culture" in Mexico allowed the state to market the nation as exotic. "Indians" were the living proof of Mexico's uninterrupted link with the past (Stephen 1991b).

The material culture of homogenized "Indianness" provides symbolic icons for both (a) forging a national identity and (b) the creation of commodities that, when converted from use articles to handicrafts, become a source of employment and foreign exchange. Following the revolution, *arte popular* (popular or people's art) was recognized officially in 1921 for the first time when the tenth anniversary of the Mexican Revolution was celebrated with a national artisanry exhibit inaugurated by Álvaro Obregón in Mexico City (García Canclini 1982:102). In the 1930s, intellectuals and artists declared arte popular to be an important part of Mexican heritage, suggesting that articles such as straw dolls, clay toys, and multi-colored sarapes were giving Mexicans "an elevated sense of race and a national conscience that was previously missing" (Novo 1932:56, cited in Novelo 1976). A program that came out of the 1940 International Indigenous Congress in Patzcuaro focused on the topic of *arte popular* and called for the protection of indigenous arts, the organization of expositions of indigenous arts, and national contests (Marroquin 1977:39–40).

Following this programatic initiative, there were economic studies done of artisanry, and the state began to set up programs to support craft production. These emphasized credit, technical assistance, and marketing cooperatives. In Teotitlán del Valle, two cooperative programs funded first by BANFOCO (Banco de Fomento de Cooperativas) and then FONART (Fomento Nacional de Artesanía) were short-lived and appear to have only benefitted a few people in the community. Local merchants as well as weavers were reluctant to participate in programs which called for additional layers of government middlemen in the marketing of crafts.

The most recent development project, *La Lanera de Oaxaca*, a wool yarn factory funded jointly by the state government of Oaxaca and the federal government on land supposedly donated by the community, has been a source of controversy since it opened its doors in 1984. Although it provoked protest initially, in 1991 it was taken over by the community and now operates successfully. The top-down structure of early state initiatives to promote craft production in Teotitlán set a pattern in which Oaxaca state officials from various departments worked only with a small subset of men who held official positions in the municipio, excluding not only women who do not attend formal community meetings, but also many men who were not closely linked to the municipio. Currently, few people in the community are interested in attempting further projects with the government.

CLASS AND GENDER RELATIONS UNDER COMMERCIAL CAPITALISM

By the mid 1980s, significant capital accumulation had taken place in Teotitlán as well as in the communities of Santa Ana del Valle and San Miguel, although on a smaller scale. All three communities are characterized by growth in their merchant sectors, with that of Teotitlán dominating those in the other two communities. While it is difficult to make absolute distinctions between merchant and weaver households, it is possible to delineate households according to their primary economic activities.[8] For the purposes of discussion here, I have separated households into three types: merchant, self-employed weavers who also sell their own goods, and piecework weaving households.

In Teotitlán, the linguistic categories of merchant and weaver have both political and economic significance. A weaver is called *rúnčilát(ši)* (maker of weavings). A merchant or *hureš̌lat(ši)* (seller of weavings) is identified by Teotitecos as the one who purchases textiles, and—through these textiles—the labor of others. They are viewed in the words of one informant as "buying what someone else labored to make. They didn't sweat for it." Similar dichotomies are found in Santa Ana and San Miguel (Cohen 1990).

The majority of merchants in Teotitlán contract weavers in local households on a piecework basis, often through kin and *compadrazgo* ties, for a certain number of pieces, designating the designs, colors, and shapes which are to be produced. Relations of production are simultaneously ties of kin and compadrazgo—the same relationships which form the basis of reciprocal labor networks used at fiestas. Merchants tend to have more godchildren than weavers. This is due to local perceptions that it is easy for them to shoulder the heavy costs of godchild sponsorship. Many merchants have their godchildren working for them as pieceworkers in a system where *padrinos* (godfathers) and *madrinas* (godmothers) provide materials and *ahijados* (godsons) and *ahijadas* (goddaughters) produce finished weaving products in their homes.

In the relations of production, respect is so inculcated into the godparent-godchild relationship that a godchild may be in a weak position to refuse a labor request from his or her godparents. From the perspective of the godchild, having a godparent with significant financial resources also makes it possible to ask for a loan in a time of financial need, often without interest. Heads of weaving households often seek out merchants as godparents for their children in the hopes that the merchants will be able to help their children economically.

Weavers often receive interest-free loans and primary materials from merchants. Because there is a shortage of weaving labor due to high market demand, weavers often have more work than they can handle. In deciding which work to do, weavers give priority to requests from relatives or *compadres*. If the compadre is not willing to pay the wage a weaver wants, however, the weaver will quietly go elsewhere to work. As long as there is a labor shortage, merchants cannot take too much advantage of their position as godfather or compadres.

A census conducted in 1986 revealed that there were approximately 110 self-identified merchant households out of a total of 1,039 households in the community of Teotitlán. Teotitecos conceptually divide merchants into three classes depending on the volume of their inventory. Approximately ten households are classified as "large" merchants and they handle the largest share of distribution, both within Teotitlán and in Santa Ana and San Miguel as well. About thirty households fall into the category of middle-level merchants with the remainder labeled as "small merchants" who purchase small numbers of weavings or sell their own production in the local artisan market.

One of the most important issues is how households move from weaver to merchant status under the present conditions of commercial capitalism. As we will see, the role of gender is important in this process. Most households which have achieved merchant status within the past fifteen years appear to have used a combination of unpaid household labor and accumulation of initial capital through migration to the United States or from land and animal sales. As analyzed by Cook and Binford (1988), the question of how petty commodity producing households become petty capitalist enterprises invokes the Lenin/Chayanov debate. My work concurs with the extensive survey research of Cook and Binford showing that household demographics can significantly affect the movement of "household enterprises from conditions of petty commodity production to those of petty capitalism" (1988:7–8). In particular, the survey found that family labor is critical to the accumulation of capital that, in some cases, allows a household to cross the threshold to petty capitalist production. As such, they represent an exception to Chayanov's emphasis on simple reproduction of the household unit (Cook and Binford 1988:8). In Teotitlán, the gender dynamics of migration to the United States were critical in this process as well.

In Teotitlán, under emerging conditions of circulation capital during the late 1940s, 1950s, and early 1960s, the labor of women sustained a significant proportion of the population while men were working in the United States. Most men did not send money home and if they returned with savings invested it in land, animals, or the means of production for weaving. Those who were able to purchase animals, land, or looms had an advantage later when they wanted to push into merchant status.

Later, the labor of women was also important in helping households to build up capital for paying non-household members as pieceworkers. As tourist and export markets for Zapotec textiles grew steadily, availability of weaving labor became a critical variable in the expansion of production. Female labor was freed through increasing the quantity of machine-spun yarn used to produce textiles, essentially mechanizing a part of the production process. Use of machine-spun yarn also freed significant amounts of labor, primarily that of women and children, which had been dedicated to spinning and carding. Elderly women, probably the most economically marginalized sector of the populations of Teotitlán and Santa Ana, continue to hand-card and hand-spin wool. The high end of the textile market in the United States and Europe that calls for hand-spun yarn provides a niche for elderly laborers who earn a wage which is three times lower than what they would earn as weavers.

Since the 1970s, girls and women have been socialized as weavers and weaving is now a normal part of their work load, probably increasing the number of labor hours they put in. In Teotitlán, approximately thirty-five to forty percent of the weaving labor force is now female.[9] Clements (1988:22–23) reported in 1988 that equal numbers of males and females are weaving in San Miguel, a community that just entered textile production in 1974 (Clements 1988:22–23).

By the 1980s, the additional weaving labor of women and girls in Teotitlán was critical in helping some households to begin functioning as employers. This had implications for the women in these households. The emergence of class relations tied to commercial capital has resulted in differences between women based on the status of their households as merchants or weavers. Women in merchant households describe themselves as managers or laborers working primarily in their husbands' businesses. Like women weavers who complain of double work loads related to weaving, merchant women have similar complaints related to the managing work they have to do for their husbands combined with a heavy domestic workload. When women in employer households discuss their subordinate position in production decision-making, they attribute it to a lack of skills needed to conduct the business aspects of the household enterprise. While many women do maintain control over a small pot of money for making purchases of household items, when a household accumulates capital and begins a business, often this money is kept in a separate pot controlled by men. In contrast to their husbands and sons, who have often spent several years working in the United States, most women have little experience interacting with Americans. Many believe that their husbands learned how to deal with Americans and accumulated capital while they labored in the United States, first as braceros and now as illegal immigrants.

In contrast to merchant women, women in pieceworker and independent weaver households characterize the production process as a team effort with their husbands and children. They have major control over production decisions such as the allocation of household labor (particularly that of children), the timing of weaving production, the number of pieces to be produced, and the negotiation of selling prices with local merchants. In weaver households women have dominant or equal control over household money, which is in the same pot as any money needed to meet the costs of weaving production (Stephen 1991a).

Women in pieceworker and independent weaver households, however, face contradictory results from the commercialization of weaving. On the one hand, they have retained significant control over the production process and family finances. On the other hand, their households as a whole are not reaping the material benefits that merchant households are. The preceding analysis of women's roles in production decision-making therefore underscores the importance of examining the impact on gender of commercialization in conjunction with class and ethnicity.

THE POLITICAL ECONOMY OF ETHNICITY

By the mid-1980s, capital accumulation had certainly taken place in Teotitlán as well as in the communities of Santa Ana del Valle and San Miguel, although on a smaller scale. This underscores the importance of class as a major dimension in local power relations. At the same time, however, what also remains interesting about the case of Teotiteco textile production is the way in which the population has historically pushed for local-level control over weaving production and distribution. Asserting an ethnically-based claim over their weavings has been an important part of this process.

As early as the 1930s, municipal authorities avoided reporting production levels to the state, yet pushed state officials to provide them with a post office and to intervene internationally to stop supposed Japanese competition. In this process the factor of ethnicity was significant as it was used by municipal officials as a way of soliciting both empathy for poor Zapotec artisans and support for the cultural inheritance of Zapotec crafts. Today ethnicity is used by merchants in their negotiations with United States importers as a basis for maintaining their legitimacy as craft producers. It is also used to mediate the relations of production and reproduction in the economic, political, and ritual life of Teotitecos.

I have argued elsewhere that the weavers of Teotitlán, as well as other indigenous groups who are economically dependent on craft production, have created multidimensional ethnic identities (Stephen 1991a). One face of that identity is produced for the consumers of indigenous cultures such as tourists, importers, and foreigners who purchase indigenous crafts. Other dimensions are defined from within indigenous communities and are accessible only to those who are members of the community by virtue of their participation in networks and institutions which form the core of this identity. The internal dimensions of this identity are mediated by kinship, compadrazgo, and the relations of social reproduction and can be used to reinforce the relations of weaving production.

Zapotec manipulation of ethnicity, both to remake the relations of production between merchants and weavers into kinship and to maintain a strong unified economic position in relation to foreign importers, is a counterforce to the commoditized ethnic identity tied to handicrafts and *arte popular.* The following excerpt from an importer's brochure on the weavers of Teotitlán typifies this commoditized and romanticized identity attributed to Zapotec weavers.

Their 2000-year-old heritage is as deep and fertile as the Oaxacan Valley of southern Mexico where the Zapotec Indians have woven a culture from the fibers of their own strong roots dyed with influences from the Mayans, Aztecs, the colonial Spanish and more recently the "modern world" as it spins towards the 21st century.

The weavers of Teotitlán del Valle, while maintaining a traditional standard of design which distinguishes them as time-
honored artisans, have evolved their wool-weaving art,
adapting and absorbing ideas from other cultures through history. The Zapotec today, in weaving each piece, still use 100%
sheeps' wool and natural dyes derived from the plants and in-
sects of this rich region. The Spanish colonial floor loom was
introduced during the conquest of Mexico and has been
adapted and maintained as the machine of the predominantly
male craftsmen. . . .

While exporters provide ready definitions for consumers not only about
the weaving process and the producers, the community continues to define ethnicity for itself in different terms, often contested among the different sectors of the population. During the 1980s Teotiteco merchants
used their claim to Zapotec ethnicity as a basis for consolidating their control over exporting.

ZAPOTEC ETHNIC MERCHANTS AND AMERICAN
IMPORTERS: CLAIMING ETHNICITY

While a majority of sales in the 1970s were to tourists in Mexico and
Mexican nationals, as the spiraling devaluation of the peso took off in
1982, the market for Zapotec textiles began to shift to an export market
centered in the United States. After 1982, neither Mexican consumers
nor Mexican middlemen—who had been an important intermediary link
between Teotiteco merchants, tourists, and American importers—could
afford Zapotec textiles. The purchasing power of American dollars rose
dramatically in Mexico in the 1980s and encouraged more Americans to
go into exporting Mexican crafts. As a result of the continued devaluation
of the peso, importers saved significant amounts of money on internal
airfare, hotels, renting automobiles, and paying guides and interpreters.
Many Mexican middlemen interviewed stated that their profit margin
has been drastically reduced since 1982 and that they cannot compete
with Americans who come to buy crafts with dollars. As Teotitecos become increasingly aggressive about marketing to foreigners and having
their prices met, they are also unwilling to sell to Mexican merchants at
lower prices.

Currently, the bulk of textiles produced in the four-treadle-loom
weaving communities of the Oaxaca Valley are funneled through the

dominant marketing structure of Teotitlán to an ever-expanding group of American importers who distribute them to privately owned import stores, chain import stores, to interior decorators, and now to wholesale department stores. Today production includes highly priced original pieces, limited editions of codices and other reproductions, high-quality geometric designs, and mass-produced simple pieces produced primarily in the subordinate towns of San Miguel and Santa Ana (Stephen 1991b).

American merchants interviewed reported selling Zapotec textiles in the United States at between 250 to 600 percent of their purchase price. However, an examination of wholesale prices in Teotitlán and retail prices in American stores suggests that in the case of department stores, retail price is often as high as 1000 percent of wholesale price.[10] Profits for American importers are quite high considering that most do not spend more than about thirty-eight percent of the purchase price for taxes, shipping, broker's fees, and their travelling expenses to get the weavings to the retail market. In 1988, the United States had an 11 percent import tax on wool goods imported from Mexico. The Mexican government has an official 2 to 3 percent export tax.

Interviews also revealed that American importers who purchase weavings in a number of places around the Third World are cross-fertilizing designs and materials between ethnic groups in an effort to reach new market niches in the United States. Several importers commented that while Mexican rugs are cheaper than Navajo, Pakistani, and Afghan rugs in the United States market, Dhuri rugs produced in India of cotton/wool blends are cheaper and compete with Zapotec rugs at the lower end of the United States carpet market. These importers acknowledged that they have contracted Indian weavers to produce "Zapotec" rugs made of cotton and cotton/wool blends. Such rugs can be found in chains such as Pier One Imports across the United States. These same importers stated that they had tried in vain to get Teotitecos to produce Eastern designs so that more of their rugs could compete in the high-end oriental rug market. Teotitlán weavers would not produce many of the designs, stating their preference for Zapotec geometrics.[11]

The concerted effort Teotiteco merchants have made to control distribution within Mexico as well as their refusal (along with that of weavers) to produce Eastern designs are assertions of their ethnically-based claim to their own textiles. The importance of asserting Teotiteco ethnic identity vis-a-vis other Mexicans and Americans is clearly a struggle for economic control, but it also invokes the construction and defense of a particular ethnicity—that which lays claim to the rugs, blankets, pillow cases, and wall hangings which are now largely produced for American consumers. Relative to the profits that American importers make from their business dealings (from 300 percent and higher) the 20 to 40 percent profit rates made by Teotiteco merchants are of a smaller scale. While their use of an ethnic claim as Zapotecs from Teotitlán to hang onto their profits is far more beneficial to them than it is to weavers, by making strong claims and pushing for higher prices, they also insure that a larger amount of the money made in marketing the textiles flows into the community. A considerable amount of that money continues to be spent within the community, on fiestas as well as on community public works, because of continued pressures on merchants to spend it this way (See Stephen 1987, 1992).

The brand of ethnic identity which merchants use to try and maintain an upper hand in the negotiating process with American importers tends to project a kin-based community producing traditional crafts tied to a glorious past. This outwardly projected identity reflects some of the same stereotypical images that municipal authorities used in the 1930s to convince bureaucrats from the National Office of Statistics that they were all "humble Indians working at simple looms." When assertions of common ethnic identity are made within the community, however, the meaning of ethnicity tends to much more contested, particularly in conjunction with the relations of production. While merchants may use their kinship and compadrazgo ties to manipulate pieceworkers, weavers use the same relations to try and improve their wages and to get wealthy merchants to make donations to community projects. Within the community, the intersection of class differences with the potential ways in which a common ethnic identity should be expressed produces a lively discourse. As the reach of international capital moves into every household economy in the community and pushes forward socio-economic differentiation, the ways in which Teotiteco ethnicity is represented both internally and externally become increasingly complex.

The current practice of weavers from India producing "Zapotec" rugs illustrates a process whereby ethnic products can be cut apart from the specific cultural context in which they originate. Such a process clearly helps American importers to fill new market niches and potentially increase their profits through larger volume sales. While the "authentic" quality of the textiles may have been compromised, their handicraft identity and exotic nature have been maintained as they continue to be handmade by far away Third World laborers who use "traditional" technology.

The producers of internationalized ethnic crafts now exist in the same international division of labor which encompasses industrial production. While such producers have little or nothing to say about the dynamics of international craft production, local-level merchants, such as those in Teotitlán, may try to extend ethnically-based claims on their products to try and prevent further loss of control over a local craft. Their action is double-edged, however, working both in their own interests as petty capitalists and also anchoring some control of production and distribution within indigenous communities.

CONCLUSIONS

As the market for Zapotec textiles changed from Oaxaca and Chiapas to international tourist and export markets, key dimensions of weaving production and consumption were reconstituted in the face of larger political and economic forces and local efforts to maintain control over production. The preceding examination of this change alerts us to the complexities of craft production in an integrated world economic system. While artisanry is often discussed solely in terms of local production and consumption, the evolution of Zapotec weaving production shows us that the very emergence of handicrafts is linked to industrialization. Such industrialization can not only eliminate regional markets for locally produced use items such as the blankets of Teotitlán, but can simultaneously create another market based on the contrast between handmade and mechanically produced commodities.

As seen in the case of Teotitlán, as commodities were transformed into handicrafts and the economic base of the community changed from merchant to commercial capital, the relations of production, gender relations, and local ethnic identity were all affected. First, a broad merchant sector has emerged which articulates with American importers to control the marketing and distribution of textiles in Mexico and the United States. Within this sector women have been marginalized because they lacked the experience and education necessary for conducting business with Americans. Cultural gender roles which make them responsible for domestic labor and child raising continue to inhibit them from obtaining education and experience equal to that of men. Merchants have also used the idiom of kinship to reinforce the relations of production.

Second, the gendered division of labor has been altered and women have moved into the weaving force in significant numbers not only in Teotitlán, but also in surrounding communities such as Santa Ana and San Miguel. In most cases this has added to the number of hours which women must work in order to complete all of their daily chores. Thirdly, the local construction of Zapotec ethnicity has been shaped in opposition to the commoditized version of "Indian" culture promoted by the state and also in a defensive reaction to outsiders who might potentially appropriate economic control of textile production. Finally, at a larger level, the case of Zapotec textiles points out the importance of exploring not only the impact of national and international political and economic forces on craft production, but also examining the ways gender, class conflict, and the construction of ethnicity feed back into the larger economic system of which craft production is a part.

NOTES

1. Fieldwork was carried out in the communities of Teotitlán del Valle, Santa Ana del Valle, and to a limited extent in San Miguel from 1984–1986, again for two months in 1987, and in the summers of 1988 and 1990.

2. With the exception of the Triqui, Mixe, and Chatino, who all have extra-community levels of political organization, most indigenous ethnic groups in Oaxaca do not have a pan-ethnic identity. Community remains the primarily level of identity. See Barabas and Bartolomé 1986 and Dennis 1987 for more discussion of the topic.

3. See Stephen 1992 for a detailed description of how class and gender differences affect the representation of kinship in the community. For example, in ritual contexts, kinship is emphasized as a basis of solidarity, while in weaving relations of production kinship is often used as a way of securing and manipulating laborers. While women generally have less power than men in relations of production, they will use their class position and kinship relations to gain the upper hand in piecework arrangements.

4. It is unclear exactly when Macuilxóchitl dropped out of weaving and shifted into full-time subsistence production. Census data suggests it may have been shortly after the Mexican Revolution in the 1920s. Interestingly enough, a few households in the community have taken up weaving again for the booming tourist and export market.

5. The documents known as *Copiadores de Oficios* contain copies of all official correspondence received from the government and the community's response as written by municipal authorities. The archives of the Teotitlán have a complete set of this correspondence for all of the 1900s and before.

6. While the restructuring of local governments as "free" *municipios* was supposed to increased the autonomy of indigenous communities, in reality it severely limited their control over local political and economic decisions (See Stephen 1990, Greenberg 1990).

7. Teotitecos were adamant in their insistence that there were no factories in Teotitlán. While homes with more than several looms might have been considered factories by the state, they were never reported as such. Factories were required to pay taxes on their production. Textile manufacturers fought throughout the late 1920s and early 1930s to reduce federal taxes on production (Secretaría de la Economía Nacional 1934).

8. Absolute delineations are difficult because there are always some households which may be involved in reselling weavings while also engaging in piecework production for someone else. At a different point in time, the same household may be involved in independent production. Most households however, will self-categorize themselves as weavers, merchants, or independent weavers, given what they view as their primary economic activity. There is a clear and consistent dichotomy between general categories of merchants and weavers.

9. This figure came from a random stratified survey of 154 households carried out in 1986. That percentage is probably higher now as younger girls continue to enter weaving production as early as age ten or eleven.

10. Comparisons were made of prices charged for the same textiles by merchants in Teotitlán and those by Pier One Imports in Boston, Filene's Department Store in Boston, and Macy's in New York in 1989.

11. Teotiteco weavers have demonstrated an apt ability and willingness to produce Navajo designs, however. In 1989 while visiting the Hubble Trading Post in Ganado, Arizona, a well-known marketing outlet for Navajo rugs, I picked up a copy of a leaflet entitled "How to Distinguish a Mexican From a Real Navajo Rug." Weavers in the trading post were quite familiar with Zapotec textiles and resented the intrusion on their market and the "stealing" of their designs.

References Cited

Acuña, Rene, ed.
1984   *Relaciones Geográficas del Siglo XVI, Antequera.* Tomo Primero. Mexico City: Universidad National Autónoma de México, Instituto Investigaciones Antropológicas.

Archivo Municipal de Teotitlán del Valle
1931   *Copiador de Oficios,* 31 Agosto.

1932   *Copiador de Oficios,* No. 113, 17 de Febrero.

1938   *Copiador de Oficios,* Agosto.

1930–   *Copiadores de Oficios.*
1940

Barabas, Alicia, and Miguel Bartolomé
1986   La pluralidad desigual en Oaxaca. In *Ethnicidad y pluralismo cultural. La dinámica étnica en Oaxaca,* ed. A. Barabas and M. Bartolome, pp. 13–96. Mexico City: Instituto Nacional De Antropología e Historia.

Barlow, Robert H.
1949   The Extent of the Empire of the Culhua Mexica. *Ibero Americana* No. 28. Berkeley: University of California.

Benería, Lourdes and Martha Roldán
1987   *The Crossroads of Class and Gender: Industrial Homework and Subcontracting and Household Dynamics in Mexico City.* Chicago: University of Chicago Press.

Bourgois, Phillip
1988   Conjugated oppression: Class and ethnicity among Guaymi and Kuna banana workers. *American Ethnologist* 15(2):328–348.

Burgoa, Fray Francisco
[1674]   *Geográfica descripción.* 2 vols. Mexico City: Archivo General
1934   de la Nación. (First edition 1674.)

Clements, Helen
   1988   Buscando la Forma: Self-Reorganization in Craft Com-
            mercialization. Paper presented at the 46th International
            Congress of Americanists, Amsterdam, the Netherlands,
            July 4–8, 1988.

Cohen, Jeffrey
   1990   Markets, Museums, and Modes of Production: Economic
            Strategies in Two Zapotec Weaving Communities of Oax-
            aca, Mexico. *Newsletter of the Society for Economic Anthropol-
            ogy.* 1990, No. 2.

Cook, Scott and Leigh Binford
   1988   Industrial Commodity Production and Agriculture in the
            Oaxaca Valley. Paper presented at the 46th International
            Congress of Americanists, Amsterdam, The Netherlands,
            July 4–8, 1988.

Dennis, Philip
   1987   *Inter-Village Conflict in Oaxaca.* New Brunswick, NJ: Rut-
            gers University Press.

Departamento de la Estadística Nacional
   1925–   *Censo general de habitantes. 30 de Noviembre 1921.* Mexico
   28   City: Talleres Gráficos de la nación.

Dirección General de Estadística
   1897–   *Censo general de la república Mexicana verificado el 20 de oc-
   99   tubre de 1895.* Mexico City: Oficina de la Secretaría de
            fomento.

   1906   *Censo general de la república Mexicana verificado el 29 de Oc-
            tubre de 1900.* Mexico City: Secretaría de Fomento.

   1918–   *Tercer censo de población de los Estados Unidos Mexicanos ver-
   1920   ificado el 27 de octubre de 1910.* Mexico City: Secretaría de
            Hacienda, Departamento de fomento.

   1936   *Quinto censo de población, 15 de Mayo 1930.* Mexico City:
            Secretaría de la Economía Nacional.

1946   *Sexto censo de población. 1940.* Mexico City: Secretaría de In-
        dustria y Comercio.

1956   *Septimo censo de población. 1950.* Mexico City: Secretaría de
        Industria y Comercio.

1963   *Octavo censo general de población. 1960.* Mexico, D.F. Secre-
        taría de Industria y Comercio.

1973   *IX Censo general de población. 1970.* Mexico, D.F.: Secre-
        taría de Industria y Comercio.

García Canclini, Néstor
1982   *Las culturas populares en el capitalismo.* Mexico City: Edito-
        rial Nueva Imagen.

Gay, Jose Antonio
1881   *Historía de Oaxaca.* 2 volumes. Mexico City: Imprenta de
        Comercio Dublán y Cía.

Greenberg, James
1990   Sanctity and Resistance in Closed Corporate Indigenous
        Communities: Coffee Money, Violence, and Ritual
        Organization. In *Class, Politics, and Popular Religion in
        Mexico and Central America,* ed. L. Stephen and J. Dow,
        pp. 95–114. Washington D.C.: American Anthropological
        Association.

Hamilton, Nora
1982   The Limits of State Autonomy: Post-Revolutionary Mex-
        ico. Princeton: Princeton University Press.

Instituto Nacional de Estadística, Geografía e Informática
1983   *X Censo General de Poblacion y Vivienda, 1980.* Mexico,
        D.F.: Secretaría de Porgramacíon y Presupuesto.

1986   *La Industria Textile y del Vestido en Mexico 1976–1985 Mex-
        ico, D.F.: Secretaría de Programacíon y Presupuesto.*

Kiser, George and Martha Woody Kiser
1979   The Second Barcero Era (1942–1964), editors' introduc-
        tion in *Mexican Workers in the United States,* ed. G. Kiser

and M. Woody Kiser, pp. 1–9. Albuquerque: University of New Mexico Press.

LiPuma, Edward and Sara Keene Meltzoff
1989   "Toward a theory of culture and class: an Iberian example." *American Ethnologist* 16(2):313–334.

Marroquín, Alejandro D.
1977   *Balance del indigenismo: informe sobre la política indigenista en América.* Mexico City: Instituto Indigenista Interamericano.

Mercado García, Alfonso
1980   *Estructura y dinamismo del mercado de tecnología industrial en México.* Mexico City: Colegio de México.

Novelo, Victoria
1976   *Artesanías y capitalismo en México.* Mexico City: SEPINAH.

1988   Las Artesanías en México. Paper presented at the 46th International Congress of Americanists, Amsterdam, The Netherlands, July 4–8, 1988.

Novo, Salvador
1932   Nuestras artes populares. *Nuestro México* 1(5):56.

Padron General de Teotitlán del Valle
1868   Archivo Municipal, Teotitlán del Valle, Oaxaca.

1890   Archivo General del Estado, Oaxaca, Oaxaca

Roseberry, William
1989   *Anthropologies and Histories: Essays in Culture, History, and Political Economy.* New Brunswick: Rutgers Univesity Press.

Secretaría de la Economía Nacional
1934   *La industria textil en México: el problema obrero y los problemas economicos.* Mexico City: Talleres Gráficos de la Nación.

Sider, Gerald
    1986   *Culture and Class in Anthropology and History.* Cambridge, England: Cambridge University Press.

Stephen, Lynn
    1987   Economic Development and Community Control: The Zapotec Weavers of Oaxaca. *Cultural Survival Quarterly,* 11(1):46–48.

    1990   The Politics of Ritual: The Mexican State and Zapotec Autonomy, 1926–1989. In *Class, Politics, and Popular Religion in Mexico and Central America,* ed. Lynn Stephen and James Dow, pp. 43–62. Washington D.C.: American Anthropological Association.

    1991a   Culture as a Resource: Four Cases of Self-Managed Indigenous Craft Production. *Economic Development and Cultural Change* 40(1):101–130.

    1991b   Export Markets and Their Effects on Indigenous Craft Production. In *Textile Traditions of Mesoamerica and the Andes: An Anthology,* ed. Margot Blum Scheville, Janet Catherine Berlo, and Edward B. Dwyer, pp. 381–402. New York: Garland Publishing, Inc.

    1991c   *Zapotec Women.* Austin: University of Texas Press.

Varese, Stefano
    1988   Multi-ethnicity and Hegemonic Construction: Indian Projects and the Global Future. In *Ethnicities and Nations: Processes of Interethnic Relations in Latin America, South Asia, and the Pacific,* ed. Remo Guidieri, Francesco Pellizzi, and Stanley J. Tambiah, pp. 55–77. Austin: University of Texas Press.

Vargas-Barón, Emily
    1968   Development and Change of Rural Artisanry: Weaving Industries of the Oaxaca Valley, Mexico. Stanford University Ph.D. Dissertation.

Young, Kate

1976   The Social Setting of Migration. Ph.D. thesis, London University.

1978   Modes of appropriation and the sexual division of labour: a case study from Oaxaca, Mexico. In *Feminism and Materialism: Women and Modes of Production,* ed. Annette Kuhn and Ann Marie Wolpe, pp. 124–154. London: Routledge and Kegan Paul.

Santo Domingo Church
San Cristóbal de Las Casas
Drawing by Christine Eber

3

Craft Commodity Production, Market Diversity, and Differential Rewards in Mexican Capitalism Today

Scott Cook

In scholarly discourse, craft production is often associated with the idea of "natural economy" (i.e., a self-sufficient economy in which material production is exclusively for autoconsumption).[1] While it is undeniable that, from the beginnings of the Neolithic, village societies have mobilized domestic skilled labor to produce artifacts for their own use, it is their involvement in systematic production for exchange that is more important for appreciating peasant-artisans' unique role in economic history. It follows, then, that the real significance of craft production lies in its role in the development and functioning of commodity economy.

Indeed, it is their commodity status which makes craft artifacts a legitimate object of economic and anthropological inquiry. Among issues that require scholarly attention are: the diversity of production and exchange arrangements for craft commodities, the differential distribution of exchange value realized from transferring these commodities from producer to user, their manifold consumption destinations, and the differential structure and content of social demand for craft commodities. All of these issues may be addressed diachronically, synchronically, and comparatively, and have multiple implications for both economic and sociocultural inquiry.[2]

In the midst of a world market economy dominated by the sophisticated products of "high tech" machinofacture,[3] how can the production of and demand for "low tech" artisan commodities be explained? Clearly, the answer to this question is two-sided, involving both supply and demand, and complex since it involves multiple interactive factors on both sides. Focusing specifically on the case of Mexico today, a prominent factor on the supply side of craft commodities is the condition of peasant-artisan labor. Peasant-artisans, the rural carriers and creators of craft-focussed culture, are situated in relatively underdeveloped, socioeconomically differentiated agrarian communities. In such communities, peasant-artisan households produce crafts as a supplement or alternative to agriculture for satisfying their subsistence or capital-accumulation needs. Simply put, craft production in present-day capitalism serves peasant-artisans as a means for meeting their ubiquitous need for cash.

On the demand side, which is empirically and analytically understudied, craft commodities are consumed either because they are cheap and useful in a utilitarian sense, because of their symbolic representational or esthetic status (which may inflate their value in price terms and put them into the "luxury" category), or due to some combination of these. The sociocultural and class origins of the demand for craft commodities correspond closely with the function they serve for consumers (e.g., as utensils, status symbols, decorative art, souvenirs), with the scale and organization of their production, as well as with patterns of marketing and value distribution. One of the notable trends in the global capitalist market for craft commodities is that as their production increases, so does the proportion of their sales to tourists and middle- and upper-income urbanites. This trend represents a new role for small-scale, labor-intensive production within capitalism and provides one important explanation from the demand side for its persistence.

As alluded to above, an extraordinary quality of craft commodities in capitalism today is that the diversity within the structure of social demand for them is, to a significant degree, mirrored by the variegated nature of their production and exchange. This cannot be said of any other category of commodities simply because the diversity capitalist machinofactured commodities display on the demand side is countered by uniformity on the supply side; they are factory-produced or -assembled and, even if their production and/or assembly is externally subcontracted to small-scale, non-factory producers or assemblers, an overarching formal business firm typically manages the process. Craft commodities, on the other hand, may be consumed as decorative art by affluent urban connoisseurs or as necessary utensils by peasants. On the supply side they may be informally produced in independently managed household workshops or in petty capitalist putting-out systems and manufactories. Whereas machinofactured commodities are by and large mass-merchandised at fixed prices, craft commodities may be made to order and their exchange value is often determined by barter in kind or by haggling in money terms. Craft commodities, then, are artifactual anachronisms that seem out of place in a world of machinofactured commodities.

The irony is, of course, that craft production remains very much an essential feature in a world economy dominated by capitalist machinofacture. This is so, to repeat, because craft commodities are relatively cheap and/or because they are unique—embodying artisan labor rather than machine-driven labor and, thus, having a capacity to satisfy a special demand for the hand-made. It is precisely here that the contradictory nature of crafts in capitalism is most exposed—along the axes pitting practical economics against symbolism and esthetics, and the material interests of artisans against consumer interests (material and otherwise). In the remainder of this chapter I will provide some examples of these contradictions in craft production and marketing from my research in the Oaxaca Valley of Mexico.[4]

There is no better illustration of the market-driven nature of craft commodity production in the Oaxaca Valley than the contrast between the *petate* (palm mat) and *metate* (quern or grindstone) industries, and the treadle-loom weaving and brick industries. The latter two industries supply two different urban-based mass markets and essentially by-pass the periodic marketplace system, whereas the former two industries supply mostly rural markets and depend heavily on the periodic marketplace system.[5] Petates and metates are utilitarian commodities that are bought mostly by peasants for daily use in their households (metates for grinding corn and other foodstuffs, and petates for bedding or carpeting). In contrast, bricks are purchased primarily by building contractors or masons for residential or commercial construction in Oaxaca City, and the various kinds of wool, cotton, and acrylic woven products (e.g., sarapes, shawls, shirts, tapestries) are mostly bought by Mexican and foreign tourists or are exported.

The diversity of craft commodities, to repeat, is not only reflected in the social demand for them, but also in the ways in which they are marketed, in the social forms of their production, and, finally, in the patterns of value distribution deriving from their sale. Table 2 compares the four

Table 2. Comparisons of Selected Oaxaca Valley Craft Industries in Four Economic Categories

Craft Industry	Social Demand	Marketing Modes	Production Forms	Patterns of Value Distribution
Palm Plaiting	utilitarian peasants working class	some marketplace sale by plaiters mostly village-to-marketplace intermediaries; no export limited store credit	household production only no wage labor; merchant buyers do not extend cash advances to plaiters	low returns to direct producers; moderate returns to intermediaries
Metate Making	utilitarian and symbolic peasants working class and others with servants	same as above except many intermediaries finish products and give cash advances to metate makers	inter-household cooperation in quarrying but then independent household production no wage labor but sharing of raw stone cash advances and product finishing by buyers	low to moderate returns to direct producers moderate to good returns to intermediaries
Treadle-Loom Weaving (wool)	tourists (natl. & internatl.) export to urbanites utilitarian styles to peasants luxury lines	work-sales shops village-to-marketplace and -City intermediaries buy-up via credit for yarn many extra-marketplace sales	independent household production + work-shops with piece wage labor some putting-out satellitization of Santa Ana export by Teotitlán	moderate returns to direct producers moderate to high returns to intermediaries and employers high returns to original design weavers

Craft	Market	Marketing/Sales	Production Organization	Returns
Treadle-Loom Weaving (cotton)	tourists (natl. & internatl.) export to urbanites few luxury lines	merchant shops & intermediaries in Mitla craft market & town center also to Oaxaca City tourist shops and marketplaces	independent household production + workshops with piece-workers satellitization of Xaagá by Mitla	moderate returns to piece-rate and independent weavers low to moderate returns to female machine sewers low returns to female shawl-knotters
Backstrap-Loom Weaving	tourists (natl. & (internatl.) export to urbanites on-demand luxury work	weavers' co-op and others sell in village and town marketplaces village intermediaries to Oaxaca City export by co-op and intermediaries some special-order production	independent household production only no workshops or putting-out weavers' co-op has marketing role only	low to moderate return to weavers moderate to high return to intermediaries
Embroidery	tourists (natl. & (internatl.) varied product style and quality some luxury lines	merchant putters-out to wholesale export buyers village-to-city merchant sales to tourist shops & marketplace stalls some sales by independents	some independent production but putting-out system predominates	low returns to direct producers moderate to high returns to putting out merchants high returns to wholesale buyers
Brick Making	urban residential (multi-class) and commercial construction	some brickyard sales by non-intermediaries most sales by intermediaries to contractors or masons	some independent household production piece-work capitalism predominant	moderate returns to piece-workers moderate to high returns to employers and intermediaries

Oaxaca Valley craft industries mentioned above (plus embroidery and backstrap-loom weaving) in these four categories: social demand, marketing mode, production form, and value distribution.

A glance at the social demand category yields a threefold pattern between palm plaiting (petates) and metate making, whose products are consumed by local/regional peasant and urban working-class households (except metates that are used in middle- and upper-income urban households with servants); treadle-loom weaving (both branches), backstrap-loom weaving, and embroidery, whose products are consumed mostly by tourists and foreign urbanites (via export); and brick making, which supplies the urban construction market. Social demand for the first group of commodities has always been focussed on the same social classes (i.e., *las clases populares*—the peasantry and the working class), which is not surprising given the historical depth of their embeddedness in "traditional" popular culture. The persisting demand for metates—artifacts that have for some time been rendered quasi-obsolete by mechanical mills and machinofactured tortillas—is especially deserving of further study. It appears that the persistence of demand for metates may be as much a reflection of their symbolic role in defining female roles in the household division of labor as it is of their utilitarian role in food preparation (see Cook and Binford 1990:74–75).

With regard to marketing modes, once again palm plaiting and metate making share the same patterns; there is some direct sale by producers but the role of village-to-marketplace intermediaries predominates, with intermediaries controlling marketing in the entry marketplace and beyond (see Cook 1982:241–294). One difference between these two industries is that merchant-storekeepers are very important as buyers and resellers of palm products, whereas the intermediaries in the metate industry are not storekeepers and tend to be involved in metate production themselves, especially in finishing semi-finished products. Intermediaries in both industries tend to use cash advances to acquire products from direct producers—although the buyers in the palm industry also accept palm products in exchange for goods (i.e., indirect barter with money as a standard of value) or credit. Both industries depend heavily on the regional marketplace system to sell their commodities. They are also characterized by a long-term trend toward the predominance of intermediaries (and the diminution of direct producers) in extra-village marketing.

The marketing situation becomes much more complex in the other industries (treadle-loom and backstrap-loom weaving, embroidery, brick-making), again in correspondence with a more complex structure of social demand. With some exceptions (especially backstrap-loom weaving), commodities are alienated from direct producers at the production sites in these industries since, as shown in the "production forms" column, capitalist piecework relations of production prevail. Again the exception is backstrap-loom weaving, where independent household production and marketing predominate, although merchants (craft shop owners in Oaxaca City) and village-based intermediaries do intervene in marketing. Another unique feature of this industry is the relative importance of a marketing cooperative, as well as the existence of a weavers' marketplace in the principal weaving village (Santo Tomás Jalieza)—both of which are significant supports for the direct intervention in marketing by direct producers.

The marketing situation in treadle-loom weaving contrasts markedly with that in backstrap-loom weaving. The most marked difference is the prevalence of shop-based merchants and intermediaries with large inventories and the less prominent role of the weavers themselves in marketing. For those familiar with the Oaxaca Valley, the magnitude of this difference is illustrated by the difference between Santo Tomás Jalieza, the principal backstrap-loom weaving community, and Teotitlán del Valle or Mitla, the two principal sites of treadle-loom weaving. The shop-lined streets and marketplaces of these two communities—open to tourists every day of the week—and the inventories of woven goods in sales shops dwarf in scale the Santo Tomás marketing situation. The merchants and intermediaries of Teotitlán and Mitla—most of whom began their careers as weavers and some of whom still weave luxury pieces—are big-time players in Oaxaca's lucrative tourist economy. Although Santo Tomás, as the production leader in a multi-village industry, has developed some degree of cliental relations in marketing with producers in neighboring backstrap-weaving villages (e.g., San Jacinto Chilateca, Santo Domingo Jalieza), these do not approach the level of satellization that exists in the treadle-loom industry. As major tourist sites, Teotitlán del Valle and Mitla have established hegemony in the treadle-loom products market; their political-administrative control of the spaces where tourists congregate enables them to exclude competitors from other villages, and the wealth and commercial success of many of their merchants and intermediaries enables the latter to buy up or otherwise control (via putting-out or supplying raw materials on credit) the supply of woven goods originating in nearby villages. Thus, Santa Ana del Valle is, for all practical purposes, a weaving satellite of Teotitlán, just as Xaagá is of Mitla (see Cook and Binford 1990:87–99, 123–136).

This pattern of satellization exists on an even larger scale in the embroidery industry where hundreds of rural households—especially in villages in the district of Ocotlán—perform piecework for merchants and intermediaries based primarily in San Antonino del Castillo (see Waterbury 1989), San Juan Chilteca, Ocotlán de Morelos, or Oaxaca City (see Cook and Binford 1990:169–175, 201–202, 210–212). Unlike the weaving situation, however, embroidery goods are marketed almost exclusively through craft stores, shops, or marketplace stalls in Oaxaca City; both merchants and intermediaries also sell outside of Oaxaca (e.g., Mexico City, resorts, border), including export. Moreover, a large percentage of sales by local embroidery intermediaries is to wholesale export buyers from the United States, Europe, and elsewhere who periodically make buying trips to the principal putting-out centers (e.g., San Antonino—see Waterbury 1989:255). There is relatively little itinerant peddling of embroidered goods by either intermediaries or embroiderers, and only a small proportion of sales to consumers is made by the embroiderers themselves.

Although most bricks move from producers to consumers through intermediaries, there are typically fewer links in the chain than in weaving. In fact, if bricks are not sold by the brickyard operator directly to the consumer, there is apt to be only one intermediate link between the brickyard and the consumer. The intermediary may also be a brickyard owner but is always a hauler with one or more flatbed trucks who specializes in supplying bricks to building contractors. Sales by special order or prior contract tend to be more common in the brick industry than in the other petty industries studied. Sales in the marketplace system, on the other hand, are uncommon (see Cook 1984a:130–139 for more information on brick marketing).

With regard to production forms, the major difference is between industries organized strictly on a household basis with labor supplied exclusively by the household, and those organized on a capitalist basis with most labor hired for a wage (usually determined by piece rate). As shown in Table 1 the palm plaiting, metate making, and backstrap-loom weaving industries are characterized by household organization in which means of production are privately owned or accessed by the direct producers themselves. It should be noted, however, that in each of these industries village-to-marketplace intermediaries play a significant marketing role as buyers of craft commodities (see Cook and Binford 1990:190–198 on the role of intermediaries in petty commodity production).

By contrast, embroidery, brick making, and treadle-loom weaving provide arenas for the development of capitalist relations of production. Embroidery is predominantly organized on a putting-out (merchant-to-outworker) basis, whereas brick making is dominated by relations between brickyard proprietors (often worker-owners or, perhaps, trucker-intermediaries) and their pieceworkers. A given brickyard capitalist may own several brickyards. Treadle-loom weaving, on the other hand, is characterized by a mixed capitalist organization: weaver-proprietors may employ pieceworkers (men employed as loom operators or women as sewing machine operators) in a workshop alone or in tandem with piece-rate outworkers (usually women employed as sewing machine operators or as clothing finishers), and merchants (non-weavers) may employ piece-rate outworkers or may operate strictly as buyers on a credit basis with "independent" weavers.

Despite the concrete organizational differences, in a formal sense the common element among these industries is the piece-rate form of remuneration—a form historically associated with incipient small-scale capitalism (Cook 1984a:124–129, 191–203). The relative invisibility of petty capitalist organization in craft industries is a reflection of this piece-rate and/or putting-out form, which is easily mistaken for independent petty commodity production. Petty piecework capitalism simulates petty commodity production by allowing the direct producer to essentially be in charge of the labor process and, therefore, of the output that will determine his or her wage. It is precisely in these petty capitalist forms where the often-ignored transition from petty commodity production to capitalism has occurred through "endofamilial accumulation" (a process of capital accumulation nourished by the employment of unpaid family labor—see Cook 1984a:199–200 et passim; Cook and Binford 1990, esp. Ch. 4). When confronted with empirical evidence of this transition, dualistic and develomentalist discourse—which posits two separate economies in articulation, the "modern" capitalist and the "traditional" peasant-artisan, and views capitalist development as originating outside the peasant-artisan economy—comes to grief (Cook and Binford 1990: Ch. 1).

It can be argued that the most critical link in the process of craft commodity production and circulation, the link that is the most sensitive determinant of the reproductive rhythm or viability of the entire process, is the distribution of value among owners and/or managers, direct producers, intermediaries, and others who participate directly or indirectly in the process. The last columns in Tables 2 and 3 provide data that bear directly on this issue.

A perusal of the data presented in Table 3 discloses three patterns of striking disparity: (1) between the incomes of separate groups of direct producers; (2) between the incomes, both for direct producers and employer/intermediaries, in each industry; and (3) between the incomes of

Table 3.   Income Data for Craft Producers, Employers, and Intermediaries

| | Monthly Income in Dollars | | | |
	Direct Producers		Employers/Intermediaries*	Income Ratio
Industry	N		N	(EI/DP)
Embroidery	236	$ 4.00	30	$ 88.00	22/1
Palm Plaiting	97	$ 10.00	1 +	$ 30.00	3/1
Backstrap-Loom Weaving	76	$ 35.00	2	$321.00	9.2/1
Treadle-Loom Weaving	155	$ 70.00	5	$133.00	1.9/1
Brick Making	17	$287.00	7	$361.00	1.3/1

*Owing to the small sample, the income figures for Employers/Intermediaries are probably less reliable than those for direct producers. However, with regard to weaving and brick making, the small size of the sample is offset by the method of data collection (intensive case study); in backstrap-loom weaving, for example, budget data was collected daily for two months in one case and one month in the other. With regard to palm plaiting, the data was collected by observation for one week only but was corroborated by other observational data. Caution is also advised regarding the reliability of the income ratio as a central tendency due to the wide variability of income data between units in particular industries, over time, and so on.

All the values in both columns are medians for net income.

direct producers and of employers/intermediaries in each industry. At the outset, it must be noted that the first pattern of disparity not only reflects a difference between industries but also the differential remuneration of male and female artisans. The two low remuneration industries—embroidery and palm plaiting—are also predominantly female (93 percent and 98 percent respectively), whereas the two high remuneration industries—treadle-loom weaving and brick making—are predominantly male (96 percent and 95 percent respectively). Backstrap-loom weaving, which is a middle-income industry, has an essentially divided work force (56 percent male vs. 44 percent female). These data show, in short, that it is considerably more rewarding to be either an employer or an intermediary than it is a direct producer in Oaxaca Valley craft industries, and that it is more remunerative to be a male rather than a female direct producer.

Even though low remuneration of direct producers generates an expectation of high potential earnings (and capital accumulation) for employers/intermediaries, the 22/1 income ratio favoring intermediaries in the embroidery industry is shocking and dwarfs the ratio in the other industries. Nevertheless, an independent study of embroidery in the Oaxaca Valley suggests that the ratio presented in Table 3 is not unreasonable as a central tendency (see Waterbury 1989:252–254; cf. Cook 1982:64–65). My research has clearly identified embroidery as a rapid growth industry that has been among a select few to thrive on the tourist trade and wholesale export (Cook 1984b:27–28; Cook and Binford 1990:210–212; cf. Waterbury 1989). The fact that embroidery merchants have relatively low fixed-capital costs, in comparison with treadle-loom shop and brickyard operators, may also have a bearing on the high income ratio in this industry.

Also surprising is the relatively high ratio in backstrap-loom weaving together with the fact that the average monthly intermediary income was second in amount only to brick making. A similar set of factors to the embroidery case also operate here, namely, relatively low overhead (even lower than that for embroidery, where sewing machines are necessary for the garment assembly process) and strong tourist and export demand. (Probably a similar proportion of products from these two industries are sold in Oaxaca City.) This ratio also suggests that the producers' marketing cooperative in Santo Tomás Jalieza should be encountering more widespread support among weavers than it has heretofore enjoyed as a marketing alternative that can provide a higher proportional return to the weavers since it bypasses local intermediaries.

By contrast, the relatively low ratios in treadle-loom weaving and brick making are not surprising, first because of the relatively high fixed-capital and raw material costs in these two industries, and second, due to the relatively high cost of labor in both (but especially in the case of the brick industry). Not only is the labor in these two industries quite demanding physically and, therefore, suited to only a selected segment of the working-age population, but competition is keen among the enterprises in these industries. This has an inflationary impact on piece rates and a deflationary impact on commodity prices, thus producing a squeeze on profits.[6]

Tentative as they may be, these data on income distribution suggest that the industries experiencing the most pervasive extension of capitalist relations of production, namely, treadle-loom weaving and brick making, are the most likely to display the highest incomes in combination with the lowest employer/worker income ratios. This reflects, among other things, the higher capital costs, the stronger market position of labor, and the keen competition among enterprises in these industries.

What are some of the implications of the material presented above for class relations and social consciousness in the Oaxaca Valley? A report

(Silva 1980:24) on the results of a household survey in the important treadle-loom weaving community of Teotitlán del Valle made the following statement which succinctly expresses the relationship between craft activity and class relations in the Oaxaca Valley:

> In reality artisan activity is what defines the community in terms of social classes, as much for the relations that exist inside the commodity production process as for the relations between producers and intermediaries or, on the other hand, the relations that exist between producers who own capital and wage workers.

If this thesis is correct, and I think it is, there is no better testing ground for it in the rural Oaxaca Valley than treadle-loom weaving and brickmaking. As reviewed above, my research on these two industries has examined in detail the objective material conditions which give rise to and sustain relations of production between direct producers of commodities and "others" who supply critical means of production to direct producers or buy-up and market the commodities they produce.

These "others," may be owners of places of employment and the necessary means of production, as is the case with proprietors of weaving shops in Teotitlán and Xaagá or of brickyards in Santa Lucía, or they may be intermediaries who either put-out raw materials for finishing or buy-up finished products (usually in exchange for supplying raw materials, cash, or credit) as is the case with intermediaries operating in both the woolen products and the cotton products branches of the treadle-loom weaving/garment industry. Under both sets of conditions, value created by the labor of direct producers is appropriated by the "others" without compensation. The shop proprietor and putter-out accomplish this by paying a piece wage that is below the value of the labor embodied in the commodity produced (i.e., bricks, cotton cloth, wool blankets, shawls) and selling the commodity for a price which exceeds the wage bill (and other production costs); the intermediary appropriates value by charging high prices for raw materials supplied or high interest on cash advanced and/or paying low prices (i.e., lower than the market value and lower than the reproduction cost of the labor contained in them) for the commodities acquired.

Having laid out the objective material dimensions of these capitalist relations of production, in which value created by artisan labor ends up in the pockets of employers or intermediaries, it is now appropriate to address the question of the subjective and ideological ramifications of those objective dimensions. The social consciousness of artisans, as well as their social relations and the value created by their labor, is also affected by the division between workers who do not profit and profit-takers who operate enterprises. My purpose in this section is to put some ideological flesh on the bones of infrastructure, essentially by looking at how relations of production, which are part of people's daily experience, are represented ideologically and expressed in opinions and attitudes.

Teotitlán del Valle, because of its preeminence in weaving and the large size of its artisan population, was selected for asking an additional set of questions to each household surveyed, including five open-ended questions designed to elicit attitudes regarding the distribution of income and wealth. An average of one-third (range from 16.7 percent to 62.3 percent) of the answers to these questions specifically cited intermediaries or employers disapprovingly as appropriators of a disproportionate share of the income produced by the weaving industry. The question with the lowest percentage of such responses asked the respondents to explain why most artisans were poor. A typical charge of those who blamed intermediaries for artisan poverty was that they "didn't pay what products were worth" or that "they know how to take advantage of the artisans." According to 21.7 percent of the respondents to this question, artisan sloth or poor quality work was responsible for their poverty; 13.3 percent attributed poverty to the will of God or to bad luck; and 48.3 percent considered it to be a consequence of various structural conditions beyond their control (e.g., lack of sales opportunities, high cost of materials and cheap prices for their products, lack of capital or means of production, lack of education).

The question which elicited the highest incidence of anti-intermediary responses was one posing hypothetical situation in which a weaver sold a sarape to an intermediary who on the same day resold it for a substantial profit. Eighteen percent of the respondents viewed the transaction as exploitation and were of the opinion that the artisan was grossly underpaid, whereas another 16.4 percent agreed but argued further that the weaver had a right to a higher price because it was his labor, and not the intermediary's, that produced the sarape ("The weaver wove the sarape and his work ought to be better paid"). Those respondents who felt that the transaction did not reflect badly on the intermediary did so mostly on the grounds that the intermediary has a right to earn whatever profit he (or she) can in a given transaction.

The theme that the direct producer has the right to the whole value of what he or she produces (and sells) emerged in several answers to a question as to whether the respondents felt that they received what they deserved when they sold their products (see Cook 1984a:113–116). Two notable responses link an emphatic "no" to this question with the above-mentioned theme as well as with specific disapproval of intermediaries, as follows:

> 1. We receive very little of what our products are worth be-cause the intermediary receives a cut. Our work is worth more but the reseller receives the other part.
> 2. The persons who earn are the intermediaries who buy from us. When they don't pay us what our work is worth that is where they are exploiting us. Since we are the producers it is necessary for us to sell directly to clients, and that way we will obtain the total value of our work.

The fact that just over half of the respondents to this question indicated that they did earn from weaving what they were due is not surprising when it is pointed out that 55 percent were "self-employed" weavers who did not buy yarn on credit. In other words, this response is skewed toward the successful household enterprises in one of the Oaxaca Valley's most lucrative peasant-artisan industries.

The last of the five questions in this series is perhaps the most telling with regard to the extent to which the social consciousness of Teotitlán weavers reflects the class divisions of their population. When asked whether they believed that there were persons (or groups of persons) in their village who had more material advantages and privileges than oth-ers, 82.5 percent responded positively. In specifying the identity of these persons or groups, 28.1 percent mentioned intermediaries, whereas the remainder cited merchants (*comerciantes,* a category which includes inter-mediaries, store owners, and business operators in general) or those who had capital to invest (*"tienen algún capital para mover"*, literally, "they have capital to move"). Also emphasized in this response was that the persons in this category had more friends, more contacts, sharper wits (*"piensan mejor"*), or better language skills (*"hablan mejor"*). One of the most note-worthy responses that, not surprisingly, came from a weaver who lived in a rather remote *barrio* in this spectacularly sprawling community made reference to "the merchants along the principal streets because they have the advantage that the tourists arrive there."

As anyone who has visited Teotitlán periodically over the last twenty-five years can testify, the commercial development along its main street and in the vicinity of its square has been remarkable and presents tangible proof of the capitalist accumulation that is alluded to in this and other informants' statements.

Turning now to the case of another Oaxaca Valley weaving community, Xaagá located in Mitla's backyard, similar questions regarding social differentiation and wealth distribution were asked to a sub-sample of weavers who were interviewed as a follow-up to the household survey. In contrast to the much larger community of Teotitlán, where there is considerable socioeconomic differentiation, Xaagá informants appropriately downplay the socioeconomic differences between households and accentuate the differences between themselves and the Mitleños. Internal differences are admitted to exist with regard to ownership of means of production (number of looms, amount of land, number of cattle), occupation (weaver, peasant, agricultural laborer), work habits (some work more diligently or more competently than others), and household size. (Surprisingly enough, informants typically associate large households with more poverty, a pattern not supported by our survey data.) A representative statement was as follows:

> We don't all live equally but according to the means of each household. There are households with many family members and the poor head only works as a day laborer (*jornalero*).

With specific regard to the garment industry, there was only one informant, a full-time pieceworker, who even came close to characterizing differences among its personnel in class terms. In his words,

> The loom owners can earn more than us because without working they still get a week's income and what we get is a week of work—but not any profit. All those who have worked here, even though with one or two looms, seem to be progressing. I, working as [an employee], don't progress—I'm just always there.

The other informants characterized intra-industry differences strictly in terms of number of looms, level of earnings, work habits, and product pricing.

On the other hand, when it came to answering the question as to whether there were others who earned profits from their products, nine of thirteen informants pointed to the Mitla intermediaries; two pieceworkers cited their employers ("The profits stay with him. One is the propri-

etor and the other works."), but even one of them also mentioned the
Mitla merchants. One of the two largest workshop owners characterized
the Mitla *regatones* (intermediaries) in the same terms employed by his col-
leagues, stopping short of accusing the Mitleños of exploitation:

> Those people dedicate themselves to selling our products,
> whether in the beach resorts or in the homes of foreigners.
> Some of them export to foreign markets. They profit by buy-
> ing at one price and reselling at another. And they don't sell
> 100 pieces like we do but 1000. That is their advantage.

The posture of the Xaagá shop owners regarding the Mitleños is that of
neophytes to expert role models; they admire, and seek to emulate, the
material success of Mitla entrepreneurs even though it is at their own
expense.

In the case of the brick industry of Santa Lucía del Camino, a large
community on the fringes of the provincial capital, Oaxaca City, social relations are conducted through a split-level idiom. At one level, the focus
is on the assymetrical nature of relations between *patrones* (employers) and
mileros (pieceworkers), and their ongoing struggle over the distribution of
income from brick sales. At the other level, the assymetrical and conflicted
nature of their relations is downplayed; rather these are portrayed as being
conducted in a spirit of family and common interest—with the latter subject to harm from impersonal market forces and government meddling.

On the first level, the principal concern is over wages and prices—
not only the price of bricks but also, from the standpoint of the brickyard
operators, the prices of non-labor inputs (fuel for kiln firing, gasoline for
the trucks which haul bricks), and from the standpoint of the pieceworkers, the prices of wage goods (e.g., tortillas, bread, sugar, beans, clothing)
and basic services (e.g., transportation, medical care, etc.). Two statements, the first by a *milero* and the second by a *patron,* illustrate this level
of ideological expression:

> 1. The boss pays me cheap but he doesn't sell the bricks I
> make cheap. He sells them for double what he pays me. I am
> losing. The bosses pay us cheap and we go to buy in the city
> where prices are expensive—starting with corn, beans, cloth-
> ing—everything is expensive. Yet one works for the same
> piece rate.
> 2. The mileros are always on top of you. If they hear that
> you sold bricks for more than the going price they ask for a

fifty-peso raise. But they forget that sometimes sales are slug-gish. If that happens one sells below the going price in order to do business and to be able to pay the mileros. They never take reductions in the piece rate but only increases. But when I see that I have a big inventory of bricks on hand, I have to lower the price of bricks to sell so I can get money to pay my mileros.

The second level of ideological expression of brickyard social rela-tions is employer-centered and reflects their response to competition—for sales as well as for pieceworkers. The following statement by an employer exemplifies this level:

If the standard price of bricks goes up then one should raise the mileros' wage accordingly. But if by chance I sell a thou-sand bricks for 3000 pesos because the clients liked them and were willing to pay that price, well in that case I don't have to raise the mileros' piece rate. On the other hand, if there is a price increase in all the brickyards, of course, I have to raise the piece rate. One has to get along (*convivir*) with the mileros. One should treat them as members of one's own family and help them with their problems. That way they will be content, and will work quietly and do a good job.

This statement shows an employer's strategy for dealing with attrition among pieceworkers who are not easily replaced. The strategy includes treating employees as equals and allowing them to go about their work with as little direct supervision as possible, as well as making them loans or providing them with assistance in family crises. The mileros expect this kind of behavior from an employer but recognize that there are limits to its exercise. They also realize that it does not change the fundamental na-ture of the relationship between them and their employers. Consequently, they do not hesitate to take advantage of paternalism without allowing it to bind them permanently to one employer.

Underlying incidents of paternalism by brickyard owners to attempt to bind mileros to them, and of opportunism by mileros to obtain income from more than one employer, demonstrate a pragmatic ideology that rec-ognizes separate class divisions and interests. This ideology is most clearly expressed by mileros. It combines a "dichotomic conception" (Ossowski 1963: Ch.2) of community social structure (i.e., split into two strata de-fined as rich and poor) with a fundamental class division in the brick industry. As one milero expressed it, "The bosses earn, they have the wherewithal, while the poor worker gets only his wage. The bosses own the brickyards. They are the ones who really earn." Although only a minority of informants in our interview sample considered the Santa Lucía population to be divided along role lines in the production process, income, and standard of living, all who did so were mileros. This bedrock class ideology has not led to cross-brickyard worker organization, however, and its political implications are contradictory to the extent that they are understood (see Cook 1984a:139–148, 162–167; 1984b:72–77).

It is clear that while participation in privatized market-driven commodity production does generate class differentiation, a majority of those who participate in it (at least in the Oaxaca Valley) may be disgruntled about the material conditions and results of their performance, but not to the point of raising doubts about the legitimacy of the system. Most of their discontent is focussed upon perceived obstacles (e.g., corrupt politicians or government functionaries, lack of credit, lack of market information, price gouging in raw materials markets, inability to determine or adjust commodity prices) to more rewarding participation rather than inequities in the reward structure. Those who would see petty producers as a potential force for radical social change should note that petty commodity production promotes the belief that hard work and enterprise are the keys to material progress and upward mobility. To the extent that a few petty enterprises in particular branches of craft commodity production cross the capitalist threshold, they serve as examples of business success to others and, therefore, reinforce the aforementioned petty bourgeois credo. This demonstration effect operates in the embroidery, treadle-loom weaving, and brickmaking industries (among others) in the Oaxaca Valley; it illustrates the mutually reinforcing nature of the relationship between petty commodity, mercantile, and capitalist forms of industry and trade (Cook and Binford 1990:230).

RECAPITULATION AND CONCLUSIONS

This article has attempted to demonstrate that by starting with the differentiated demand for craft commodities we will inevitably be led to a corresponding differentiation of supply, and that this will, in turn, lead to unevenness in the distribution of value—a process that is, perhaps, the crucial determinant of the viability of production itself. Unfortunately, the sources and structure of social demand—and the entire question of craft commodity consumption—are poorly researched. What passes currently for analysis of these issues is mostly anecdotal, impressionistic, or speculative and has little systematic empirical basis—though in some cases authors compensate for this lack of data with thoughtfulness, imaginativeness, and sophistication (e.g., Novelo 1976:233–242; García Canclini 1982). My statement that the persisting demand for craft commodities in a global capitalist system dominated by machinofacture is a function of the crafts' cheapness or uniqueness is a distillation of scholarly opinion on the topic. To my knowledge, however, theoretically informed, analytically sophisticated, and comprehensive studies of craft commodity consumption designed to analyze past and present sociocultural and economic sources of consumer motivations, attitudes, and tastes have not yet been undertaken.

Considerable documentation shows the importance of tourism in stimulating the production of craft commodities, although once again our knowledge about why tourists buy crafts does not go much beyond the notion of "souvenir." By contrast, we have a plethora of detailed studies on the supply side of the tourist market—including products ranging from hammocks (Littlefield 1976) and embroidery (Waterbury 1989) to bark-paper paintings (Good Eshelman 1988) and silver jewelry (Stromberg 1985), to cite but a few. There is also a great deal of documentation, in these and a host of other studies, of a linkage between a tourist demand for craft commodities and the exploitation of artisans by petty capitalist workshop operators, putting-out merchants, or buyers. Some studies have also pointed out the positive impact of tourist markets on the livelihood of artisans and intermediaries (e.g., Good Eshelman 1988; Cook 1988; Ehlers 1989).

Craft commodity production, or—more broadly—skilled, labor-intensive forms of industrial commodity production, is part and parcel of the wider commodity economy (which happens to be dominated by capitalist relations), not a remnant from a precapitalist epoch or an element in a separate and subsumed peasant- or petty-commodity economy with its own logic. This is supported by research on the production and exchange of craft commodities. The research record also demonstrates that the need for cash operates as a pervasive material incentive for craft commodity producers regardless of whether they are self-employed or employees. A significant proportion of producers' income is spent on wage or producer's goods of capitalist origin—thus comprising part of the social demand necessary for the expanded reproduction of capital. On the other hand, craft commodities themselves satisfy a special demand within the capitalist economy that either cannot be satisfied through machinofacture or capital-intensive production processes (e.g., for handicrafts imbued with particular symbolic or esthetic content), or cannot be satisfied at prices competitive with those at which petty producers sell (thus rendering such markets unprofitable for capital-intensive enterprises). In short, craft commodity production is thoroughly integrated into the circuitry of the present-day world capitalist market economy.

NOTES

1. An example from Mexican studies of identifying craft production with natural economy or autoconsumption and, thus, ignoring its precapitalist commodity status is found in García Canclini's otherwise imaginative and stimulating book, where he characterizes the "traditional function of handicrafts" as "supplying objects for autoconsumption in indigenous communities" (1982:90; cf. p. 145).

2. "Crafts" are artifacts produced through labor processes of low organic composition of capital (i.e., low proportion of capital to labor.) While many classifications of artifacts produced by artisans can be posited—with criteria such as type of raw material, use value status, and so on—the labor that creates these artifacts, regardless of their class or type, is more or less skilled and selectively recruited. Artisan labor is specialized and special, and depends upon unmechanized technology. The relations of craft production are not restricted exclusively to family/household units or domestic groups; they may also be wage-based relations. Craft commodities, therefore, may be produced in independent households, in dependent outworker households, or in petty capitalist workshops (cf. Novelo 1976:241–242). Keith Hart has succinctly defined a commodity as "human labor embodied in a good or service offered to society rather than consumed directly by its producer" (1982:40; cf. Cook 1976:396; Engels 1967:897). There is general agreement among students of economic evolution that commodity production appeared prior to petty commodity production (i.e., private household production for market sale) which, in turn, preceded but is subsequently subordinated to capitalist production (Godelier 1968; Mandel 1970; Friedmann 1980; Scott 1986). Petty commodity producers, as joint owners/workers in household based enterprises, combine characteristics of capitalists and wage laborers in a single contradictory social location (Gibbon and Neocosmos 1985; Bernstein 1988).

3. "Machinofacture" is a term introduced by Karl Marx in *Capital* (Volume 1) to refer to capital-intensive, machine-driven, large-scale modern factory industry. It is used effectively by Marx in contradistinction to

"manufacture" that denotes a labor-intensive, small-scale type of industry employing hand tools rather than machines (see Bottomore, T., et.al., 1983: 296–8).

4. Field work and data analysis in the Oaxaca Valley was conducted in 1977 with a grant from the Social Science Research Council, and between 1978 and 1983 with funding provided by the National Science Foundation; field work in November 1985 was supported by the University of Connecticut Research Foundation. All told, survey data were collected from 1008 households in 23 communities in three districts: Ocotlán, Centro, and Tlacolula. For a more detailed description of this research, see Cook and Binford 1990:243–249.

5. The Central Valley region of Oaxaca has a seven-day periodic marketplace or *plaza* system in which district head towns (*cabeceras*) host a large market once a week, drawing participants from villages in the district and beyond, on a designated day. The system also includes several satellite markets in smaller communities. Further information about this system may be found in Malinowski and de la Fuente 1982, Beals 1975, and Cook and Diskin, eds., 1976.

6. It should be noted that the figures for treadle-loom employers are from the cotton products branch of the industry in Xaagá, which is a satellite of the more affluent commercial center, Mitla. I believe the income ratio would be substantially higher if it included a sample of Mitla merchants/intermediaries. The same would also hold if a sample of Teotitlán del Valle merchant-weavers/intermediaries in the wool products branch of treadle-loom weaving were included.

References Cited

Beals, R.
    1975   *The Peasant Marketing System of Oaxaca, Mexico*, Berkeley and Los Angeles: University of California Press.

Bernstein, H.
    1988   Capitalism and petty-bourgeois production: class relations and division of labour. *Journal of Peasant Studies* 15 (2):258–271.

Bottomore, T., et. al.
  1983   *A Dictionary of Marxist Thought.* Cambridge: Harvard
          University Press.

Cooks, S.
  1976   Value, price, and simple commodity production: the case
          of the Zapotec stoneworkers. *Journal of Peasant Studies*
          3(4):395–427.

  1977   Beyond the *Formen:* towards a revised Marxist theory of
          precapitalist formations and the transition to capitalism.
          Journal of Peasant Studies 4(4):360–389.

  1982   *Zapotec Stoneworkers.* Lanham, Md.: University Press of
          America.

  1984a   *Peasant Capitalist Industry.* Lanham, Md.: University Press
          of America.

  1984b   Peasant economy, rural industry, and capitalist develop-
          ment in the Oaxaca valley, Mexico. *Journal of Peasant Stud-
          ies* 12(1):3–40.

  1988   Inflation and Rural Livelihood in a Mexican Province: an
          exploratory analysis. *Mexican Studies/Estudios Mexicanos*
          4(1):55–77.

Cook, S. and L. Binford
  1986   Petty commodity production, capital accumulation, and
          peasant differentiation: Lenin vs. Chayanov in rural Mex-
          ico. *Review of Radical Political Economics* 18(4):1–31.

  1990   *Obliging Need: Rural Petty Industry in Mexican Capitalism.*
          Austin: University of Texas Press.

Cook, S. and M. Diskin, eds.
  1976   *Markets in Oaxaca.* Austin: University of Texas Press.

Deere, C. and A. de Janvry
  1979   A conceptual framework for the empirical analysis of
          peasants. *American Journal of Agricultural Economics* 61:
          601–611.

Ehlers, Tracy Bachrach
1989   *Silent Looms.* Denver, Colo: Westview Press.

Engels, F.
1967   "Supplement to Capital, Volume Three." In K. Marx, *Capital,* Vol. 3, pp. 889–910. New York: International Publishers.

Friedmann, H.
1980   Household production and the national economy: concepts for the analysis of agrarian formations. *Journal of Peasant Studies* 7(2):158–184.

Fröebel, F. et. al.
1978   The new international division of labour. *Social Science Information* 17(1):123–142.

1980   *The New International Division of Labour.* Cambridge: Cambridge University Press.

García Canclini, N.
1982   *Las culturas populares en el capitalismo.* México, D.F.: Editorial Nueva Imagen.

Gibbon, P. and M. Neocosmos
1985   Some problems in the political economy of "African socialism." In H. Bernstein and B. Campbell, eds., *Contradictions of Accumulation in Africa,* pp. 153–206. Beverly Hills, Calif.: Sage Publications.

Godelier, M.
1968   *Las Sociedades Primitivas y el Nacimiento de las Sociedades de Clases segun Marx y Engels.* Medellin, Colombia: Editorial La Oveja Negra.

Good Eshelman, C.
1988   *Haciendo La Lucha.* México, D.F.: Fondo de Cultura Economica.

Hart, K.
1982   On commoditization. In *From Craft to Industry,* E. Goody, ed., pp. 38–49, Cambridge: Cambridge University Press.

Hobsbawm, E.
   1965   Introduction. In *Pre-Capitalist Economic Formations*. Karl
             Marx, New York: International Publishers.

Littlefield, A.
   1976   *La industria de las hamacas en Yucatan, México*. México,
             D.F.: SEP-INI.

Malinowski, B. and J. de la Fuente
   1982   *The Economics of a Mexican Market System*. London: Rout-
             ledge and Kegan Paul.

Mandel, E.
   1970   *Marxist Economic Theory*, Vol. 1. New York: Monthly
             Review.

Marx, K.
   1967   *Capital*, Vol. 1. New York: International Publishers.

Nash, J. and M. Fernandez-Kelly, eds.
   1983   *Women, Men, and the International Division of Labor*. Al-
             bany: SUNY Press.

Novelo, V.
   1976   *Artesanías y capitalismo en México*. México, D.F.: SEP-
             INAH.

Ossowski, S.
   1963   *Class Structure in the Social Consciousness*. New York: Free
             Press.

Portes, A.
   1983   The informal sector: definition, controversy, and relations
             to national development. *Review* VII (1):151–174.

Schmitz, H.
   1982   *Manufacturing in the Backyard*. London: F. Pinter.

Schneider, J. and A. Weiner, eds.
   1989   *Cloth and Human Experience*. Washington, D.C.: Smithso-
             nian Institution Press.

Scott, Alison M.
  1986   Rethinking petty commodity production. *Social Analysis* 20:93–105.

Silva, G.
  1980   *Examen de una Economía en Oaxaca, Estudio de Caso: Teotitlán del Valle.* Estudios de Antropología e Historia 21, INAH Centro Regional de Oaxaca.

Stromberg, G.
  1985   *El Juego Del Coyote: Platería y Arte En Taxco.* México, D.F.: Fondo De Cultura Económica.

Waterbury, R.
  1989   Embroidery for Tourists. In *Cloth and Human Experience,* Schneider and Weiner, eds., pp. 243–271. Washington, D.C.: Smithsonian Institution Press.

Drawing by Christine Eber

4

Coyotes *and Culture Brokers: The Production and Marketing of Taxco Silverwork*

Gobi Stromberg-Pellizzi

The popular arts of the Third World are being catapulted into metropolitan centers through a vast network of commercial and cultural avenues. The New York public experienced a wave of exhibits and events related to Mexican art that began with a number of shows on the Maya during the mid-1980s, before swelling to the over 260 cultural events that accompanied the blockbuster, "Thirty Centuries of Splendor" at the Metropolitan Museum in the fall of 1990.[1] The conference and exhibit of Highland Maya craft production at the City University of New York Graduate Center, which generated some of the articles in this book and was among the first of events, addressed recent developments in arts and crafts production within the world context, rather than the exclusively ethnographic one. As participants in a conference tracing the recent changes in art objects, we found ourselves strategically situated in New York to discuss changes stemming from the exhibition and sale of the objects that we study.

The reception of these artforms, in places like New York, is conditioned by the practices engaged in by the various types of intermediaries. In Mexico, intermediaries are known as *coyotes,* because of the power they hold over the producers. Their counterparts in the United States might be found among wholesalers, dealers, retailers, or even individuals in museums and corporations that patronize the arts and artisan production. Both the clientel and the marketing strategies can have a decisive effect on production. This is especially the case when the profit motive prevails, to the detriment of other considerations, and aspects such as quality in design and execution suffer accordingly. Furthermore, the negative effects often surpass the immediate deleterious consequences, reaching far into the entire structure of production.

At another level, the dialogue, or relationship, between the producers and the consumers of arts and crafts is charted by forces that extend beyond the intermediaries, encompassing the larger economic and political realities. Thus, the constellation of events in New York highlighting Mexican art could be seen as a surge of interest that accompanies recent changes in trade and migration policies. While the artisan conference and other events reflect the growing need to address changes in Third World culture and art traditions, these changes must also be analyzed in terms of their meaning and significance for Western consumers. As both participants in this conference and ethnographers, our role is, ideally, to bridge the two worlds; the one in which the art originates and the one in which it is viewed and consumed. We do, of course, formulate our observations and interpretations within a framework and a language that reflects the changing perspectives within our own society. Likewise, the cultural, political, and economic forces that shape our perceptions are also active in the formation of our society's aesthetic expression and taste. Therefore, when we allude to the changes in non-Western arts that stem from their reception and consumption, we are aware that they do not take place within a closed system, separate from the processes prevailing in Western contemporary art itself. These arts are even affected, no doubt, by our ethnographic formulations, which, for example, may be transmitted into the shared pool of attitudes that find expression in the marketplace.

The interpretation of the exchanges that I have mentioned so far also involves a more specific task: the examination of the exchange itself. In this essay, I will trace the objects' course from the context of production to the Western public (via markets, museums, etc.) and back again to their creators. It is the complex relationship between the conditions of the origins, production and marketing that affects, and often determines, the nature of what emerges from these encounters.

In what follows, after having mentioned a few pertinent aspects of non-Western art production and consumption, as they appear from the perspective of New York, rather than from "the field," I will discuss a specific case, that of the Taxco silver industry, which will help illustrate the complexities of the market, particularly as it interacts with the processes of production.

While for "us" as the First World consumers an important aspect of these popular art forms lies in the understanding gained from such a confrontation with exotic artistic expressions. For the producers the meaning could be quite different: the artistic production of non-Western societies is not only an individual, but also a tradition-bound activity. As bearers of a distinct culture, the artisans find a means of expressing their ethnic identity. Through the exchange of their production, the individual creators, along with their society, enter into a dialogue with the rest of the world from which both sides emerge affected, if not transformed, in a process that is manifested aesthetically.

In social and political terms, we could say that the artisan conference indicated the renewed interest in and relevance of "traditional," "primitive" and "popular" art to Western society. Within this context, the role of the national governments in promoting the production and the export of the popular arts and crafts can, and often does have a widespread impact upon the course that the artform takes. Over the years we have seen a multitude of permutations as these arts have entered new arenas with greater and expanded consumption. During the past few decades they have also begun to appear in settings where they would not have been previously found. Expanding beyond the prior association of some genres with the souvenir, ethnic, curio type of marketing, they have penetrated a wider and more sophisticated market, as well as appearing in museums and art galleries, and in some cases even being exhibited as "contemporary art." The case of Taxco silver jewelry production illustrates the fact that this process is far from random, and that what might be dismissed as the whims of the market, are determined by the interaction of specific spheres of craft production and marketing.

THE TAXCO SILVER INDUSTRY[2]

The issues that have emerged as Western society and traditional cultures interact within the international marketplace are complex, particularly for the artisan communities. The Taxco silver industry illustrates the transformation from incipient traditional craft production into an internationally prominent industry. I will examine the complexity of this process on the basis of some of the findings of my fieldwork. I began to study the role of design innovation and technique within the framework of the interactions between production, marketing, and consumption in Taxco, Guerrero, from 1972 to 1974, and resumed this research again in 1979.

Because of its recent origin and the magnitude and complexity of its development, the silver industry provides an opportunity to examine the interaction among consumer tastes, marketing demands (including price and volume), and the constraints in production that generate the various alternatives available to the artisan. Design and design innovation play a crucial role in this context.

The Dynamics of the Market

The extent to which certain elements are pursued by the West has, needless to say, a determining influence on the course that particular art objects take as they come into the sphere of the Western markets. For example, the vehemence with which Westerners have rejected the polished look of industrial production in different periods has been rapidly met with an expedient production of rustic, exotic, and almost archaic-looking objects. In the case of the Taxco silver industry, this reaction dealt an almost devastating blow to a large and complex industry that had for decades been producing sophisticated jewelry that was well executed, both aesthetically and technically. Nonetheless, this industry had the resilience to produce an ethnic and a "Mexican" line that had enough appeal to the tastes of its "jaded" capitalist consumers.

Since the bulk of arts and the crafts that make their way into the Western marketplace are so dramatically affected by extrinsic forces, the consumers' tastes, and the producers' visions and creative impulses have been almost incidental. These forces refer to the complex nature of marketing considerations (beyond those of profit, competition, large volumes and large-scale appeal, logistics, etc.) as well as the interplay among complex chains or networks of individuals and institutions that are affecting—sometimes in a determinant fashion—the course that the product will take. In certain instances, the government and/or other intermediaries can take some of the prevailing prejudices (if one can refer to some types of aesthetic preferences in this way) so much to heart that by the excessive promotion of the most mediocre forms of expression or production, they risk or sometimes even succeed in squelching variety, spontaneity, and innovative or experimental occurrences.

In my research on the Taxco silver industry, I developed a method of analyzing the relationship and dynamic of design innovation, the market, and the organization of production in a fairly large sample of up to 200 workshops. It soon became clear that both the design and the expressive attributes of the medium functioned independently from the processes of its production and commerce. The analysis of these processes in the industrial context allows us to discern all the conditions that propel craft production toward its maximum technical and creative expression and, in the opposite case, those that suffocate it.

Background and History

In the 1930s the virtually insignificant silversmithing activity of a small mining village was radically catapulted into prominence. Its position is due not only to the magnitude of its productivity (10,000 silversmiths transform up to four tons of silver into jewelry and ornamental objects each month), but also to its achievements in jewelry design, technical innovations and excellence, the artistic quality intrinsic to the work, and the multiplicity of markets where it is destined.

The silver commerce is carried out through a wide variety of settings, ranging from the 420 silver shops in Taxco and countless small stalls of silver that stand in the plazas, markets, and streets of cities and towns throughout the country, to the large department stores and the prestigious jewelry shops, including Tiffany's and Cartier.

Taxco silversmithing can (and perhaps should) be distinguished from other handicraft traditions in that since its origins, it has focused on international markets. Its vast repertoire of designs is constantly renewed by a continuous generation of designs, formats, and techniques that have superseded the "traditional" format to include elements of modern abstract, pre-Hispanic, and "popular" art. This variety of styles has provided the Taxco smiths with a wide market that covers a broad range of consumer tastes in jewelry.

With the revitalization of a small silver industry came a new "tradition." Catalyzed by a certain entrepreneurial "know-how" as well as by the often-crucial ingredient of intense or passionate personal involvement, when American architect and designer from Louisiana, William Spratling initiated the first silver workshop, "Las Delicias." Modeled on a small factory, hierarchical in organization (though within a style replete with feudal-type elements), Don Guillermo, as he was called, encouraged the growth of a solid generation of highly trained silversmiths, some of whom were themselves able and astute entrepreneurs, and others who were very talented artists and designers. A number of these men were to supersede his own efforts.

Figure 12. A large-scale taller *can sustain a polishing department. (Photograph by Gobi Stromberg-Pellizzi).*

Among the outstanding Spratling and Coco disciples were Antonio Castillo, Antonio Pineda, Jorge "Chato" Castillo, Sigi Pineda, Salvador Teran, Enrique Ledesma, and Hector Aguilar. Together with an ever-growing community of smiths they forged a climate of unbridled experimentation in design and technique. They experienced a phenomenal rate of growth for several decades that brought with it success and international fame. By the late 1940s, Antonio Castillo had over 300 silversmiths and workers in his employ, producing over one ton of jewelry on a monthly basis. By the late 1950s, though, this situation came to a halt, and after a series of cataclysmic declines and ruptures, an entirely new structure began to emerge.

Although the large-scale production units, known as the talleres grandes ("large workshops" which were really more like factories), had a notable capacity for growth, they lacked certain elements, which appear in their more "modern" capitalist counterparts. When the boom in demand for silver jewelry and flatware began to wane in Europe, the talleres were virtually unable to address the new conditions of labor and work out the needed arrangements with the newly forming unions. The strength of the large-scale talleres was essentially undermined not as much by the unions as by the new group of entrepreneurs, intermediaries (a loosely emergent

Figure 13. Silversmiths specialize and achieve mastery in an array of techniques. (Photograph by Gobi Stromberg-Pellizzi).

form of a merchant-like class) that began to contract individual smiths on a putting-out or piecework basis.

At the time when production was down, the intermediaries, known locally as "coyotes," would purchase individual silversmiths' production outside of the taller, from their home-based workshops. At this time, many silversmiths began to follow the few who had already started "moonlighting" by setting up small, somewhat makeshift operations at home, often selling the same lines of jewelry that they made at the taller.

Soon, the market was being supplied with ever-increasing volumes of cheaper, more light-weight and less well-executed production. The potential for greater profit margins made this venture highly appealing to many, and soon the large established talleres, already in financial straits, began to slide into bankruptcy as they saw their formerly "exclusive" lines of silver undergo the process of malbaratada whereby the pieces are cheapened (figuratively, in quality or literally, "badly cheapened") through imitation and the use of poorer workmanship and materials. As this process spread, the family talleres were popping up everywhere, providing endless volumes of increasingly cheapened production, though still with vestiges of Taxco distinctiveness. The situation of the large talleres was further

Figure 14. Master polishers give the final touches to the finished pieces. (Photograph by Gobi Stromberg-Pellizzi).

aggravated by government policies, especially regarding exports (particularly silver), and its laws applying to less industrial types of production (taxation and worker benefits payments and the ensuing sanctions).

Design

The aesthetic and plastic development of the industry was early on characterized by an intense and pervasive level of experimentation, unique and varied individual approaches to design, and the emergence of an appealing and refined "Taxco" style. The artistic and creative dimension of silver production changed dramatically, as both the manifestation and the result of the structural changes that began to take place within the industry, particularly in the spheres of production and marketing. When the structure of the large factory units eroded, giving way to production in family shops, design innovation took on a different character, one that can be considered "innovative creativity." Even though there are still different levels of design creation, it generally consists more in the ordering and readjustment of the already existing design elements. It is no longer a creative act that gives origin not only to new forms, but to new concepts of form.

Figure 15. A silversmith cuts out an intricate design that will be filled in with feathers and covered with resin. (Photograph by Gobi Stromberg-Pellizzi).

This change in creative orientation increased with the growing shift in the control of production, first out of the talleres grandes and then as the intermediaries strengthened their position vis-a-vis the silversmiths. This situation, in turn, exercised a highly restrictive influence on production and markets, shifting the industry toward massive production of standardized pieces. The designers, subject not only to the whims of the market, but also to contraction in production, could no longer continue with the experimentation that had contributed to the notable expansion and development of the previous years. What were the reasons for these changes? I shall consider the question in relation to changes in production and sales.

Most craft and artisan production takes place on an individual basis, within the household unit. In the case of Taxco, production has been characterized by a more complex situation. Two levels of plastic expression in Taxco are accompanied by two different structures in production: that of the "large workshop" and the subsequent "family workshop." Once the basic means of production, which include the worktable, the tools, and the elementary techniques of silversmithing, are acquired, the silversmiths or the workshop must have a line, a design or group of designs, plus a client. The silversmith may use a design learned in the workshop where he began to work, the wholesaler may provide him with the designs, or the craftsman may develop them by himself. However, a silversmith's or workshop's possibilities for selling will be good only as long as no other silversmith or workshop produces those same designs at a lower price.

The contrast between these two large and the family workshops indicates the dialectical relation between production and design. Within the more recent context of the family workshop, we can see the processes and dynamics that have imposed serious restrictions on the conditions of production and creative expression. In the market, designs are subject to the competitive aspects of innovation. When a market is oriented to volume production, the fact that a design is produced simultaneously in many workshops is of little importance. The wholesalers simply buy the pieces from the silversmith or the workshop that is able to produce them at the lowest price.

The "name" or brand of the designer or workshop is not an issue for these wholesalers. Even though the elements of design and technique are taken into consideration in the sales transaction, price inevitably remains the determining factor. In this context, it is not surprising that the accelerated competition for clients among small scale producers also gave rise to an acceleration in the copying of designs.

The ease with which the silver market accepts duplication of a piece at a lower price, without considering the quality of execution and design, intensifies competition. This is why the less innovative silversmiths devote themselves mainly to producing copies at lower prices. These two propensities, the one of the market and the other of the silversmith-producers, are essentially what has given rise to copying and to malbaratada. The first refers to the active copying of designs, to which many silversmiths are dedicated; the second refers more specifically to the economic undervaluation of the copy's designs. It means the price has been lowered on the basis of the low quality of goods.

The prevalence of copying and malbaratada in Taxco leaves silversmiths two options: either to accept a decrease in earnings and continue producing a design that has already been copied at the lower rung of the price range that the intermediaries are willing to pay, or to produce a new design. Thus, innovation represents a way of temporarily escaping from the vicious circle of copying and malbaratada. If it is possible for a silversmith to produce a design that is easy to sell and widely accepted in the market, the profits derived from this sale, at least at the beginning, are maximized since the lack of competitors forces the client or the wholesaler to pay a high price for the piece. In this sense, economic competition and copying act as catalysts that force more ingenious and creative silversmiths to constantly create new designs. Innovation constitutes an important economic advantage as long as it provides the innovator with a competitive margin in the market.

Even though the actual training in design creation was nonexistent among the small workshops, or talleres, many of the craftspeople interviewed pointed out that they were actually forced to look for new designs. Another common response to this situation is for many creative and innovative silversmiths to stop creating their own designs, or even to hide them. Since they are not able to obtain an economic profit from their designs, they prefer to not even expose them to the malbaratada.

For many silversmiths, the possibilities for protecting their designs and profiting from them are factors that define their disposition toward innovation. This may also be influenced by the craftsman's opportunity to achieve large or massive production rates. Yet, the increase in production through the employment of more workers may have negative effects for the workshop owners.

An example of this process was described by Samuel Rodriguez, who had been producing a successful line of rings with amethyst stones. He sold the rings for a period of two years at 65 pesos each, until one of his workers—on his own—found a client who paid 55 pesos for the ring. The worker left Mr. Rodriguez's workshop and established his own. He began to produce numerous rings until Rodriguez's client realized that other wholesalers were buying the same piece at a lower price. When this client began to buy the rings from Rodriguez's former worker, Rodriguez decided to lower the price of his own merchandise by 10 pesos each, but the new merchant had already reduced his rings by 5 pesos more. Mr. Rodriguez could not compete against this price and faced the need to develop another line. This new design combined plastic and raw stones. The new rings were relatively cheap and required a very specific knowledge about plastic work. When Rodriguez was interviewed he expressed his reservations about whether he should increase production incrementally through other workshops or keep it "exclusive" by maintaining the production in his workshop alone. Thus, we can see that the ways in which traders and wholesalers modify and change the relationship between the silversmith and his clients or customers are important to the innovative process. Because of priorities of supply and the great volumes that intermediaries acquire at low prices, the public is given only a limited version of the creative and technical potential of the silversmith. At the same time, intermediaries subject silversmiths to the production of objects that neither mesh with their artistic production, nor with their productive possibilities.

The analysis of the relationships of production reflects the ways through which the commercial sector controls production as well as technical, aesthetic, and productive techniques. The kind of aesthetic expression fostered by these conditions incorporates what are termed "modifications" and "stylization" rather than design creation. This process produces changes not only in the object itself but also in the silversmith's perceptions regarding the more salient qualities of design. Among the conditions that most directly determine the expressive possibilities, I found the following: the smith's level of technical capacity, the economic space within the productive context for experimentation, margin of utility, income, pressures of production, and the level of control that productive entities exert over their market.

The impact that the loss of creativity and innovation might have on the industry is of great concern. The silversmiths consider that one way to overcome these difficult obstacles lies in the reappropriation of their production. This, of course, would entail their achieving economic independence from the intermediaries in order to form direct contact with their markets. The strategy that the silversmithing unions have adopted is precisely the one that gives priority to the acquisition of economic means substantial enough to obtain and sustain their independence.

Alternative Development Strategies

Contrasting policies within the Mexican government concerning the development of craft industry are reflected by the fact that while silversmiths (as well as other craft industries) are thrust toward massive production at low prices, the growth in the scale of workshop operations is not supported. In this situation, the craftspeople lose the control over their production and become dependent upon the conditions established by the intermediaries. The actual growth of operations (i.e. size of production units), as well as the quality and design of production are not specifically addressed. Where competition undermines the value of quality and innovative design, silversmiths lose control over their production, and become subjected to the conditions established by the intermediaries. In addition, instead of acting as managers of family workshops, silversmiths now become pieceworkers for the intermediaries. This situation has become so widespread in the craft producing sector that in recent years, an increasing number of artisans have organized collective alternatives to overcome the limitations imposed by the prevailing marketing systems. Taxco organizations have not as yet developed markets on the scale of cooperatives elsewhere in Mexico.

In San Cristóbal de Las Casas, Chiapas, the Sna Jolobil ("House of the Weaver") the investment in aesthetic and technical quality has been central not only to the success of sales and profits for weavers but to preserving and even enhancing the standards of production that are deeply embedded in their traditional arts. The decision of the collective to appeal to a more refined collector-oriented market for the authentic "look" led the weavers (with the encouragement of their outside supporters and advisors) to promote a full-fledged revival and research of many almost extinct weaving techniques, formats, designs, and natural dyeing processes. This proved to be a marketing coup for the organization. Another example is that of the Nahua Amate bark-paper painters who have succeeded in creating a market for more gifted individual artists by exhibiting and selling their work through art galleries in Mexico City and North America.

In the past, the government's approach to promoting artisan production often failed to value the achievements of the most sophisticated craftsmen. The government promotes the silverwork of Taxco at an international level, but by dealing with it as a mass-production type of craft, it fails to promote the best work. Local initiatives have not received full-fledged support. The most outstanding example of neglect in this area is the National Silver Fair which has been, from its origins at the Spratling workshop "Las Delicias," a local initiative that should have obtained ample governmental support. When in 1979, through considerable local efforts, the community initiated a full-fledged attempt to change the fair into an international event, the federal government failed to provide the support they needed in order to make the project a success.

During the past few years, the State has given greater support to small communities in various places, some of them even near Taxco. Whereas these programs provide support to communities in need, thousands of silversmiths in Taxco do not receive any at all, and their situation is worsened by the competition from their neighbors. The intense competition that has taken place within Taxco will continue to be a chronic situation due to the nature of production, the dynamics of monopolization in the market, and the ease with which additional workshops can be formed. Unless all the workshops are integrated, associated, and subject to a series of agreements and rules in relation to prices and the copying of designs, the current economic situation will continue to threaten the very survival of the industry.

In the case of craft production, where its development is as much a community endeavor as it is an individual one, several aspects come to light when considered within the national context. In a country such a Mexico, where the government is characterized by a centralization of power, the communities become virtually obliged to engage in a struggle for autonomy. Here, the role of craft production has been essential in achieving a level of political and economic autonomy. The government's neglect in supporting this sector, particularly in the 1930s through the 1960s, when it could have expanded significantly, as in the case of India, is conceivably linked to a conflict of interests generated at this level. Nonetheless, it is ironic that as the negotiation of the Free Trade Agreement approaches, in which a large portion of the Mexican business and industrial sectors appear concerned, there are some indications that the craft producing sector, that has been largely neglected, may emerge as the least scathed. Additionally, it is clear that the heightened interest in Mexico, in part fueled by the Free Trade Agreement, will also favor the traditional craft industries.

Independently of governmental or institutional intercession, Taxco silver has been making its way into galleries and museums, particularly the silver jewelry that was produced in the 1940s and 50s. This development is due to numerous factors, including the rising interest in design, ornamentation, and the decorative arts, which have heightened the appreciation of jewelry design. The approach to design during the early Taxco period, when the silversmiths were experimenting with both traditional and incipient modern concepts, has become appreciated in the past decade. Silver metal itself has gone through a process of revaluation relative to gold, and silver objects are increasingly displayed within the museum context, as was the case with the prominent display given to the silverwork of the Colonial period in Mexico at the Metropolitan Museum's show in the Fall of 1990.

This movement of Taxco jewelry within the market also reflects the public's willingness to look at Mexican—as well as non-Western art in general in a more appreciative light than in the past. At the same time, Taxco silver has had to find its particular niche, because it has not fallen into some of the other more easily categorized ones, such as the so-called primitive, ethnic, or traditional. Rather, it developed as a product of the modern age, yet with its own aesthetic parameters that reached into the past for inspiration and into the contemporary art orientations for a modern thrust in design. While this represented an immense challenge, it did achieve a character in design and craftsmanship that is unmistakably its own.

CONCLUDING NOTE

In this chapter I have focussed upon the dialogue that takes place through the commercial exchange, and its effect on the object. I have also described the dynamics within the community of craftsmen that are generated under differing circumstances, as well as those of the societies that consume these crafts. The significance of the changing perspective on the popular (and so-called 'lesser') artforms, as opposed to the 'Fine' arts does have immediate implications for the course which these artforms will take. The rise in the public's interest in popular artforms, as well as that of contemporary artists, is also evident in the art market itself. The particular inspiration that the younger artists are finding in these popular artforms may provide a retroactive enrichment for craft production, by inspiring the artisans to strive for another level, in terms of really pursuing the limits of design and quality. Such an example would be the experiences of the weavers of Sna Jolobil and the Taxco silversmiths who propelled their work into a gallery context and to museums as well.

In concluding, I would like to point out, at the risk of contradicting my initial treatment of the conference that led to this essay, that although the ethnographer's role may be one of interpreting the cultural exchange between societies of differing worlds, we (the ethnographers) are also actors and initiators, even brokers. Personally, I consider one of the overriding elements that gave the impetus for this conference and the accompanying events, to be the personal involvement of the organizer, June Nash, and of most of the participants.[4] If we consider this conference in ethnographic terms as I have suggested, it was fitting that it took place within New York; and that the members of the Maya communities themselves were present. Their presence clearly underscored the importance of the reciprocity in the dialogue and the exchange between the cultures. Yet, it took the individual interest and desire to make the connection between these two worlds, in order to facilitate the actual presence of the artisans. While it was initially striking to see the presence of the Maya Indians in New York, garbed in their extraordinary costumes, I was reminded, inevitably, that they have been engaged with the Western, and specifically New York public for years, through the exhibition and sale of their weaving. With each commercial exchange, ideas, values, taste have been conveyed back and forth. This exchange has been a dialogue in itself.

NOTES

Acknowledgments: I would like to express my appreciation to June Nash for her painstaking editorial work, which superseded the bounds of duty; as well as Penelope Yungblut, Roseann Cane, and Francesco Pellizzi for their helpful editorial comments.

This essay is dedicated to the memory of Guillermo Bonfil Batalla.

1. As could be expected over 60 commercial ventures, primarily the sale of Mexican art, followed suit, profiting from the interest that was generated by these events. (Source: The Mexican Cultural Institute of New York)

A survey of the public's response to the Metropolitan Museum's Show, in ideological and aesthetic terms, is forthcoming in, "Art and Attitudes: the Public's Response to Thirty Centuries of Splendor," by Brigitta Buvelan, Jean Herbst, and Gobi Stromberg.

2. These research findings were written as a dissertation, *The Marketing and Production of Innovation: the Taxco Silver Industry,* Berkeley, University of California, 1976. The subsequent research was published in *El Juego del Coyote: Platería y Arte en Taxco,* México, D.F., Fondo de Cultura Económica, Colección Popular, 1983.

3. The presence and significance of popular art in modern art was the theme of the Beaubourg Museum's major show of the decade, "Les Magiciens de la Terre," in 1989. This issue was also specifically explored in the conference (and forthcoming edition), "Popular Art and Identity," which accompanied the "Rooted Visions" show at the Museum of Contemporary Hispanic Art in New York, in 1988.

4. My participation in this event also had the personal dimension, primarily through a long association with Sna Jolobil, involving the Pellizzi Textile Collection, and my Escuela Nacional de Antropología e Historia students' research with and of the cooperative, as well as my and my family's close friendship with Pedro Mesa, the administrator and original inspirer of Sna Jolobil.

References Cited

Graburn, Nelson H.H.
    1976   *Ethnic and Tourist arts: Cultural Expressions from the Fourth World,* Berkeley, University of California Press.

Chenalhó, Chiapas
Drawing by Christine Eber

5

Mexican Museums in the Creation of a National Image in World Tourism

Flora S. Kaplan

INTRODUCTION

Mexican museums have played an historic role in local and national artisan production and in the creation of a national image in world tourism. As repositories of material culture and its symbols, museums have stimulated artisans to re-create forms and designs and contributed, generally, to modern craft production. The role of museums is rooted in the dual cultural heritage of the country, in the indigenous and in the European traditions, collected, conserved, and interpreted within museum walls. These traditions, colliding in the conquest of the New World, took forms and expressions that were both like and unlike the old ways, and became something else entirely—something *mestizaje,* a combination of Indian and Spanish heritage that is distinctly "Mexican."

In the aftermath of the 1910 Revolution, the quest for a national identity embraced the idea that Mexicans could be united by the same cultural patrimony—that folk art and folk lore, *artesanías,* have positive value which the non-indigenous population should learn to love and respect—

and that one nation would emerge from this union. The promotor of this idea was Dr. Manuel Gamio ([1916] 1982: 221–334). He believed the "fusion of races, convergence and fusion of cultural manifestations, linguistic unification, and an economic equilibrium of social elements [conditions which] should characterize a Mexican population before it constitutes and embodies a powerful state with a coherent and well defined nationality" (1923:221). The role to be played by museums in the 20th century, may be found in the intellectual and political life of New Spain in the late eighteenth and early nineteenth centuries (Kaplan 1980; 1992a), and in the economy that was directed towards capitalism and tied to a world system of production. These underpinnings support the growth of nationalism and incipient modern nation-state formation (Kaplan 1992b). Other developments contributing to the creation of a national image in museums include the objectification and codification of knowledge, and its dissemination to a wider public; and the commoditization of the products of social relations. The latter include artifacts of all kinds, from ideology and culture, to things, items made and used (Kaplan 1988). Thus, in museums—where widely held ideas and values manifest themselves in a series of powerful visual symbols, in art and material culture—groups seeking to gain or to maintain power within the culture find the stuff with which to create and clothe a national image.

The creation of national images may also be stimulated by outside forces. For example, foreign tourism may stimulate internal demand for imagery and group identity on local, regional, and national levels. This phenomenon, associated with the development of nation-states, is accompanied by the formation of museums and cultural institutions and has until recently, been largely overlooked (Kaplan 1992b, 1991, 1987, 1980). This chapter calls attention to museums as places where social, ideological, and cultural changes are manifested, and where representation of ruling elites is promoted and politically legitimized. In selecting, preserving, and presenting past and present artisan production in museums, the prevailing elite views of cultural heritage and national history are both re-created and reflected anew. Museums give such a group the chance to present themselves to themselves, as well as to others who may sojourn among them. Subsequently, elite views of themselves are re-formed along with their views of "others," by outsiders. "Others" are defined as other groups within society, as well as sojourners, who may be classified, collectively, as "tourists." Each of these groups has a differential impact on artisan production, museums, and their collections (Kaplan 1988) that will be explored below.

HISTORICAL BACKGROUND OF TOURISM AND MUSEUMS

Tourism and tourists refer to more than simply "others" abroad. They must be distinguished from the travel of soldiers, traders, and missionaries who frequently initiate contact or interact with groups other than themselves to attain specific national, commercial, and institutional purposes. Rather, the term "tourist" should be reserved for those travellers who seek to learn, to experience, or to simply enjoy another place, either inside or outside their own locale, country, and continent (See the accounts of such travellers: Catherwood 1844; von Humboldt 1814, 1824, 1970; Nebel 1836; Stephens 1841, 1843). The impact of behavior and ideas that derive from the use of leisure time and the search for something new and novel is unique and intrinsic to the notion of "tourist," as employed here. While travel has been a part of every generation, it is perhaps the nineteenth-century "grand tour," in which Americans went to Europe and Europeans went to the Americas and both went to other continents, that set forth a process of personal transformation based on travel, among members of upwardly mobile groups seeking entry to the ranks of new and existing elites. In the twentieth century, more leisure and ease and speed of transportation have accelerated "tourism" worldwide.

The impact of modern tourism has been profound in many countries—increasing income and creating service jobs in related sectors. It also directs attention to artisan production. It may stimulate innovation and production of new and different artifacts for national image and identity, and it may lead to production and alteration of traditional works and forgeries. This is not a new development. W. H. Holmes of the U.S. Bureau of Ethnology noted in 1886 and 1889 that archaeological fakes and reproductions were being made in old molds and sold to American and European tourists at the pyramids of Teotihuacán outside Mexico City.

MUSEUMS IN MEXICO

The late eighteenth century saw nascent interest developing in Indian cultures via antiquities that had been found from time to time during excavations in the capital and elsewhere. Of course, some individuals and early missionaries, like Sahagún and Bartolomé de Las Casas, had taken a serious interest in the cultures they encountered; Cortez had sent back detailed reports on the Indians to the Spanish monarch in the sixteenth century. It was not until about 1775, however, that the foundations for future museums were laid: Viceroy Bucareli, the colonial governor, took official action locally and ordered the documents collected earlier by Lorenzo

Boturini, together with some relics, transferred to the University (Ramirez Vázquez 1968; Solana 1981). In 1790 the monolithic sculpture of "Coatlicue," (Figure 16), discovered in Mexico City's main public square, the Zocalo, was also taken there and later that same year, the "Aztec Calendar Stone" was found and added to the University's treasures. These two stones became the subject of a serious study by Antonio de León y Gama, together with four other stones found in the Zocalo between December 1791 and June 1792. These and a few other finds became the core of the collections of the future national museum (García 1909), and León y Gama's studies were the first based on ancient finds (Ramirez Vázquez 1968:10). Later, Viceroy Iturrigaray established a Board of Antiquities. Shortly after the wars of independence from Spain in the early nineteenth century, an archaeological museum was founded by the decrees of two presidents, Guadalupe Victoria and Anastasio Bustamante. The editor and historian, Lucas Alamán, who has been called the "founder of the Mexican museum," by Carlos María de Bustamente, was instrumental in these efforts (Museo Mexicano 1843–44). Emperor Maximilian had the museum moved to its first separate quarters in 1865, at 13 Moneda Street, Mexico City (Garcia 1909; Ramirez Vázquez 1968:11–12). The present and world famous Museum of Anthropology was begun in 1963, in Chapultepec Park, and dedicated on 17 September 1964 by President Adolfo Lopez Mateos.

The Transformation of Museums in Mexico

This extraordinary modern museum is notable not only for its architecture, directed by Pedro Ramirez Vázquez and a sizable force of engineers, architects, artisans, and laborers, but for its museography and conceptual force. Ramirez Vázquez has detailed and documented their labors over nineteen months (1968), which is recounted here. As the project director, he supervised forty scientific consultants, sponsored archaeological and ethnographic surveys, transported large archaeological pieces from several regions, transferred the entire contents of the old museums, classified and catalogued the pieces electronically, installed galleries, trained bilingual guides, and issued publications and various commemorative works. Making use of open space, the building itself was visually innovative and harmonious with its setting; the rectangular floor plan, ornamentation, and sense of proportion reflected the architectural features of ancient Indian culture as well as some of the colonial churches. The scientific and educational mission of the museum was central in its

Figure 16. "Coatlicue," Goddess of the Serpent Skirt. Aztec culture, Tenochtitlán (Mexico City), 14th–15th century A.D. *Collection, National Museum of Anthropology, Mexico City.*

planning, and full use was made of available technology and media to provide the results of intensive research as well as services and amenities for staff and visitors.

The museographic purpose of the museum was to recreate the past and present civilizations of Mexico as accurately as possible. With regard to ethnographic displays, materials were brought from all parts of the country, and traditional folk artists were used to decorate the walls; Indian laborers from the major regions each built exact reproductions of their own houses, household furnishings, and tools of everyday life and work. They used traditional techniques in building and decorating these structures and items. For the first time, then, the inhabitants of the various regions built their own habitats for a museum (Figure 17). The museum was planned so that the second-floor rooms for ethnology were located, where possible, directly over the corresponding rooms for archaeology on the ground floor. The methods employed in organizing the galleries of the new museum derived from museography, the techniques of presenting collections so that the visitor's appreciation and understanding of them is enhanced: incorporating models, architectural elements, audiovisual aids, dioramas, etc. The museographers were guided also by their grasp of museology, the latter defined as the history and theory of museums and their role in society. The installation took into account all aspects of the environment (social, physical, and historical) in the rooms devoted to archaeology, physical anthropology, and linguistics.

This comprehensive, anthropological view adopted by the new museum made the prior neglect of the ethnographic collections evident. The rapid change in traditional patterns of Indian life gave urgency to the need to represent living cultures. Within a year some seventy ethnographic expeditions were mounted to survey and obtain the necessary background data and materials needed for the projected ethnographic exhibitions. As a result, thousands of domestic and ritual items were cataloged, more than 15,000 photographs were taken, hundreds of drawings were made, tape recordings of languages and music, films, and observations were gathered for use in future research. On a more limited scale, excavations were also carried out; many gifts, donations, and purchases expanded the collections still further (Ramirez Vázquez, 1968).

The bringing together of this vast array of knowledge, art, and culture under one roof opened a panorama of Mexican prehistory and diversity before a wide public audience. The direct involvement of the Indians was seen not only in the creation of the exhibitions themselves, but in their visits to the museum in the years that followed. All Mexicans were to be given an opportunity to learn about each other and themselves within

*Figure 17. Huichol Indian chief discusses details of installa-
tion of Huichol houses during construction at the new National Museum, 1963. Photograph courtesy of the National
Museum of Anthropology, Mexico City.*

an overarching conceptual framework that linked past with present and gave visible representation to the notion of *mestizaje* (the fusion of the races toward a single people). In this process, leading artists also played a major role: Gonzales Camarena created a mural for the section "Introduction to Anthropology;" and José Chavez Morado depicted the millenia of pre-Columbian cultures in the Mesoamerica Room (Figure 18). Pablo O'Higgins painted the valleys and legends and mountains of ancient western Mexico; the main lobby of the museum was enriched with an allegorical mural by Rufino Tamayo, representing the struggle between good and evil, between the plumed serpent and the tiger, between the ancient Aztec deities *Quetzalcoatl* and *Tezcatlipoca* who represented these forces. Other artists made imaginative use of indigenous colors and materials to convey ancient and contemporary traditions. In housing these ideas within the National Museum of Anthropology, the president, the government, scholars, students, artisans, citizens, and visitors alike, from Mexico, the Americas, Europe, and elsewhere partook of a national vision and imbibed a national ethos that was set before them in time and space. The effect was to shape and reshape their ideas and values. It remains a profound experience, and it remains to see what vision is presented in the new renovations of the museum, currently underway.

MEXICAN ARTISTS, FOLK ART, AND MUSEUMS

The 1920s saw three artists play major roles in rediscovering and popularizing Mexican Indian art by means of texts and exhibitions, and by the formation of collections: Gerardo Murillo (1922), or "Dr. Atl," as he was widely known, Roberto Montenegro (1940, 1948), and Adolfo Best-Maugard (1926). Also, Rufino Tamayo made enduring and sensitive use of pre-Columbian and folk art in the subject matter, color, and design elements of his work, as did Diego Rivera, Orozco, and Siquieros. Before them, José Guadalupe Posada, the nineteenth-century graphic artist, led the way with mass dissemination of popular "sayings" and imagery that drew on Indian, Spanish, religious, and contemporary events and themes (Figure 19). His genre engravings and etchings affirmed Mexico's unique cultural heritage in the period of the "Porfiriato," when European manners and styles were being widely emulated (Diaz de Leon 1938; Museum of Contemporary Hispanic Art 1988).

Intellectuals and artists of the 1920s praised popular folk art as having pure Mexican value: Othon de Mendízabal, Moises Saenz, Alfonso Caso, Salvador Novo, Diego Rivera, David Siqueiros. The symbols of this new ethnic identity emphasized the cultural products of the mestizaje. In

Figure 18. View of Mesoamerica Room, with mural tracing the development of pre-Classic, Classic, and post-Classic ancient cultures, by José Chavez Morado, 1964. Photograph courtesy of the National Museum of Anthropology, Mexico City.

Figure 19. *Calaveras de Artesanos metal engraving,*
(1902–1909), by José Guadalupe Posada. Collection, The
Museum of Modern Art, New York.

1922, the government gave voice to its admiration for popular arts, and by order of President Álvaro Obregón, the Secretaría de Industría y Comércio published a second edition of Dr. Atl's original work, *Popular Arts of Mexico* (1921). In 1932, in the magazine *Nuestro Mexico,* Salvator Novo wrote, " . . . now we discover the petate dolls, the "jicaras," the clay toys, the polychrome serapes, are not only admired by us because they offer us a spiritual and aesthetic message which gives us a sense of racial pride and a conscience of nationality which we lacked before, when we limited artistic imports and habits, but are also cherished by countries far away. . . . "

ARTISANS AND THE COMMODITIZATION OF CULTURE AND "ETHNICITY"

Since the 1920s, when the revolution of 1910 was effectively brought to a close, the Mexican government, its exhibitions, publications, and museums, have all played an active role in developing and preserving traditional folklore and crafts by establishing a wide range of activities and institutions for their protection and production (Romero 1986). The Dirección de Antropología, first created in 1917 and headed by Gamio, carried out studies that gave evidence of the great creativity of the indigenous peoples (Comas 1953:92–97). Intellectuals and artists advised the government to recognize the value of folk art, and then to protect and disseminate it (Comas 1953, Gamio 1923, Starr 1899). As director of the Dirección de Antropología, Dr. Gamio considered the educational system and SEP (Secretaría de Educación Pública) to be important means of doing this; he saw to it that a number of works on *artesanías* or popular arts, were published ([1916]1982:55–65). Initially, official efforts went toward protecting, preserving, and collecting authentic traditional craft productions. These were exhibited in museums and offered for sale at fairs, government outlets, private stores, and other places (Toor 1947, 1936). Museum shops exhibited and sold crafts, and became important outlets for modern works as well as reproductions of ancient ones. Museums provided models for artisans to see and copy.

In time, and with the growth of the tourist industry, crafts became increasingly commercialized and an important source of income for the country, especially as the rural population became marginalized economically (Daniels 1938). Between 1950 and 1960, 80 percent of the general income from agriculture was earned by 3.3 percent of the farm population, those who held 72 percent of farming surface/lands and 75 percent of the machinery. Thus, an increase in the capitalist sector led to poverty in other sectors of the economy and created a need for new sources of income. Crafts became a major source of employment, encouraged by the government, which saw crafts also as a way to stem the flow of people from the rural areas to the cities. The relatively simple technology and low capitalization needed for craft production encouraged its development as an alternative source of employment during debt crises.

Tourism has been a powerful economic force in Mexico. The Banco de Comércio Exterior estimated that tourists spent about 18 percent of their monies on crafts and popular art works or *artesanías* in Mexico (Romero 1986). In the balance of payments, tourism has been second only to oil. The revenues from tourism rose 27 percent in 1987, continuing the rapid expansion begun in 1986 and reached a surplus of 1.5 billion dollars. In the same year, tourism generated an income of 2,274 million dollars, and the number of visitors reached 5.4 million people. Of those visiting Mexico in 1987, 85.4 percent were from the United States, 6.2 percent from Canada, 4.1 percent from Europe, 3.8 percent from Latin America, and 0.5 percent from Asia and other areas. The tourist industry employed an estimated 1.825 million persons; in 1987, it produced 4,000 jobs directly and 10,000 indirectly. Further, an estimated 8 percent of the population of Mexico, or 1 in 12 people, depends on the production and sale of folk art or crafts of either traditional or modern types (Banco de México 1988:125–126).

The Instituto Nacional de Antropología e Historia (hereafter referred to an INAH), which conducts research and maintains archaeological and historical sites, puts the number of visits to archaeological sites, museums, and historical monuments, administered by INAH at 6.3 million in 1987. These figures include both Mexican and foreign tourists. It is worth noting that nationals accounted for 73 percent of the visits and foreigners 27 percent. INAH reports visits in 1987 were distributed as follows: museums 55 percent, archaeological zones 33 percent, and historical sites 12 percent. (These figures represent an increase in museum visits in recent years, from 49 percent in 1984 to 55 percent in 1987). Of the total number of visits in 1987, museums were visited by 3.4 million people; 2.1 million visited archaeological zones; and 775,000 people visited historical monuments. The Federal Districts had the most visitors with 36 percent of the total; they also received 33 percent of all visits by foreign tourists and 38 percent by nationals. Other frequently visited places included the states of México, Morelos, Oaxaca, Puebla, Vera Cruz, and Yucatán.

Today there are over fifty institutions and official agencies that promote popular art in Mexico. The number alone attests to the important role of artesanías as an economic option and source of employment in some sectors of society, and to the market for national imagery and identity created by tourism among people both outside and inside the country (Figure 20). These markets each have a different impact on the crafts produced (Kaplan 1988). The four most important institutions and agencies created were: Instituto Nacional Indigenista (INI), Fideicomiso para el Fomento de Las Artesanías (now the BANFOCO), Secretaria de Trabajadores no Asalariados y Artesanos de La CNOP, and Instituto Mexicano de Comércio Exterior (IMCE).

Founded by the First Indigenous Interamerican Congress, Mexico, in 1940, INI was created to promote indigenous culture, in particular the popular arts that gave expression to it. Later, as a branch of the Instituto Indigenista Interamericano created in 1948, it endeavored to protect the positive values of indigenous people while assimilating them into the wider society (Figure 21). To protect and promote commercialization of popular art, INI led to the creation of the Patronato de Artes e Indústrias Populares. The Muséo Nacional de Artes e Indústrias Populares was founded in 1951, in Mexico City, Distrito Federal. The role of the Patronato was to advance loans and to buy the best produced objects. Between 1951 and 1963, the Patronato bought 11.5 million pesos worth of crafts. The Museum, however, has been independent of the Patronato since 1968, covering its expenses from tax-free sales income.

The Fomento (BANFOCO) was created to provide technical assistance, credit, and help with commercialization of the products of artesanias. It funds and buys surplus production. In 1972 Fomento gave five million pesos credit and bought crafts worth fifteen million pesos. The most credit was given in the Federal Districts (15.7 percent), and in the three poorest states: Michoacán (12.1 percent), Tlaxcala (11.3 percent), and Guerrero (10.9 percent). Fomento (BANFOCO) organizes contests, festivals, and expositions to publicize new products and to help less popular artists. It exports abroad to the biggest importers of popular art: United States, Japan, Spain, and Germany. It also sells to other distributors nationally. Like FONART, it became a major buyer, monopolizing the industry but spending 60 percent of its income on operations, and running a deficit despite its sales.

The Secretaría de Trabajadores no Asalariados y Artesanos was created in 1947, but functioned only in 1971. It was part of the National Confederation of Organizations, and had some 250,000 artisans affiliated with the Secretaría.

IMCE was created by law on 30 December 1970 and began operations in February of 1971. It studies and makes policy, plans, and programs to develop foreign commerce; it coordinates public and private

Figure 20. Tree of Life, painted ceramic, 1972, by Aurelio Flores, Izúcar de Matamoros, Puebla, Mexico. The artist decorates a traditional folk candelabra used in marriage ceremonies with Christian and Indian figures and motifs. His candelabras are exhibited in museums and fairs (ferias) and sold to tourists. (Photograph by Flora S. Kaplan).

Figure 21. Traditional women potters, Juliana Perez and her sister, firing an outdoor kiln in Amatenango del Valle, Chiapas, Mexico. This firing included hearth or horno they copied in the style of Oaxaca potters, as well as candlesticks and pottery based on European models to sell to tourists. Photograph by Flora S. Kaplan, 1979.

entities to work with the foreign sector; it promotes association among producers, merchants, distributors, and exporters; and it also promotes exports of artesanías. IMCE created the Commission of Craft Houses in 1973, to coordinate all agencies working with folk art. Most of the fifty large enterprises that carry out 65 to 70 percent of all craft exports are American-owned. Indeed, some 75 percent of all Mexican artesanias are exported to the United States. The scale of these exports reached 117,518,051 pesos in 1971, of which 88.7 percent went to the United States; in 1972 it reached 142,784,325 pesos exported, of which 96.6 percent went to the United States. Most of the products were clothing, jewelry, musical instruments, glassware, and pottery (private communication, *Consulado General de México*, New York, September 10, 1988).

"MEXICAN" FOLK ART AND MUSEUMS IN THE UNITED STATES

Mexican artists who were part of the muralist movement following the 1910 revolution extolled Indian heritage, the pre-Columbian and folk traditions. Their connections with North Americans led to growing interest in native, as well as contemporary, works by collectors and museum professionals. For example, Nelson Rockefeller began to collect folk art on his first trip to Mexico in 1933. His interest was stimulated by Miguel and Rosa Covarrubias. Through them he met Roberto Montenegro, painter, muralist, editor, and graphic artist. He also met and sought the advice of several people connected with popularizing Mexican crafts and contemporary art in America: Fred Davis, collector, shop owner, art expert, and adviser; William Spratling, a Taxco silversmith; and Frances Flynn Paine, a student of folk arts. In the mid-1930s he also met René D'Harnoncourt, who had collected for the American Federation of Arts (AFA) and put together a Mexican show that toured fifteen U.S. cities. The impact of these works and of contemporary Mexican artists on artists and intellectuals of the period in the United States is presently being reassessed (Museum of Contemporary Hispanic Art, 1988). Thereafter, D'Harnoncourt assisted Nelson Rockefeller in collecting pre-Columbian and folk art, despite the fact that many museums in America showed no inclination to collect, conserve, and exhibit such works. In 1939, Nelson Rockefeller tried to interest New York's Metropolitan Museum of Art in "primitive art," the art of the New World, Africa, and Oceania, without success. Forty years later, in 1979, his collections were finally acquired to create the Michael Rockefeller Wing of that museum. In 1940, however, as President of the Museum of Modern Art (MOMA) in New York, in cooperation with the Mexican government, he initiated a travelling show of 5,000 works, "20 Centuries of Mexican Art," for which Roberto Montenegro helped select the pieces. In 1969, Rockefeller once again held an exhibition of Mexican folk art, this time at his private Museum of Primitive Art in New York. The museum was founded in 1954, opened to the public in 1957, and the collections made part of the Metropolitan Museum in 1979, after Rockefeller's death. In 1985, his ethnographic Mexican collection went to the Mexican Museum in San Francisco, as a gift of his daughter, Ann Rockefeller Roberts. Some museums on the West Coast and in the Southwest focus their collections and exhibitions on Mexican folk art *artesanías* and its influence on Latin American modern artists. These include: the International Museum of Folk Art, Santa Fé, New Mexico, the Museum of Contemporary Folk Art, Los Angeles, California, and the most recent was the Museum of Contemporary Hispanic Art, New York City.

DISCUSSION AND CONCLUSIONS

The sources of new national ethnic identity in the twentieth century lie in the colonial past of the sixteenth century, when political and religious dominion over the Indians was established, and a largely unsuccessful attempt was made to keep the Indians and Europeans in separate economic and social spheres. Independence from Spain in the early nineteenth century enhanced the growing self-consciousness of a new nation. The French intervention that followed made European influence fashionable, although the full impact of foreign influence was felt only toward the end of the nineteenth century, with rapid capitalist expansion during the period of the Porfiriato (1876–1910). The revolution of 1910 brought that period to a close in a series of events and violent conflicts that lasted until about 1920. The intellectual ferment and renewed self-awareness ushered in by the revolutionary period, were followed by increasing official recognition of Indian traditions. The modern notion of *mestizaje* that one nation could be welded by engendering respect and love for a common cultural patrimony, guided various efforts to preserve Mexico's ancient and indigenous past. This past and its presentation were given a major role in Mexico's museums. Artesanías were also presented and perpetuated through museums.

Other factors have also led to the perpetuation of artesanias in Mexico—and their representation, collection, and sale through state and federal museums, tourist offices, and other outlets. These include: innovation and change as a result of customer and tourist preference or government and distributor activities and demands; continuity of traditional modes of production and techniques of teaching (Figure 22); values and uses among producers and consumers; and the existence of at least two tourist markets (internal or domestic and external or foreign). All of these factors affect the products which are made and sold, where and; they also affect the degree of continuity and change exhibited over time (Kaplan 1992b). Things used in the country for daily and for ritual purposes tend to be conservative, whereas those made for tourists may not: they respond to fluctuating market demands, permit more innovation, adopt European conventions in art, and accept the importance of novelty and individuality along with "Mexican" sensibilities (Kaplan 1988:22).

It is somewhat ironic that the customs, dress, and artifacts of agricultural workers and artisans, who are mostly marginal producers in rural areas, have come to be seen as symbols of the Mexican "nation." Incorporation of their rural economies into a world capitalist system has disrupted these same people from their traditional way of life, from reinvestment in ritual cycles, from funds for prestige and community, and from kinship obligations. At the same time, industrialization and political, social, and economic change have left them even more marginal. Craft production of popular arts, encouraged by the government, provides them alternate and supplementary employment. The artisans engaged in traditional modes of production have become the producers of "ethnicity," and the keepers of traditions around which the nation gathers and gains a sense of local, regional, and national identity (Martinez Pẽnaloza 1971, 1972; Ramirez Vázquez 1981; Solana 1981). Their products, art and artifacts, have become commodities that may be bought and sold. Nonetheless, they retain their impact because they have old meanings attached to them that convey widely held values, and new meanings have come to adhere to them.

Those who attach new meanings include international modern artists for whom the museums and the motifs and metaphors of ancient and folk Mexico have become sources of inspiration and ideas. These artists have imbibed a sense of mestizaje from the country's educational system and public works and institutions, but they also look to western European and North American models in literature, criticism, art, and art history. As artists they seek to express their dual heritage in new ways, and in so doing find their distinctly Mexican "voice" (Museum of Contemporary Art 1988). Their search is part of a tradition that goes back to the 1920s.

The dynamic role of Mexican museums in collecting, conserving, and interpreting cultural heritage has created a national image in world tourism as well as markets for craft production. The image or images of

Figure 22. Potter decorating miniatures with his sons watching and helping in Barrio de La Acocota, Puebla, Puebla, Mexico. Observing and learning about pottery making begins early in craft families, which fosters continuity in the tradition. (Photograph by Flora S. Kaplan, 1972).

"Mexicanness" imparted by museums are literally carried away through craft production by tourists, in their heads and hands and, I might add, most importantly, by the Mexicans themselves.

REFERENCES CITED

Arceo, Rene H.
  1988   *José Guadalupe Posada Aguilar.* Chicago: The Mexican Fine Arts Center Museum.

Atl, Dr. [Gerardo Murillo]
  1922   *Las Artes Populares en Mexico.* 2 vols. 2nd edition. México: Secretaría de Indústria y Comércio.

Banco de México
  1988   *The Mexican Economy.* Annual publication of the Direccíon de Organismos y Acuerdos Internacionales de Banco de México. Mexico D.F.

Best-Maugard, Adolfo
  1926   *A Method for Creative Design.* New York & London: Alfred A. Knopf.

Catherwood, Frederick
  1844   *Views of Ancient Monuments in Central America, Chiapas, and Yucatán.* London.

Comas, Juan
  1953   *Ensayos Sobre Indígenismo,* III. México: Instituto Indigenista Interamericano.

Daniels, Josephus
  1938   Americans in Mexico. *Mexican Art and Life.* Introductory Issue. México D.F.: D.A.P.P.

Diaz de Leon, Francisco
  1938   Mexican Lithographic Tradition. *Mexican Art and Life,* No. 3, July, Mexico D.F.: D.A.P.P.

Espejel, Carlos
  1986   *The Nelson A. Rockefeller Collection of Mexican Folk Art.* San Francisco: The Mexican Museum, Chronicle Books Editions.

Gamio, Manuel
    1923   Nacionalismo e Internacionalismo, *ETHNOS,* Vol. 1, No. 2, Febrero-Abril. Mexico.

    [1948] Consideraciones Sobre el Problema Indígena. 3rd edition.
    1966   Mexico: Instituto Indigenista Interamericano.

    [1916] Forjando Patria. 3rd edition. Mexico: Editorial Porrua,
    1982   S.A.

García, Genaro
    1909   Introduction. *ANALES.* Museo Nacional de Arqueología, Historia y Ethnología, Vol. 1. México.

Kaplan, Flora S.
    1980   *Una Tradición Alfarera: Conocimiento e éstilo.* México D.F.: Instituto National Indigenista. Editorial Porrua, S.A.

    1981   The "Meaning" of Pottery. In *The Anthropological Use of Museum Collections,* ed. A. M. Cantwell, J. Griffin, and N. Rothschild, pp. 315–324. Annals of the New York Academy of Sciences, vol. 376, New York.

    1987   *Museology and Museums: Reflections on the boundaries of disciplines, social institutions, and nation-state formation.* ICOFOM Study Series, No. 13. Stockholm and Paris.

    1988   The Two Faces of Tourism: The relative impact of internal vs. foreign tourism. Paper presented, Symposium, Artesanías y Sociedad, at 46th International Congress of Americanists, Amsterdam, The Netherlands. July 5th.

    1992a *A Mexican Folk Pottery Tradition: Cognition and Style in Material Culture in the Valley of Puebla.* Carbondale: Southern Illinois University Press.

    1992b Museums and National Identity. In *Museums and National Identity: The importance of objects in the formation of nation-states,* ed. Flora S. Kaplan. Leicester: Leicester University Press. pp. 1–10.

Martinez Peñaloza, Porfirio
1971   Arte Popular en Mexico. *Anuario Indigenista,* III, Vol. XXXI, diciembre. Mexico.

1972   *Arte Popular y Artesanías Artísticas en México.* México: Secretaría de Hacienda y Crédito Público.

Montenegro, Roberto
1940   *20 Centuries of Mexican Art.* New York.

1948   Museo de Artes Populares, Colección Anahuac de Arte Mexicano, 6. Mexico.

Museum of Contemporary Hispanic Art
1988   *Rooted Visions: Mexican Art Today* (Exhibition catalog). With contributions by Teresa del Conde, Fernando Gamboa interview with Andres de Luna, Carla Stellweg, and Gobi Stromberg de Pellizzi. March 17–May 8. New York.

Museo Mexicano
1843–   Volumes I-IV. México D.F.
44

Nebel, Carl
1836   *Voyage pittoresque et archeologique dans la partie la plus interessant du Mexique.* Paris: M. Moench.

Novo, Salvator
1932   *Nuestro México.* México D.F.

Ramirez Vázquez, Pedro
1968   *National Museum of Anthropology:* Mexico. New York: Harry N. Abrams, Inc.

1981   *The Future of Heritage and the Heritage of the Future. Proceedings of the 12th General Conference and 13th General Assembly of the International Council of Museums (ICOM),* Mexico City, October 25–November 4, 1980. Paris: ICOM. pp. 48–52

Romero, Hector Manuel
  1986   *Enciclopedia Mexicana del Turismo*. 3 vols. Mexico D.F.: Editorial Limusa. Instituto Politécnico Nacional.

Solana, Fernando
  1981   Inaugural Address by the Minister of Public Education of Mexico. *Proceedings of the 12th General Conference and 13th General Assembly of the International Council of Museums (ICOM)*, Mexico City, October 25–November 4, 1980. Paris: ICOM. pp. 17–21

Starr, Frederick
  1899   *Catalogue of a Collection of Objects Illustrating the Folklore of Mexico*. London: Published for The Folklore Society by David Nutt, J. B. Nichols and Sons.

Stephens, John L.
  1841   *Incidents of Travel in Central America, Chiapas, and Yucatán*. 2 vols. New York: Harper Brothers.

  1843   *Incidents of Travel in Yucatán*. 2 vols. New York.

Toor, Frances
  1936   *Mexican Popular Arts*. New York.

  1947   *A Treasury of Mexican Folkways*. New York: Crown Publishers.

von Humboldt, Alexander
  1814   *Political Essay on the Kingdom of New Spain*. Translated by John Black. London. 4 vols.

  1824   *Selections from the Works of the Baron de Humboldt, Relating to the Climate, Inhabitants, Productions, and Mines of Mexico*. (With Notes by John Taylor) London.

  1970   *Tablas Geográficas Políticas del Reino de Nueva España y Correspondencia Mexicana*. Los textos de Humboldt reunidos en éste volumen han sido recopilados e interpretados por Miguel S. Wionczek con asistencia de Enrique Florescano. México: Dirección General de Estadística.

Collecting water off the tin roof, Chojollá, Chenalhó, Chiapas, Mexico
(tz'una Pablo Perez Perez)   June 1987

A Home in Chenalhó, Chiapas
Drawing by Christine Eber

6

Maya Household Production in the World Market: The Potters of Amatenango del Valle, Chiapas, Mexico

June Nash

In 1982 I returned to Amatenango del Valle, a pottery producing Maya community in highland Chiapas, Mexico, after fifteen years absence. The town had grown from three to five thousand but it still looked familiar, though there was evidence of greater prosperity. The plaza was paved in tile with ornate benches to accommodate visitors that now included tourists along with the civil officials sobering up from a bout in the town hall. Cement block houses with tile or metal roofs were interspersed with the wattle-and-daub mud houses with thatch or wood slat roofs that predominated when I lived there. The most striking feature was a multiple-unit government building that housed a cooperative of women potters for over a decade after I left town. When I asked why it was no longer in operation, I was told that the president, Petrona Lopez, had been killed and other women who were active in the cooperative had fled town.

Fieldwork in 1986 and 1987 was funded by the Professional Staff Congress City University of New York Research Office. I am grateful for the assistance of Gerrie Casey and Maximo Leon in carrying out the updated census.

I had known Petrona as a girl when I visited her father, the major-domo of the church, to learn about ritual practices during my first field session in the community in 1957. Shortly after her marriage in 1964 when she was 17 I attended a "curing" ceremony in her parents' home. I found her hefting 100-pound bags of wheat before the ceremony began, and this made me realize that, following the logic of curing practices in this town, Petrona's troubles with her young husband were the "sickness" that required a cure. For a week after the cure the couple slept on the path of pine boughs laid between "altars" with four candles to mark the path of the soul from the center post of the back and center walls of the house.

The "operation" was a success, but the marriage failed, and Petrona developed into a strong-willed matron. She had a child by a married man whom she took to court to gain a settlement of an acre of land. Other lovers followed as Petrona built her own career organizing the cooperative of potters. With the connections she made with the government museum agents and the Party of the Institutionalized Revolution (PRI) she ran for mayor, an unprecedented act for a woman in this or any other Indian community. During her candidacy she accused her opponent of embezzling funds given for local projects. Shortly thereafter her assassin followed her home one evening and shot her dead. The local authority made no attempt to apprehend her killer, but it was clear to the women in the cooperative that she was killed because of her role in the cooperative. Several fled town and remained in exile throughout the eighties.

Upon my return to do fieldwork in 1986 I asked the mayor of the town why Petrona had been killed. He denied knowledge but went on to assert that she had done wrong by parcelling out orders for pottery only to single women and that married women were being prejudiced. Theories as to who had done it and why she was killed abounded. One asserted that the brother of a lover whom she had abandoned and then hired someone to kill had himself killed her. Another claimed that the wife of the father of her child had her killed for claiming a piece of the land in court. But by 1989 most agreed it was done by a man hired by a former president of the town who was her running mate in the election. He had left his wife and children and gone off with another woman to "hot country," the lower altitudes where commercial agriculture offers job opportunities for Indians. Yet when I asked some of the women who had worked with her in the cooperative what they thought about the killer getting off free, they quickly reiterated her sexual misdemeanors, implying that this flouting of customary behavior for women was reason enough for her untimely death. One woman added that Petrona was disrespectful to her mother, ordering her around like a man orders his wife, calling for food as soon as she arrived home and abusing her for her negligence and laziness.

Petrona was clearly a threat to a patriarchal order of households wherein women's production was controlled by their fathers or husbands. All men in the community were threatened by the autonomy women gained in the cooperative and condoned the act that released them from the threat. Women too felt that her behavior flaunted the mores that bound them to communal traditions and that she was therefore beyond the pale that established the privileges and protection (as well as the subordination) accorded to women.

The explosive consequences of Petrona's challenge to male authority were unpredictable in a theoretical model of indigenous families as egalitarian households where income earned was pooled and shared. In assessing what led up to the murder, the structured inequality in the complementary roles of men and women must be recognized. The way in which people in this community are responding to the new pressures let loose by intensification of production reveals some of the implicit contradictions in the relations in domestic production that affect most Indian communities of the area.[1]

ARTISAN PRODUCTION IN THE DEBT CRISIS

Household production for use and exchange is becoming ever more important in the current debt crisis in Latin America. As the available capital for investment is reduced, semi-subsistence producers have to pay higher interest for loans to buy fertilizers and pesticides to raise productivity on a shrinking land base. When the increasing dependence on the cash economy involves people of the "Fourth World" who have not forgotten traditional arts, they frequently resort to the intensification of artisan production. At the same time, the growing gap in wealth among sectors of the same society and nations in the global order creates a demand for exotic products that preserve the very features destroyed in the globalization of world production. In the 1980s over a billion dollars worth of artisan work was exported annually from Third World countries to industrial centers, with Latin American countries, chiefly Mexico, exporting $100,000,000 worth (Sistema Economica Latinoamericana, cited in an editorial of American Indígena 1981:191). Uncalculated quantities of artisan products are sold to tourists within the countries to which they travel.

Given the interlocking conditions resulting in the new encounter of artisans in the Fourth World and world tourists, new market forces are being released. These have repercussions on the domestic mode of production that threaten to change the balance of power within families and the relations between families and government agencies mediating the market encounter.

Intensification of production done in the home has occurred in rural areas throughout Mexico as a result of the shrinking land base for indigenous communities and a rising population. In the 1970s a highly capitalized agricultural sector relying on irrigation, chemical fertilizers, pesticides, and herbicides was supported by official credit and the legal structure (Collier 1990; Rabasa 1981). It drew its labor supply from a base of small and medium producers that cultivated poor lands and sold at low prices to popular sectors that entered into the agro-industrial work force. Those very same laborers were forced to sell their labor in order to buy the chemical fertilizers, pesticides, and herbicides that were being introduced into semisubsistence agriculture (Cancian 1972; Collier 1990). In some areas such as the Yucatán, government policies promoting commercial crops resulted in the loss of thousands of hectares of corn and beans held by small-plot farmers, forcing them to work in the large plantations producing cotton, hennequin, and vegetable oil (Rabasa G. 1981). Agricultural workers were again caught short when the value of these crops dropped. These conditions set the stage for government promotion of craft production in the late seventies as a retreat from their own policies impoverishing the peasants (Littlefield 1978; Villanueva de V. 1981). Yet even in areas such as the Yucatán where artisan production abounds, analysts continue to deny them a future (Castro 1981).

The crisis has affected the rural economy in such a way as to threaten the hegemonic power of the ruling Institutionalized Revolutionary Party (PRI). Until the decade of the 1980s the PRI allowed a large degree of autonomy to local *cacicazgos* (power elites) of Indian leaders provided that they deliver the vote to the national party. The repartition of *ejido* plots, communal lands granted in the Land Reform Act of 1927, along with national funds for road construction and electrification projects ensured the allegiance of these local leaders. Although land was always in short supply and Indians were forced to migrate to the plantations and to construction sites for the growing tourist trade, the expanding population far exceeds the capacity of the communal land base to absorb labor. Limited credit and high interest rates threaten the intensive agriculture that Indian communities throughout the highland Chiapas area adopted in the seventies in an effort to overcome the pressure on limited land resources (Collier 1990). In some towns local cacicazgos are pursuing a policy of expelling Protestant converts and political opponents. The growing numbers of peasants thrust out of the communities with ejido lands have turned to the informal economy in cities, selling their labor or products in the plaza or streets. Those who remain within the domestic group have turned to artisan production in order to increase cash income.

The increasing importance of artisan production in the present crisis is intensifying the ties between the domestic producers and the capitalist economy to which they relate. The resulting tensions threaten the domestic relations in which such production is contained. The fact that many of these producers are women means that the newly generated sources of money are not controlled through the patriarchal relations that have developed in the domestic economy. Rising prices for raw materials, particularly those used by weavers, reduce earnings at the precise moment when families have begun to rely on these sources for more than half their income. As a result, they are compelled to raise prices or abandon the standards that tradition dictated. Forced to expand production of traditional artisan goods in order to increase cash incomes, indigenous producers are spending more of their time in the alien culture of the market economy. This threatens the very craft technique that identifies their art as unique and stemming from autochthonous sources of inspiration (América Indígena 1981:190). In the crunch of rising prices for raw materials and transportation, they are often forced to repress the standards of production that make their goods competitive with industrial products. Since many of the producers are women whose products enhanced their identity as mothers and wives, their new market roles threaten the sources of their inspiration to produce these goods.

In order to understand the dynamic of these changes on the domestic unit that continues to be the main basis for production of artisan products, we have to question what are the conditions influencing the form of articulation of capitalist expansion in rural artisan production and then relate these to cultural predilections to make decisions in one or another direction. Smith (1983/84) provides a basis for the model that follows.

First there are the conditions defining domestic relations of production in the context of community-controlled norms of conduct. These are so linked to the gender ideology that any change in the levels of production and means of commercialization affects marital relations, reproduction rates, and norms of male/female interaction in ways that are not predictable in advance.

Second there are the capital-to-labor requirements influencing the differentiation of artisan populations into owners and workers. The lower the costs for capital goods, the greater the possibility for entry into production on one's own.[2] Traditional procedures are often retained much longer in the activities carried out by women since they have more limited alternatives for earning income.

Third there are the changing market relations that affect men and women differently as they relate to local, regional, and national markets. Highway construction and improved transportation can link previously isolated subsistence economies into market systems, opening new roles for men as truck drivers and even owners of trucks.

Finally there is the intervention of state agencies that mediate between rural households and capitalist markets. In Mexico's corporatist form of government, the state is trying to integrate women in political positions that were formerly denied to them in an effort to bolster the waning power of the central party. Women artisans are currently drawn into nationally organized conferences, competitions, and programs to promote their production and sales. In these contexts, women leaders are identified and—for the first time—enter into minor roles in the state government in a way that challenges male control in the home as well as patriarchal power in the nation.

I shall spell out these conditions affecting the process of commodification in the township of Amatenango del Valle, Chiapas, where women have traditionally made pottery for domestic use and for sale for over a millennium. Changing relations within the household and community respond to and in turn influence national policies and even international markets based on tourism.

CHANGING RELATIONS OF PRODUCTION AND EXCHANGE IN AMATENANGO DEL VALLE

Household units of production are reproduced within indigenous communities where powerful constraints persist in defining the appropriate roles of men and women. The daily production of women potters recreates cultural patterns that are still distinctively Mayan. Near the present center of Amatenango is a post-classic fifteenth-century site containing a ball court and sherds of pottery produced with the same techniques and even embellished with designs similar to those of contemporary pottery production (Adams 1961). This continuity is related to an intermeshing of cultural practices and ideological premises that identifies gender roles with economic production.

The agricultural crisis was less dramatic in highland Chiapas, where subsistence producers had legitimized their claims to land seized under the agrarian law in the thirties and forties (Cancian 1972; Wasserstrom 1977), than in Yucatán (Littlefield 1976; Rabasa G. 1981; Villanueva de

V. 1981). Wheat was introduced in the 1960s as a rotation crop that enhanced the fertility of *milpa* (corn-producing) lands and provided cash income. It was only late in the seventies that widespread use of chemical fertilizers, pesticides, and herbicides increased the costs of agricultural practices. "We had a hard time promoting credit with the Indians until after 1976," a manager in the Rural Credit Bank told me in an interview in 1987, "but after that we couldn't get them enough." By the 1980s the costs for that credit had become exorbitant, 55 percent and over even for government-subsidized lending agencies, yet the farmers of the area were committed to the new agricultural techniques that demanded high inputs.

Artisan production has been a complement to small-plot semi-subsistence farming of corn, beans, and fruits in a gender division of labor in which women produced utilitarian ware that men carried on horseback to sell or barter for corn in Indian towns in the area. Men helped by bringing wood for firing the pottery and occasionally assisted in the last stages of firing when the burning planks are removed from the pots stacked in a pyramid, but women carried the clay from the pits on tumplines and performed all of the production processes from molding the base to painting the designs.

The conservative tradition in pottery production derives from the gender-specific identification of economic production in the household. Girls learn to make pots from their mothers from about the age of eleven, and they are expected to produce pottery for home use and sale throughout their lives. A woman who fails to do so, just as a man who fails to work in the milpa or bring home wood, is criticized by her kin and neighbors and may even be denounced in court when a family dispute is being aired (Nash 1985). Her identity as a wife and manager of a household is assessed not only in terms of her overall production but also in terms of what kinds of pottery she produces. In my earlier field work in 1963 to 1967, women were expected to produce water carriers, storage jars, cooking pots, and *comales* (griddles for toasting tortillas). One older woman who produced very imaginative vases, ash trays, and other items sold in the neighboring town of Teopisca was ostracized for her unconventional line of goods, and most younger women interested in getting or staying married did not venture into these fields.[3] One elderly woman who admitted to knowing how to make the huge ceremonial cooking pots tempered with ground stone was asked to do this in the homes of the captains of fiestas. She received food and liquor but no cash payment during the days that she worked.

In betrothal rituals the prospective bridegroom was enjoined to provide his future wife and children with food from the milpa and firewood

*Figure 23. Potter "mines" clay in fields near Amatenango
del Valle. Low capital-to-labor requirements enables traditional crafts to survive.*

and the bride to feed her husband and family and perform her wifely duties. Pottery was not specified in formal speech, but women who did not
help supplement family income from the sale of the cash crop of wheat
were criticized by their husbands or neighbors who charged that "she
was out looking for lovers." Judging from court cases, men were more
often delinquent than women in fulfilling their household responsibilities, and when a wife or her parents brought a man to court for negligence
in his husbandly role, the judges exhorted him to fulfill his obligations.
I observed numerous cases of men who had been condemned in court
bringing home piles of wood so that it overflowed the patio. Even with
male assistance in this chore, in my earlier field trip in 1957–58 and
1963–66 I observed many women carrying their own wood on a tump-
line. This never once occurred in my return trips in 1988 and 1989 when
I saw only boys carrying wood on wooden carts or men leading horses
laden with wood.

These patterns have been influenced but not subverted by the increase in pottery production. The major change in household production
in the period from my first field trips until my return in 1987 is the increased role men have in helping women with the gathering of raw ma-

terials—clay and wood—for pottery production. With their entry into such roles, they usually hire one of the dozen trucks operated by Indians in the community or use horses to bring in major supplies that will last for months.[4] Women still accompany them to the clay fields to test the quality of the clay and indicate where it should be dug, but they rarely carry the 50- to 100-pound balls the two- to three-mile walk to their homes. One man has undertaken pottery production, working with his wife and mother in their extended household. He specializes in the production of complicated animal figures using wire frameworks that are more like sculpture than the usual ware. His wife took over the production of doves as they gained a larger market and became a more standardized operation, while he innovated with other forms. The most elaborate was a dragon with bared teeth which I thought might have been inspired by the ancient Maya glyphs but which he told me was modeled after a likeness appearing on the trademark of firecrackers sold for fiestas. Because of his greater mobility he travels frequently to the departmental capital of San Cristobal de las Casas where he sells the work of other potters as well as his own. He often represented these works as his own; an instance of this was a large tiger molded on a wire base that won first prize in the annual exhibition of the Chiapas Artisan Institute which I discovered to be the creation of a woman who rarely travelled to the city.

The following tables based on censuses I made in 1957 that were updated in 1987[5] indicate the retention of household forms of production even with an increase in output. Table 4 relates the ratio of agriculturalists to potters with production levels.

Although the ratios of agriculturalists to potters are similar from 1957 to 1987 in the middle ranges, the remarkable changes come with the upper ranges. In 1987, women were more likely to continue to produce pottery even when there are three or more men working in agriculture. This demonstrates the increasing importance of income from pottery even in households with many agricultural workers, and it is clearly related to higher earnings from such production. In 1957 a water carrying jar sold for $2.50 to $5 pesos depending on season and market supply, whereas in 1987 a similar jar sold for $900 to $1500 pesos and by 1991 it could command $15,000 pesos. The exchange ratio of the peso to U.S. currency has gone from $10 to $2900 pesos in the same period, but even if we were to translate the terms of monetary exchange to current rates, the price such a water jar commands in the market is about thirty times greater in the dollar value for each unit. Furthermore, the high cost of credit enhances the value of immediate cash for pottery that can be used to subsidize agriculture. Comparison of 1957 and 1987 production shows that there is

Table 4.   Household Production According to Ratio of Potters to Agriculturalists, 1957 and 1987

| Agriculturalist/Potter Ratio | Production Levels | | | | | |
| | Household Use | | Sale | | No Pottery | |
	1957	1987	1957	1987	1957	1987
0/1						18
0/2					7	6
1/1			6	19		
1/2			113	116		
1/3			17	17		
1/4	2		4	5		
1/6				1		
2/2	1		8	12		
2/3	1		33	33		
2/4	1		23	29		
2/5			3	10		
2/6			1	3		
3/3			2	1		
3/4			2	1		
3/5			11	15		
3/6			4	17		
3/7			7	8		
4/4				3		
4/5			1	1		
4/6				3		
4/7				7		
5/6			2	3		
TOTAL	5		237	304	7	24

no pottery made for domestic use only in 1987 compared with 5 households in 1957. Since the few households that produced pottery only for their own use in 1957 were in the middle range of agriculturalist-to-potter ratios, it is clear that pottery production was an adjunct to income from agriculture, and women occupied with household tasks of food preparation when there were several adult men working in the fields did not have to sell pottery. Today the need for cash forces all households capable of producing pottery to engage in production for sale. Women living alone, a residence type that was not found in 1957, are limited in their production since they have to buy wood, yet even these women occasionally do make pottery.

I then tested Chayanov's (1966) thesis that the motivation to produce varies in accord with the availability of land and the ratios of consumers to producers. These correlations are shown in the following two

Table 5. Pottery Production in Relation to Producer-to-consumer Ratios, 1957–87

Producer/Consumer Ratio	Agriculture and Pottery				No Agriculture				No Pottery			
	1957	%	1987	%	1957	%	1987	%	1957	%	1987	%
Equal or more Producers to Consumers	200	79	260	82	8	80	12	40	2	100	10	40
More consumers	51	21	55	18	2	20	18	60	—	—	12	60

Table 6. Pottery Production of Households According to Number of Women in Each Household, 1987

No. of Potters in hh	Number of Households Producing:							
	Canteros	Tinajas	Macetas	Incenceros	Animalitos	Ollas	Palomitas	Other
1	135	125	125	81	46	1	23	1
2	75	68	64	52	23	4	4	1
3	55	39	43	36	21	2	5	—
4	11	13	12	9	6	—	3	—
5	2	2	2	2	1	—	1	—
TOTAL	278	247	246	180	97	7	36	2

tables. Chayanov's thesis that there will be more artisan production when there are more consumers in relation to producers is probably based on the assumption that the producers are men. When they are women, it means that their household tasks are increased when there are more consumers, i.e. children and or old people who no longer work, and they have less time for pottery. The Amatenango data show this in the reduced production in high consumer-to-producer households.[6] In comparing the 1957 with the 1987 data, the higher producer-to-consumer ratios are a result of the increased pottery production activity on the part of all women in the household. The patterns are remarkably similar except for the higher consumer-to-producer ratios in the few households with no agricultural activity. This indicates the potential for female-headed families

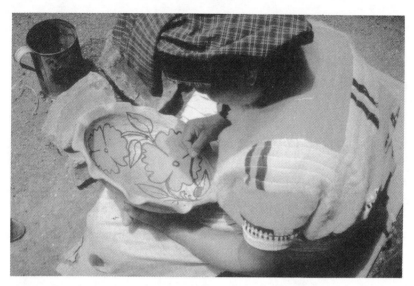

Figure 24. Amatenango del Valle potters introduce new forms, embellishing them with designs introduced by Instituto Nacional Indigenista (INI) agents, yet still use natural pigments. (Photo by Marielle Flood).

supporting children without the help of men. In the past, these households would be integrated with parents and in-laws, a resolution that occurred several times in my earlier field study in 1964. There are more potters relative to agriculturalists in 1987, a reflection in part of the greater outmigration of men as well as the increased number of women within each household contributing to pottery production. The following two tables show the activities of women potters and male agriculturalists. Of the 278 households in which pottery was censused in 1987, all made *canteros,* the basic utility water-carrying jar that was the traditional product. Most of the households also made the *tinajas,* or water-storage jars, and *macetas,* large open pots now often used as flower planters. Two-thirds of the households still make the *incenseros,* or incense burners, but the other articles introduced primarily for tourist trade are restricted to fewer than one-third of households where women work full time on pottery and are highly tuned in to the markets for tourists.

The comparison of 1957 with 1987 demonstrates the growing importance of pottery sales still contained within a domestic mode of production. The greater number of potters relative to agriculturalists reflects both the greater outmigration of men as well as the increased number of women within each household contributing to pottery production. Whereas in 1957 there was a greater division of labor among women within the household, with young mothers and old women doing far less pottery production, today almost every woman, regardless of age or number of children, produces pottery regularly.

Chayanov's (1966) expectation concerning levels of artisan production are not borne out in the Amatenango data. In his model, artisan production was treated as a residual activity undertaken "when the farm does not have the land or capital needed to develop an agricultural undertaking optimal as to the relationship between farm and family size." (Chayanov 1966:5). Similarly when men are the principle artisans, their production increases in accord with their rising responsibilities to increases in consumers. These conditions were more evident in 1957 when agricultural production was given priority in subsistence activities, but they no longer prevail since artisan production has emerged on a par with agriculture. Given the fact that women are the principle producers, we would not expect his model to be predictive of production levels. At the same time that we must pay close attention to the gender issues within the family, we must look beyond the composition of the household labor force to understand the dynamics of the domestic production. Chayanov's theory of the peasant economy as a closed system limits awareness of its articulation with the larger economy (cf. Bartra 1976).

The changing value of women's contribution through the greater intensity of artisan production is affecting betrothal customs, marital relations, and the redistribution of wealth within the family. The choice of marriage partners was customarily arranged by the parents of a young man. Although he might express an interest in any particular girl, their assistance was necessary because of the costly gifts exchanged with the parents of a girl in a series of visits that often took place over a year. When parents failed to assist a young man in his suit, it was the cause of severe friction and in one case that occurred when I was in the field in 1964, the reason given for patricide.[7] Sometimes young men went to work in the coffee or sugar cane plantations to acquire some of the cash necessary to buy liquor, bread, meat, and dowery price to gain the consent of the girl's parents (Nash 1973). Indians of the area often commented that women of Amatenango could command a high betrothal gift, equivalent to a year's income in the fincas, because of the value of their pottery production. In the 1960s, girls were asked in marriage anywhere between the ages of eighteen and twenty-five. This was considered to be an advance over previous generations when girls were betrothed shortly after puberty, and

Table 7. Marital Status by Age Group of Men and Women,
1957 and 1987

| Age Group | % of Men | | | | % of Women | | | |
| | Married | | Unmarried | | Married | | Unmarried | |
	1957	1987	1957	1987	1957	1987	1957	1987
15–20 years old	47	10	53	90	69	18	31	84
15–25 years old	65	45	35	55	86	52	14	48

were integrated in their mother-in-law's pottery production since most of
their training came after marriage. Upon my return, the majority of men
between the ages of fifteen and twenty-five remained unmarried, an increase from 35 to 55 percent as shown in Table 7. Marriage is later for
both men and women, but the change is even more dramatic for women,
with a drop of 53 percent being married in the fifteen- to twenty-year-old
group compared with a drop of 37 percent of men being married in the
same age group in the thirty-year period. During the same period,
women were gaining a degree of autonomy through their income-earning
potential that in some cases was being used as leverage to escape familial
obligations. Frequently they expressed a preference for remaining single
indefinitely so that they could enjoy their freedom and control their own
earnings. Young couples often eloped, thus escaping parental decisions
as to whom they should marry and the expensive exchanges between families of the betrothed that often required young men to work in the
plantations.

In rural agricultural societies such as Amatenango del Valle, families
are the chief means of redistributing social resources to which individual
members have different access. So long as semisubsistence, small-plot cultivation persisted (until the late sixties), most cash income came from the
sale of surplus corn or wheat sold by men in neighboring towns and later
to CONASUPO, the government supply stations. The money earned by
men from these sales was customarily turned over to women for family
needs. In betrothal ceremonies, this message was continuously reiterated
by elders to the youth. Family disputes usually revolved around the issue
of other sources of wealth. In the sixties, this consisted in earnings from
nearby sawmills or the fincas. The young men who worked outside the
town often claimed their wages as individually disposable income until
they were brought to court by their wives or parents.

These tendencies toward individualization of control over income
initiated by men in the 1960s can now be seen among women in the

1980s. Even without the development of capitalist relations of production in the home, Amatenango potters who exploit only their own labor are nonetheless threatened with the loss of kin and community ties when they can no longer expend time in fulfilling customary obligations incumbent upon them as wives, mothers, sisters, or women speakers in charge of festivals.

As their earning capacity increases, women are becoming caught up in the contest of envy and competitive personal advancement that was restricted to men when I first worked in Amatenango. Petrona was not the only victim of homicide; another young woman who was a successful potter with a wide range of orders from hotels and museums was the victim of homicide by her jealous brother-in-law in 1988. These are not isolated events, but rather a struggle involving structural realignment of gender relations as I shall try to show in the discussion of government intervention in pottery through the introduction of cooperatives.

LIMITS ON CAPITALIZATION AND PROFITS

Domestic organization of pottery production in Amatenango persists in part because of the availability of raw materials at no cost except labor expenditure and because of lack of technological inputs. The only tools women use are the digging stick to extract clay, a wooden board to turn the pot upon, and a knife blade to scrape the pots once they are sundried. Kilns were introduced by the National Indian Institute (INI) cooperative in an attempt to upgrade products and reduce the cutting of wood, but it was discovered that the clay could not be fired at high temperatures. Wood for firing the pots is available on communal lands at no cost except for the labor of men to cut it and bring it home. With the intensification of pottery production in the past decade, some better-off families hire a truck to bring home the clay and wood that they extract. This has led to higher productivity among families with greater resources, but it has not as yet created a class of entrepreneurs competing for the labor of others in pottery production. While men work for wages for other Indians and Ladinos (people of the region who do not identify themselves as Indians, speak Spanish, and wear European style clothing) as yet no women living within the community work in other households.

Capital accumulation is limited in the production of pottery as a result of these conditions. Where it does occur is in trucking interests that have grown around the transport of pottery. The first truck was purchased in 1965 when I was still working in the community. The owners formed a cooperative of thirty-one members who contributed capital for the downpayment and signed the loan. The principal owner felt that the co-operative gave him security from witchcraft, directed against members of the community who had acquired wealth. It also proved an effective means for pooling resources to gain major capital goods. When I returned to the town in 1986 there were thirteen trucks, three of which were owned by members of the same family. Since all of these owners had served as mayor, most people suspected that they had embezzled public funds to buy the trucks. Truck ownership became the principle means for accumulating wealth, some of which these owners invested in corn-grinding mills and in the purchase of cement-block houses, which were becoming increasingly desired as an alternative to wattle-and-daub thatch houses. These wealthier families undertook the more expensive *cargos* or burdens of the saints' fiestas, outdoing each other in lavish celebrations. These cargos, which had been avoided in the sixties, seemed to have ac-quired the function of validating their new wealth much as Cancian (1965) described for the "prestige economy" of Zinacantan, though Am-atenangueros did not have long waiting lists for the privilege.

Pottery production has always served as a complement to small-plot cultivation of ejido and privately held lands. With a shrinking land base, the increasing costs of intensified agriculture with the use of pesticides, chemical fertilizers, and herbicides—combined with rising interest rates for credit—enhance the value of immediate income from pottery pro-duction. The greater involvement in the cash economy accounts for the expanded production of pottery by all households, regardless of landhold-ing, and of the greater involvement of men assisting women in artisan work. By the same token, expansion of pottery production enables fami-lies to survive with small-plot cultivation, diminishing the trend toward class divisions based on landowners and wage earners.

CHANGING MARKET RELATIONS

As peasants become caught up in wage-earning employment, cash income is evaluated more highly than products made for home use in the household. When women put their products on the market, their labor is evaluated on this lower scale. In Amatenango del Valle, this tendency pre-vailed until women's products entered into a wider market arena. Before the Pan American Highway was extended from San Cristóbal to Comitán in the 1950s, men, sometimes accompanied by their children, walked with horses laden with pottery to neighboring Indian communities and to the urban centers of the highlands and down to hot country near Venustiano Carranza or Ocosingo to market their wares. Most of the exchanges were

Figure 25. Amatenango del Valle girls sell pottery on Pan American Highway.

in-kind, giving pots for corn and beans that were harvested earlier in the year at the lower altitudes, or for the cotton textiles that were woven in these areas. These trips, sometimes over a hundred kilometers, lasted days and even weeks. Recalling her struggle to keep up with the three horses burdened with pots that her father led on the trail, a woman potter, now sixty years old, said that she loved one old mare that slowed them down enough so that she could keep up with her father and brothers.

When the Pan American Highway that skirted the town center was paved, men continued to market the pottery, taking it atop second-class buses and trucks to the large market cities of San Cristóbal de Las Casas, Comitán, and Tuxtla Gutierrez. The direct exchange in local Indian towns was abandoned as Amatenangueros began to sell their products to middlemen and shopkeepers. The first truck owned by an Indian cooperative proved that it was a profitable enterprise and as a result the number expanded to thirteen. Wealth differences are now related more to the ownership of trucks than to land ownership. During the seventies when busses and trucks transported pottery to the main market centers, women were beginning to enter the market directly, sometimes alone or accompanied by their husbands. In these trips they were becoming aware of the fluctuations in price in response to the supply, but they did not adjust their production to these changes since they entered the market primarily when they needed the cash for a festival or celebration of a wedding or baptism (Nash 1985).

The decisive change in marketing relations came about in the 1970s as wholesalers from national museum shops and tourist outlets in Oaxaca bought pottery on order and sent their own trucks to pick it up. Since they dealt directly with women in their homes, this upset the men's intervention in sales and their control over the income from pottery in a way that threatened the balance of power in the family.

The growing importance of tourist markets compared with indigenous markets lends a special dynamic to the emerging commodity production. Amatenango is now the locus for tour buses to come with tourists from all over the world. In 1982 when I returned to Amatenango del Valle after 15 years absence, I noticed that, instead of fleeing from strangers, little girls flocked around incoming cars to sell small pottery items and animal figures which were an entirely new product.

Later when I returned in 1986 there was an active trade in pottery sold on the highway by householders living nearby. The highway had always been shunned, partly because of fear of traffic since some pedestrians had been killed on it, but even more because of the feeling that evil spirits traversed it. In a town that discouraged the sale of land to outsiders, I was offered a site to purchase that fronted on the highway in 1957. The growing commercialization of pottery by women who lived adjacent to the highway enhanced the value of this land as houseowners maximized their location to increase sales. In 1988 I noticed for the first time that certain householders set small tables with pottery items at the gate to their yards.

In the process of selling the objects they make, the women of Amatenango del Valle are gradually beginning to sell their culture despite powerful inhibitions.[8] The tourists pay for pictures as well as pots and, as Amatenangueros often complain, they take with each negative a part of the spirit of the producers. In the minimal cultural interaction there emerges in tourist art what Graburn (1976:17) calls "a minimum system reducing the semantic level of traditional forms to a cross-cultural code rather like pidgin language." The object purchased must symbolize to outsiders a few central beliefs about the makers. Amatenangueros have not yet reduced their repertoire to tourist-inspired jargons, but they have expanded their utilitarian ware to include flower pots and pitchers that do not hold water because of the porosity of the clay. In addition they make the decorative figures and animals prized by tourists. In the cooperative introduced by INI, young women learned to paint naturalistic flowers on large water holders and carriers that echo a colonial rather than

Figure 26. Weavers of San Andres produce huipiles for themselves and the market, and in similar form and design, a distinctive feature of Chiapas tourist sales.

Indian culture, but most of the old forms and designs are retained along with the new.

When peasant producers sell their products, there are few constraints on competition (Tax 1950). This exacerbates the unequal exchange that characterizes their relationship as buyers and sellers in national and international markets. Thus, although they appear in a double guise as both capitalist entrepreneurs and producers (Marx 1969:407, cited in Bartra 1976) they are in fact dependent on forces beyond their control. Bartra (1976:62–64) attributes their low returns to the fact that they do not form a class at the national level, although they share interests in common with other peasant entrepreneurs at the local level.

A gender perspective is necessary to go beyond the unexplored paradox of peasants' position as entrepreneur, merchant, and producer persisting in production when returns are below the costs of reproduction. Given the usually low returns, particularly in recent years, the remarkable persistence may be directly attributed to the division of labor within the family, where the masked exploitation of women—whose work is often marketed by men in the family—is maintained within patriarchal structures. The failure to assess the contribution women make in the production of products used in the family carries over and influences the decisions regarding their production of artisan products for sale. Opportunity costs (the term economists use to consider calculation of alternative possibilities when any economic activity is undertaken) are not taken into consideration as they might be with male activities. This in itself can act as a conservative force in retaining traditional production. But along with this is a division of labor where men receive returns on their wives', mothers', or daughters' labor, which is culturally devalued despite its growing importance. The powerful reaction of men to women's increasing autonomy in marketing with the government-stimulated cooperative reveals the nature of this internal exploitation within the household.

GOVERNMENT MEDIATION

All of the conditions discussed above that influence the development of commoditized social relations are in turn affected by government mediation. The framework for intervention in the 1950s was the ideology of *indigenismo*. Recognition of Indian arts and their contribution to the Mexican nation became a basis for promoting entry into capitalist markets (Novelo 1976, 1981). The government attempted to stimulate new channels for marketing Indian goods, adapting pottery, weaving, woodwork, and metalwork for tourist consumption and displaying it in the Museo de Artes Regionales in Mexico City. Programs and projects promoting the kind of production that, according to an editorial in *América Indígena* (1981) "both satisfies the criteria of the great elitist tradition without destroying the cultural canons the artisan learns in the socialization into his/her craft" (my translation) were undertaken by the Mexican government. However they were underfunded and netted little for the producer after the bureaucratic costs and commercial profits were subtracted (Novelo 1981).

In Amatenango del Valle the INI undertook a project to raise the level and quality of crafts in the fifties. Heyman (n.d.) did a chemical analysis of the pottery in Amatenango from which he concluded that improvements could be made with a simple kiln. However experiments made through the years indicated that existing clays could not withstand the higher heat of any of the experimental kilns. Instead, the INI concentrated on finding a market for the products made with the existing materials in its regional museums. The very primitive nature of coil pottery made without molds or the wheel enhanced the value of the pot. At the same time, the INI began to promote the sale of textiles woven on the backstrap loom and using natural dyes rather than encouraging technological innovation. A few households in Amatenango del Valle began to respond to the new market despite the fact that production of anything other than standard utility wares was discouraged by social ostracism. The innovators were generally widows or divorced women driven by necessity to respond to the new markets and independent of patriarchal control within the house. Some of these goods had already found a market in Teopisca, San Cristóbal, and Tuxtla Guitiérrez before INI intervened, but the volume of trade grew.

The INI also began to establish cooperatives in the predominantly Indian communities in the 1950s and 1960s. Amatenango del Valle had a cooperative store in a building that also housed a clinic in 1957. The notion of cooperatives to accumulate and invest capital took off, and a few Amatenangueros used this technique to invest in phonograph players, opening bars that catered to the young men of the town who worked in the nearby lumber camp and who returned to town on Saturday nights. A cooperative of thirty-one men purchased a truck in 1965, a number of participants large enough, the founder told me, to offset the threat of witchcraft or homicide instigated by envy (Nash 1966). Their principle customers were pottery producers taking their wares to the urban markets.

The success of these ventures probably convinced INI promoters to respond to the initiative of young women producers to set up a cooperative in 1973. They converted a building in the schoolyard for pottery production, installing a kiln to conserve fuel used in open-hearth firing and to lighten the task.

The effect of this first major attempt to restructure pottery production around a cooperative controlled by the women themselves challenged control by men over the marketing, and hence the proceeds, of pottery. Although the cooperative ceased to exist when Petrona was killed, one of the former members continues to receive and distribute orders from the national museums and INI, but it is within a network of relatives, neighbors, and friends. Some of the women who were involved in the cooperatives are still afraid to return to live in the community and the killer remains at large. Even her close associates in the cooperative condone the murder and disparage the personality and life style of the victim as the basis for justifying the act.

The experience of the cooperative promoted by the government in Amatenango del Valle is unusual in the violence of the outcome and the consequent repression of women. Yet gender antagonism has erupted in other townships within this context, indicating the importance of the perceived challenge. The entry of PRI into programs to stimulate artisan production through their Program for the Integration of Women will open up the political process in the future. Although women do not vote in the Indian communities, those who have left the village are beginning to vote in the cities. The potential for change is as yet unpredictable.

CONCLUSIONS

Pottery production in Amatenango del Valle demonstrates the potential for survival and intensification of the domestic mode of production without internal differentiation into capitalist classes of exploiters and exploited. Its persistence has been explained in economic terms as related to the low capitalization costs combined with minimal per-unit profits limiting the potential for the development of an entrepreneurial class. Yet the profits from pottery production have enabled some households to accumulate sufficient capital to buy cattle, horses, and increasingly trucks. It is also invested in the education of sons, some of whom have become teachers in the Indian schools. Once considered ancillary to the household income to care for ceremonial expenditures in the annual cycle of religious festivals, pottery production is now more central to meeting basic subsistence needs. Men devote more labor to pottery production than in the 1960s at the same time that women are assuming more responsibility for marketing. Change in the division of labor within the household is affecting the position of women within and outside of the domestic sphere, necessitating more powerful means of suppression exercised by men than in the past to preserve the patriarchal relations in the family.

The preservation of small-plot, semisubsistence household production supplemented by artisan production in the context of the growing economic crisis is a cultural preference that cannot adequately be explained in economic terms alone. I suggest here that the reason for the high preference for domestic mode of production lies in the exploitative relations in production within the household where men can exercise control over women not only economically but also sexually. This ideologically condoned domination that is defended as a "traditional way of life" is a compelling dynamic in holding together an economic unit that yields a low return but high levels of satisfaction for men accustomed to a dominant position within the indigenous family and community. Severe sanctions exercised against those women who challenge their dominance warn others to accept a traditional position in the domestic economy. Yet the increasing number of women heads of household and the rising age for marriage allow women more autonomy in the economic sphere that may eventually be translated into political power. At the same time, they lose the protection offered by men in the household and community, becoming victims to the violence and abuse that characterizes many interpersonal relations.

In the development literature of the 1960s, the choice to pursue small-plot cultivation and artisan production using simple technology would have been considered irrational opposition to the inevitable course of agro-industrial expansion or industrialization. This potential is only now being promoted by the government when it lacks the funds for the capital-intensive projects preferred in the past. Preservation of a way of life is presented as one of the objectives, yet little is said about the exploitative conditions existing within the household nor the potential for profit by intermediaries. Neither government officials nor anthropologists have adequately assessed the explosive consequences of intensified artisan production with the increased autonomy of women as producers and sellers. As the class struggle moves from the arenas of formal production to the household, it becomes increasingly evident that this must be analyzed and incorporated in policies for change.

NOTES

1. Brenda Rosenbaum (1988) explores the gender implications of these changing social relations in the nearby town of Chamula, where women, forced to augment domestic earnings by selling artisan products in the local market and streets of San Cristobal de las Casas, are beaten and often abandoned by their husbands.

2. Based on her study of artisan production in Totonicapán, Guatemala, Carol Smith (1983/84) suggests that where the amount of labor involved in production is high and the productivity of labor is relatively low despite a high price for labor, and where the cost of entry into production is low, there is little opportunity for the crystallisation of class interests in a group of entrepreneurs and workers. These factors, along with the ideological predilection for domestic production in male-dominated households, seem to hold for Amatenango del Valle.

3. Ruben Reina (1962/3) observed a similar tendency in Chinautla, Guatemala, when he asked a young woman why she did not make the angle figures that she had sold successfully in Guatemala City during his previous stay and she replied that she wanted to get married.

4. In 282 of the households censused on who and how they got clay, more than half (51 percent) of the women who went alone to get clay

still carried it with the *mecapal* and 44.8 percent used the wheeled cart or hired a truck, but when men went with women, only 20 percent used the mecapal, 60 percent used the wheeled cart or truck and 20 percent used horses. Typically when men assume tasks done by women in peasant societies they are more likely to introduce more advanced technology. This is further evidence of the power they exert within the domestic group and the consequent control over capital.

5. Censuses were done with the assistance of local policemen. In 1987 I was assisted by Gerrie Cassey and Maximo Lopez, the son of one of my close associates in Amatenango del Valle.

6. Cook (1984) also failed to see the correlation of producers to consumers and points out the need to consider specific historical conditions that affect this ratio.

7. Patricide, as Jean La Fontaine showed in her analysis of cases among the Gusi (1959) occurs when obligations that are societally structured between father and son are not fulfilled. The explosive consequences of this in Chiapas are insightfully drawn by Carter Wilson (1967) in his novel based on fieldwork in Chamula, near Amatenango del Valle.

8. Geshekter (1978) asserts that promoting tourism within the framework of competitive international capitalism involves selling a country as a product. The transcultural character of the tourist sector (D. Nash 1978) distorts the relationship between producer and consumer. The resulting "commoditization of culture" may induce other undesirable effects: the abandonment of traditional occupations to participate in the tourist industry and dependence on nonlocal retailing organizations that undermine community owned production. They further deplore the increasing inequality disrupting communities affected by tourism. One can read the history of commoditization in tracing the course of exchange of material objects, as Igor Kopytoff (1986) points out.

REFERENCES CITED

Adams, Robert M
    1961   Changing Patterns of Territorial Organization in the Central Highlands of Chiapas, Mexico. *American Antiquities.*

América Indígena
    1981   Editorial La artesanía, arma de doble fila. 41,2: 89–94.

Bartra, Armando
  1976 *Investigación Economica No. 3.* México, D.F.: Nueva Epoca.

Cancian, Frank
  1965 *Economics and Prestige in a Maya Community: A Study of the Religious Cargo System in Zinacantan, Chiapas, Mexico.* Palo Alto, Calif.: Stanford University Press.

  1972 *Change and Uncertainty in a Peasant Economy: The Maya Cornfarmers of Zinacantan.* Stanford: Stanford University Press.

Castro, A., José Luis
  1981 Breves Apuntes Geograficos de la Artesanía Chiapaneca, *Reunión Estatal para la Planeación.* Chiapas. Tuxtla Guitierrez: PRI.

Chayanov, A. V.
  1966 *The Theory of Peasant Economy,* ed. Daniel Thorner, Basile Kerblay, and R. E. F. Smith. Homewood, Il.: Richard De. Irwin, Inc.

Collier, George
  1990 Seeking Food and Seeking Money: Changing Productive Relations in a Highland Mexican Community. United Nations Research Institute for Development, Occasional Paper.

Cook, Scott
  1984 Peasant Economy, Rural Industry, and Capitalist Development in the Oaxaca Valley, Mexico. *Journal of Peasant Studies:* 3–39.

Geshekter, Charles L.
  1978 International Tourism and African Underdevelopment: Some Reflections on Kenya. In *Tourism and Economic Change.* Mario D. Zamora, Vinson H. Sutlive and Nathan Altshuler, eds., pp. 57–88. Williamsburg, VA: Department of Anthropology.

Graburn, Nelson H., ed.
  1976 *Ethnic and Tourist Arts: Cultural Expressions from the Fourth World.* Los Angeles: University of California.

Heyman, Arthur
    n.d.   Analysis of Amatenango Pottery. Chicago Chiapas Project.
              (ms. in Nabalom Library).

Kopytoff, Igor
    1986   The Cultural Biography of Things: Commoditization as
              Process. In *The Social Life of Things; Commodities in Cul-
              tural Perspective*, ed. Arjun Appadurai, pp. 3–64. Cam-
              bridge University Press.

La Fontaine, Jean
    1959   *The Gusi of Uganda*. London: International African Insti-
              tute.

Littlefield, Alice
    1976   Exploitation and the Expansion of Capitalism: the Case of
              the Hammock Industry of Yucatan. *American Ethnologist*
              5:495–508.

Marx, Karl
    1969   *Theories of Surplus Value*. Moscow: Progressive Publishers.

Nash, Dennison
    1977   Tourism as a Form of Imperialism. In *Hosts and Guests*, ed.
              Valene Smith. Philadelphia: University of Pennsylvania
              Press.

Nash, June
    1966   Social Resources of a Latin American Peasantry. *Social and
              Economic Studies* 15, 4:353–67.

    1967   The Logic of Behavior: Curing in a Maya Indian Town.
              Human Organization 26:132–9.

    1985   *In the Eyes of the Ancestors: Belief and Behavior in a Mayan
              Community*. Waveland Press. First published in 1970 by
              Yale University Press.

    1973   Ideology and Behavior: The Betrothal in a Tzeltal Speak-
              ing Maya Indian Community. In *Drinking Patterns in
              Highland Chiapas*, ed. H. Sivert, pp. 89–120. Bergen, Nor-
              way: University Sitetsforlager.

Novelo, Victoria
    1976   *Artesanías y Capitalismo en Mexico.* Mexico, D.F.: Editorial
                Nueva Imagen.

    1981   Para el Estudio de las Artesanías Mexicanas. *América Indí-
                gena* 41,2:195–210.

Rabasa G., Manuel
    1981   La Politica Agraria en Chiapas, Pioneros y Consecuentes.
                In *Mesa Redonda Tomo 3. Investigaciones Recientes en el Area
                Maya,* pp. 21–7. San Cristóbal de Las Casas: Sociedad
                Mexicana de Antropología.

Reina, Ruben
    1962/3 The Potter and the Farmer: The Fate of Two Innovators in
                a Maya Village. *Expedition,* V, 4:18–31.

Rosenbaum, Brenda
    1988   With Our Heads Bowed. Ph.D. dissertation submitted to
                the Department of Anthropology, SUNY Albany.

Smith, Carol A.
    1983/84 Does a Commodity Economy Enrich the Few While Ru-
                ining the Masses? *Journal of Peasant Studies* 60–95.

Tax, Sol
    1950   *Penny Capitalism.* Washington, D.C.: Smithsonian Institute.

Villanueva de V., Nancy B.
    1981   La Acción Estatal en el Fomento y Promoción de las Ar-
                tesanías en Halacho, Yucatán. In *XVII Mesa Redonda, Tomo
                3: Investigaciones Recientes en el Area Maya.* San Cristóbal
                de Las Casas, Sociedad Mexicana de Antropología.

Wasserstrom, Robert
    1977   Land and Labour in Central Chiapas: A Regional Analysis.
                Development and Change 8:441–63.

Wilson, Carter
    1967   *Crazy February.* Berkeley: University of California Press.

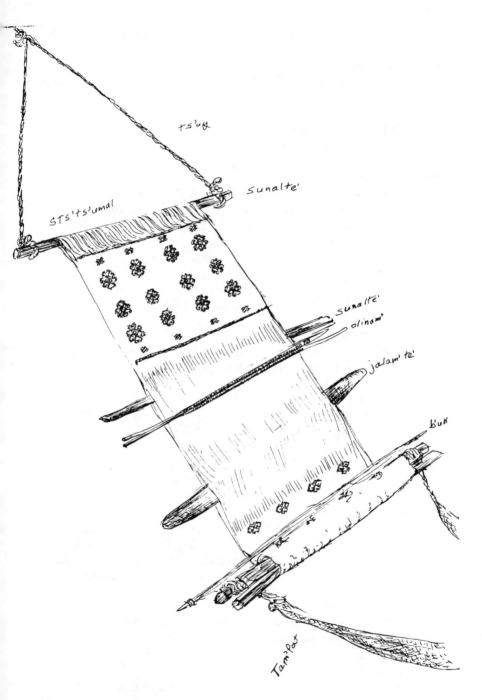

ts'ug

Sunalte'

STS'ts'umal

Sunalte'
olinam'

jalam'te'

b'uh

Tam'pat

A Loom with Serireltas from Chenalhó
Drawing by Christine Eber

7

"That we may serve beneath your hands and feet": Women Weavers in Highland Chiapas, Mexico

Christine Eber and Brenda Rosenbaum

Please, holy flowery woman
Please, holy flowery Ladina
Come and prepare the three tips of your loom
Come and prepare the three tips of your cloth
That I may find something to eat
That I may find something to drink
That I may be useful
That I may serve
beneath your hands
beneath your feet.

While conducting research in two highland Chiapas townships between 1983 and 1989,[1] we often heard indigenous women pray to their gods to help them in their work. In prayers like the one above young girls ask the moon virgin to help them learn to weave and be useful to their people. The designs girls eventually weave into cloth represent deeply rooted ideas about serving their communities beneath the guidance of their gods.

Although neither of us focused on weaving nor women's household production in our fieldwork, we were impressed by the ways women worked together to increase production of traditional weaving in order to support their families. Despite exploitation, women proudly defended their traditional roles as *campesinas* (farmers), mothers, shamans, and weavers. It became clear to us that as anthropologists and friends we need to listen to these women's analyses of their changing lives and support them in ways they request.

In this paper we discuss women's activities in weaving cooperatives in Highland Chiapas in the 1970s and 1980s as one response to economic domination by *Ladinos,* a cultural category that includes descendants of Spanish colonists, as well as Mestizos and acculturated indigenous people. We explore how women's intensified household production and collective activities are affecting household and gender relations and complicating increasingly tense social relations. We also touch on cross-cultural work to expand weaving sales in which some indigenous women and outsiders, like ourselves, are engaged. This work has made us painfully aware of the many thousands of women weavers in highland Chiapas to whom obstacles to organizing and dealing with alien markets seem formidable.

ANTONIA AND DOMINGO

When I, Christine Eber, was in San Pedro Chenalhó in September of 1989 I made an unannounced visit to my *comadre,* representative of a weaving cooperative. I realized immediately upon arriving that I was interrupting an argument between Antonia and her husband, Domingo. The next hour or two we spent discussing and trying to resolve their conflicts taught me more about women's relation to economic change in the Highlands than many of my systematic attempts to study these changes.

Antonia's agitated movements, Domingo's lowered head, created a tension I wasn't used to feeling in their home. Once I was seated by the fire, Antonia began to tell me what was happening.

> Today I feel like giving up weaving. The president of Chenalhó and his wife have asked me to be an advisor for all the weaving groups, to help them unify. But I am already the representative of two. I don't have time to go to more meetings. Domingo is angry because I am neglecting the housework. I have to leave the children alone to go to meetings. But I don't want to abandon the women in my groups. They depend on me. Domingo says I want to be an advisor for my pride, but I

have to do it because the president chose me. It is *my* responsibility. In time this burden will pass, too.

Antonia was frustrated because she could not move on in her life without an agreement with her husband about their respective responsibilities. Tzotzil-Maya couples place a great value on shared decision making in marital relations and in service to their community. They also say that one should accept *cargos,* work on behalf of one's community. Traditional cargos include service as shamans, midwives, weavers of festival garments, leaders of fiestas, and offices in hamlet and township government. Older women shamans, weavers, and past cargo holders are highly respected members of their communities. Although women do not hold political offices, with the growth of cooperatives women are now taking on nontraditional political cargos, as well.

To Antonia's relief an agreement between Domingo and herself was to take only a few weeks. The couple began to work it out the day the President of Chenalhó came to find Antonia to take her to San Cristóbal de Las Casas, the urban center of the Highlands, to meet with a lawyer to discuss unifying the cooperatives. Domingo had to concede that his wife's cargo was as important to their survival, possibly more important, than his cargo as a Catholic lay leader.

THE HIGHLANDS TODAY

Today in highland Chiapas, 500 years after the first European invasion of the Americas, indigenous men and women are struggling to keep themselves and their traditions alive. Scarce or distant water supplies, depleted or nonexistent land, hunger, illness, inadequate shelter, and religious and ethnic conflict are problems indigenous families confront on a daily basis. In 1975 Wasserstrom (1977) found that about 50 percent of Chamula families barely survived. With little or no productive land these families eked out a living by combining different economic activities, e.g. wage labor, peddling, selling artisan goods, and planting miniscule plots. More than a decade later Rus (1990:13) found that one-fourth of Chamula children in one hamlet died before age five. In Eber's census (1988) of a hamlet in Chenalhó, twenty-five women of the forty-five women interviewed had lost seventy-five children from illness. Although indigenous couples value large and close families, they have a tenuous hold on their children.

During trips to San Juan Chamula and Chenalhó in 1988, 1989, and 1990 the majority of homes we visited did not raise enough corn and beans to feed household members and had no money to buy these foods.

If a household raised eggs they sold them for cash. Chicken was a luxury eaten only during curing ceremonies or other rituals. Beef and pork were rarely affordable. Many people told us that in order to feed their families they had to exchange their labor for food or work on plantations for several months a year. Plantation work has been an option for indigenous people for some time, but many still do not consider it as honorable as supporting their families off their land.

In most highland townships men's role as principal breadwinner has been weakening. The lack of enough land, or sufficiently productive land, to feed their families has been driving men into the ranks of wage laborers, making them dependent on the demands of cities such as San Cristóbal de Las Casas and Tuxtla Guitierrez, the state capital, as well as plantations on the west coast. Going to the lowland sugar, cotton, or coffee plantations for a few months a year used to earn Chamulas just enough money to stay on their land, but as a reserve labor force that the cities could use without having to provide them with decent services (Rus 1988). Today work on plantations and in San Cristóbal is no longer readily available. Many indigenous people become part of the salaried work force, travelling long distances for long periods of time looking for work. In the past in neighboring townships like Zinacantán people solved the population explosion and consequent land scarcity with migration to lowland plots. However, as lowland ranchers are turning to cattle ranching they no longer want to rent out plots (Collier and Mountjoy 1988).

In Chenalhó, where there has been less outmigration, many men still work in their own corn and bean fields while women work in and around the home gathering and preparing food, hauling water, washing clothes, tending children and animals, and weaving or embroidering. Many women work in the field during some part of the year, and some men assist in child care and household chores. An increasing number of men are planting coffee and some are only growing coffee as the panacea for their problems. But they are discovering that coffee prices fluctuate. At the beginning of 1988 one kilo of coffee sold for $2,500 pesos, about one dollar. By September the price had fallen from $2,500 to $2,000.

In most townships women are playing a more significant role as steady providers through weaving and piecework embroidery and also through selling firewood or agricultural products. But, like their husbands, they too are more or less dependent upon the demand of cities. Weavers trying to benefit from tourism have discovered that there is considerable risk in making one's own products to sell (Rus 1990). For example, women must consider the cost of materials. With inflation the price of thread is increasing as is that of the cotton cloth that women in Chenalhó buy from Ladinos to make skirts. The latter cost about $50,000 pesos per skirt length in 1989, up from $12,000 pesos in 1987. Transportation to town to sell their work is another cost. Arrangements for child care and the possibility of increased marital tension are additional risks for most women. Some women in Chamula have chosen to stay at home and sell to an intermediary, but in 1988 a woman could only expect to make about $1,000 pesos a day (less than forty cents) for embroidery. At that time the minimum wage was $7,000 pesos (about $3.20 U.S.) a day.

Indigenous people have watched credit dry up and prices soar as the Mexican debt crisis has deepened. These factors, added to rapidly rising population, threaten the intensive agricultural methods that they adopted in the seventies in an effort to maximize productivity of their land. Confronting this crisis for men has meant either selling their labor or increasing the time spent as wage laborers on coffee or cattle plantations far from home. As these kinds of work opportunities have decreased for men, many women have had to intensify their artisan production and increase their contacts with an a lien market economy in order to support themselves and their families.

Indigenous people know that the economic domination under which they suffer is not just. They do not sit by passively as their corn supply runs out, their children die, and religious conflict spreads. Since the Spanish invasion in 1528 (Calnek 1962) indigenous men and women have attempted to bring social justice to their lives. In some respects the problems that they confront in the 1990s do not seem as awesome as those they survived during the last five hundred years. Nevertheless, the leap they are making from a life more technologically primitive than village life in Europe in the Middle Ages to a modern technological world is staggering.

Women say that to go on living well, as their ancestors have dictated, they can't afford to lose their children, their land, their animals, and the traditions through which they show respect to each other and important spiritual entities. Weavers who belong to cooperatives say that organizing themselves is one way through which they can hold onto these important aspects of their lives. Whether in cooperatives or independently, many women are turning to household production of traditional crafts for sale. Weaving for sale, in the context of their household roles, has the potential to bring moral and economic support to indigenous women in stressful times.

HISTORICAL BACKGROUND

The incorporation of new techniques and designs in traditional weaving in response to market demands during the past twenty years in highland Chiapas has many precedents. Since the Spanish invasion in 1500s through the invasion of international capitalism in the 1900s, Maya have embued alien forms with content reflecting their Maya traditions. As background to show how women work with traditional symbols and beliefs about their roles as women to build their organizations, we briefly sketch the history of gender and economic relations in the townships where we studied.

Before state societies became full-blown in Mesoamerica, women lived in kin-based societies in which they had equal rights in law and economics. They possessed property, planted crops, hunted small animals, participated in warfare, and were priestesses and curers (Bernardino de Sahagún cited in Nash 1978). Nash suggests that the structural changes the Aztec created in forming their state did not undermine women's importance in the domestic economy. They did, however, keep women out of the new predatory economy of war and tribute. Changes that the Aztec instituted included: polygamous, agnatic royal lineages which superseded the *calpulli* kin-groups that insured equal access to land and other community resources; denying women any access to warrior roles, thus cutting them off from new sources of income (in fact making them booty from war); an intensified sexual division of labor making women's tools and materials, especially the spindle and loom, metaphors for subordination; and an ideological shift in cosmology, matched to changes in daily life, which transformed a complementary pantheon of androgynous gods, first into paired bisexual deities, and finally into four male deities at the apex of a pyramid of supernatural beings (Leacock and Nash 1977).

While patriarchal tendencies became highly developed in Aztec society, it seems that classic Maya society did not restrict women as severely nor devalue their power as much. Among Yucatecan Maya a woman could become a regent, unthinkable among Aztec. Proskouriakoff's analysis of pre-Columbian clay figurines and murals (1961) suggests that, contrary to colonists' reports and some archaeologists' findings, Maya women participated in bloodletting, sat on thrones, and officiated at arraignments of prisoners. Prior to Proskouriakoff's work art historians and archaeologists thought that skirted figures were male penitents or priests and that portraits were of gods, not people. Proskouriakoff suggests that as hereditary aristocracies began to stress lineage bonds in the late classic period, women became more involved in ceremonial affairs. Yaxchilán murals depict women bloodletting, weaving on backstrap looms, and sharing the center stage with men. One Yaxchilán lintel pictures Lady Xoc, a noblewoman of the classic period, wearing the diamond-shaped designs of the universe that women still weave into ceremonial blouses used in highland Chiapas today. The remarkable continuity in women's clothing over the last 450 years has resulted from women studying old blouses of saints and weaving new ones that contained these designs for the saints (Morris 1988:113). Before the Spanish conquest Maya dressed statues of their gods. After the invasion Dominican friars enlisted indigenous women in dressing statues of saints. With this change anyone could wear the colorful blouses that previously only nobility or the gods could wear.

Peasant women continued to have important productive roles while living under state domination. With the Spanish invasion and "development" strategy, which drew their men off into tribute labor, women often took over much of their husbands' work, and in addition intensified their own spinning, weaving, and pottery work in response to forced production for Spanish tribute. The culture these women and their offspring helped create (and we would add, still create) owes much to their continuance of such traditional activities as weaving, pottery making, collecting fruit, cultivating corn, beans and vegetables, feeding their households, and treating physical and emotional disease (Nash this volume).

During the colonial period colonists imposed a system of forced labor on Indians called *repartimiento* (Wasserstrom 1983:43). They forced Indian women to weave *manta,* cotton cloth, and to sell their thread and cloth at below cost. Later women had to buy back the cloth at inflated prices. Colonists forced Indian men to work for them transporting heavy loads or farming several days out of each week. In return men received rations of food, the right to purchase goods on credit in the owner's store, and permission to plant *milpa* on small plots, barely enough to feed their families after half of the harvest went to the *patrón.*

In spite of their privileged position, from the colonists' point of view Chiapas was not highly coveted territory. It lacked mining and other entreprenuerial possibilities. What it had was a labor force. Initially colonists followed the strategy of enriching themselves off of native production, principally native trade of cocoa. However, by the mid-1500s, as indigenous populations declined, they realized that the road to riches did not lay in indigenous products and markets but in cattle raising, cotton, and sugar cane production. At first colonies forced indigenous people to produce cotton and sugar cane and return them in tribute, but as native populations declined they created large plantations to control production of these crops.

While colonists exploited indigenous labor, Catholic priests and nuns imposed Christian morality and gender concepts on them. *Marianismo,* the Spanish concept which ascribes moral superiority to women for being faithful and pure, and its counterpart, *machismo,* negatively affected indigenous women's status as did the patriarchal relations that Spaniards brought with them. Christian morality affected clothing styles as well. Short pants with a belt replaced the mantles and breech cloths indigenous men wore before Spaniards arrived. In lowland areas where indigenous people worked on plantations in slave-like conditions, they had no time to weave and adopted European peasant clothing. Nuns taught women how to embroider European designs; Spaniards introduced sheep and the foot loom on which Ladino men continue to weave cotton material that indigenous women in several townships purchase to make skirts. Despite the imposition of Spanish ideology, technology, and materials, indigenous people did not accept these without combining them with their own. Today each highland Chiapas township is known for its distinct products, clothing styles, brocaded symbols, speech patterns, and traditions.

By 1911, the end of the despotic reign of Porfirio Díaz, Ladinos in Chiapas had succeeded in depriving most indigenous communities of their lands. In the process they forced many Highlanders to migrate to lowland fields, and forced those who remained on their lands to rent them. Although the revolution, which began in 1910, arrived late in Chiapas and both revolutionaries and reactionaries used and abused Indians, followers of the revolutionary leader Venustiano Carranza instituted sweeping reforms on behalf of indigenous people. They outlawed debt peonage and abolished Indians' debts.

Notwithstanding these gains, revolutionaries withdrew after the revolution, leaving reactionary plantation owners to interpret the constitution of 1917. During the 1920s and 30s throughout highland Chiapas Ladinos privatized administrative functions that the state controlled before Díaz' era.

Politics in Chiapas since the revolution have been dominated by coffee plantation owners, lumber companies, cattle ranchers, and the landed elite. Despite the wealth of Chiapas with its lush rainforests, cattle ranches, and rushing waters trapped in hydroelectric dams, it is one of the poorest states in Mexico. Development efforts of the 1970s and 80s have not been successful in solving the problems that plague Chiapas—rising population, land reform delays, increasing concentration of private farmlands, soil erosion, deforestation, rising prices, stagnant wages, and labor exploitation (Benjamin 1989:230). A popular misconception about the current economic crisis in Mexico is that the rural poor are not suffering as much as the urban poor because they can grow their own food. But, as we have demonstrated, the ability to feed one's family off the land is not a given for indigenous people in highland Chiapas. The current debt crisis in Mexico has only intensified their already marginal existences.

Most Maya throughout Mesoamerica depend to some extent on trade and household artisan production to support their families. Maya excelled in these activities before the Spanish invasion and, as with other valued traditions, turn to them in times of crisis. After limited credit and rising interest rates in the 1980s thwarted efforts to remedy pressure on limited resources by intensifying subsistence agriculture, many indigenous people turned to selling their labor or products in highly competitive urban markets. Many of those remaining in their households turned to artisan production to increase cash income. Increasing artisan production defies predictions that the development of industrial production would eclipse artisan activities (Nash, this volume).

HOUSEHOLD RELATIONS DURING THE LAST DECADE

Household relations in highland Chiapas today have both egalitarian and patriarchal aspects. Each township is unique in the ways it has combined these aspects and stresses one over the other. Despite local differences, most indigenous men and women say that ideal household relations demonstrate fidelity in marriage and complementarity between sexes and generations.[2]

Ideal relations between humans and spiritual entities residing in sacred places on the earth and in the sky mirror cooperation between humans. In contrast to Ladinos, who often demonstrate little responsibility for women with whom they have sex and children and only a little more for the saints who guide their spiritual life, indigenous men generally demonstrate a strong sense of responsibility to women, children, and spiritual entities—and obvious pleasure in their presence. Married couples often behave like best friends in the privacy of their homes. They help each other with child care and chores and spend long, animated evenings around the fire discussing the smallest details of their own and others' lives.

Despite the importance of cooperation within households and between humans and spiritual beings, social friction is increasing in highland communities. Tension is increasing in all social relations, but the greatest tension seems to be between husbands and wives and between followers of traditional beliefs and members of Protestant groups and Catholic Action. While tension is increasing in Chenalhó, from our observations it has always been more intense in Chamula. This may be due to a combination of factors. Chamula's greater dependence on plantation work necessitates that men be away from home for long periods and that women provide for household needs in the meantime; this may have created a greater dependence on alcohol through its historical connection to debt peonage and plantation work. Other factors include the development of a class of powerful men and greater proximity to San Cristóbal de Las Casas, the urban center of the Highlands where acculturation to machismo ideology may have influenced Chamulas to adopt a symbolic system predicated on women's weakness and subordination.[3] For Chamula women, proximity to San Cristóbal has given them access to a source of nontraditional economic opportunities and markets for their products, making them less dependent on men.

While social relations tend to be more antagonistic in Chamula than in Chenalhó, like Pedranos Chamulas say that fathers, husbands, and older brothers should honor their wives, daughters, and sisters—that is, should not scold them nor use harsh voices and should provide them with corn and beans, medicines, clothes they can't make, and special foods they like. Good husbands help with household chores.[4] Some men hesitate to help when they could, but they know that they can count on their wives to help in the corn and bean fields and therefore mutual help is in everyone's best interests. Both men and women acknowledge that a woman can survive without a man by selling agricultural products or weaving to buy the corn and beans he would produce for them. Few say, however, that men can live without women. Single men living in hamlets have to buy hand presses to make tortillas and they cook their own beans. They say that they feel pitiful and others see them that way, as well.

In Chenalhó, where men have not been engaged in wage labor as extensively and where the female earth and the male sun receive equal veneration, men generally have strong ties to their wives and children and feel responsible for their welfare. Community councils of men punish other men harshly for adultery. Wives feel justified in leaving their husbands if they are habitually drunk or adulterous. Parents of abused women take their daughters in and parents of marriageable girls look unfavorably upon petitions from known drunks or adulterers. Nevertheless, heavy drinking and domestic violence have been problems in Chenalhó as well as Chamula.

Most younger women in Chamula and Chenalhó do not question their father's and husband's authority. They conform to expectations that they will stay close to home and not deal with strangers. This has kept marital friction down along with clear role expectations, acceptance of others' limitations, and a sense of humor. Nevertheless, as women are becoming more economically important to the survival of their families and communities, power relations are changing. Women's relative economic independence increases their leverage; men know that they need their wives' contributions to support their households and that their wives do not have to put up indefinitely with unjust treatment. To some extent women have always had permission from their relatives to leave a husband who was abusive. But recently a trend to not marry at all or to delay marriage is evident in communities closer to San Cristóbal or the Pan American Highway, including Chamula, Zinacantán, and Amatenango (Collier and Mountjoy 1988; Nash and Casey 1987). Even in Chenalhó where increasingly more young women are going beyond primary school and some are becoming capable of earning independent incomes, some young women are eloping or deciding not to marry. When the thirty-seven-kilometer-long dirt road between Chenalhó and San Cristóbal is paved, women will be able to go to San Cristóbal and return easily in one day, thus increasing their awareness of options for indigenous women in Ladino culture.

At the same time as they produce for the market women still weave, or pay other women to weave, much of the clothing household members wear. They weave these on back-strap looms like their ancestors used. Girls usually learn to embroider at around age eight, advancing to weaving soon after. If they show an interest and aptitude in these skills their older kinswomen will encourage them. If they show little interest or do not try hard, their mothers might threaten not to weave for them if they do not learn how to make their own clothes, but usually mothers will not force girls to continue something they don't enjoy.[5] Most women say that weaving is enjoyable and work that women were meant to do. Older women continue to teach younger women new designs and critique their work throughout their lives, but by the time girls are thirteen or fourteen they can often weave well enough to sell their work. Whether or not her family can still support itself off the land, when a woman knows how to weave she feels capable and productive; she carries on women's work in a time-honored way and others admire and appreciate her skills. Women whose mothers or grandmothers did not teach them how to weave often regret this and envy women who have the skill.

Townships have distinct styles, designs, and materials which strengthen traditions through their identifying functions. For example, Chamulas raise sheep and make wool tunics for men and wool skirts for women. They buy women's factory-made shawls and blouses as well as men's shirts and pants from stores in San Cristóbal. Pedranos, who live at lower altitudes, wear cotton clothes. They must purchase cotton thread to make women's skirts, blouses, and shawls and men's tunics. As they do not raise sheep they must also buy from neighboring Chamulas men's wool ponchos and wool thread with which to brocade designs on women's blouses. They buy cotton cloth to make women's skirts from Ladino shops or travelling salesmen.

While most women and girls do not own nontraditional blouses and skirts, young women do enjoy wearing earrings, hair ribbons, sweaters, and shoes if they can afford them. Men frequently wear nontraditional clothing, which they usually purchase used, to protect their legs in the corn and bean fields or to blend in with Mestizos. But at public gatherings where they assert their township unity, most men wear traditional clothes. Most women and men prefer to wear their traditional clothing to show solidarity with each other, but it remains to be seen if they can continue to afford to weave these. Not only is the price of thread increasing but when women are weaving for sale they have less time to weave for themselves and their families.

THE WEAVING REVIVAL AND COOPERATIVES

The revival of weaving in highland Chiapas is a response to the burgeoning tourist industry in Chiapas. San Cristóbal's daily newspaper, *El Tiempo,* (August 13, 1989) reported that in July 1989, 8,748 tourists, primarily from Europe, visited the highland town. Most tourists buy at least one and often many woven bracelets, cloths, or garments.[6]

Cooperatives have been at the forefront of the weaving renaissance. The National Indigenous Institute, INI, organized the first cooperatives in indigenous communities in the 1950s and 60s in response to a national policy of *indigenismo*. In relation to native arts, this policy recognized that indigenous arts and their part in Mexican culture provided a natural entry point into capitalist markets (Nash this volume). INI held its first weavers' fair in 1972 and opened its first potters' cooperative in Amatenango in 1973. In 1973, under the direction of anthropologist Marta Turok, non-native women set up the first nonprofit store for Indian weavers in San Cristóbal. PRODECH, a State/UNICEF agency, and an artisan's fund, funded this group. In 1974 FONART, *Fondo Nacional de Artesanías* (Foundation for the Promotion of Folk Art) opened an office in San Cristóbal to purchase artisan products. It organized 3,000 weavers into production groups in eighteen communities, gave credit, and supplied materials at cost. However, these government programs did not give artisans direct access to the market nor stable, continuous support (Morris n.d.). In 1977, Sna Jolobil (House of the Weaver) evolved out of an independent artisan's organization started by non-Indians. Fifty of the more active members of the FONART production groups joined Sna Jolobil and became the first native women to run their own cooperative. Sna Jolobil is now the oldest existing cooperative and, with over 700 members, is the largest.

Before cooperatives developed, the only outlets available to indigenous women were direct sales to tourists or tourist shops that lined the colonial streets of San Cristóbal. Then and now Ladino store owners rarely pay indigenous women what their work is worth and often make large profits. When women artisans begin to expand their markets into the growing capitalist sector wholesalers and purchasers consistently value their labor and products on the lower price scale (Nash this volume). However, as the Amatenango del Valle case indicates, and as we have seen for Chamula and Chenalhó, when women receive income from selling pottery or weaving, they use it directly to meet household needs. Women say that money they earn from selling artisan or agricultural products is theirs; however, they discuss with their husbands how to use it to supplement their husbands' small-plot cultivation or wage work.

The main reason women sell to stores is to receive immediate payment. Well-meaning Ladinas who try to pay indigenous women fairly for their work by selling on consignment have frequently had to make them wait to be paid, eliminating the main attraction of selling to stores. Women continue to use all available outlets although they might prefer to sell only within cooperatives if they didn't have to wait so long to be paid. Due to operating costs and slow periods weavers have to wait as long as six to eight months to be paid. Women impressed upon us that when the cooperative leaders in San Cristóbal or shop owners tell them they have no money, that day *those* people's children eat well. In contrast, the weavers go home without food or medicine for their children after spending what little money they have on the bus trip to town.

In Chenalhó as of 1989 there were four cooperatives. Two are connected to political parties, one is under a government agency, and one is private. The latter, Sna Jolobil, is one of the oldest and most respected of the cooperatives. The other cooperatives are under the direction of *La Confederación Nacional Campesino* or CNC, (The National Peasant Confederation formed by Cárdenas in 1938), *El Partido Revolucionario Institucional* or PRI (The Institutional Revolutionary Party, the ruling party in Mexico since 1946), and the *Instituto Nacional Indigenista*, INI.

Antonia is representative of the Chenalhó group connected to Sna Jolobil. The eighteen women who belong to this group live in three contiguous hamlets and come from the three religious groups in Che-nalhó—Traditionalist, Catholic Action, and Protestant. Women who have been with Sna Jolobil for several years, like Antonia and her mother and sisters, see it as more stable than other cooperatives because it is not con-nected to any one political party and it is "their house": members con-tribute a small amount each year to the organization, the way family members contribute to households. The decentralized structure of Sna Jolobil allows women to stay at home while still earning money. Through their local group affiliation women are connected to the larger group. They attend frequent local meetings in representatives' homes and also one or two full membership meetings yearly in San Cristóbal. This struc-ture seems to work well for most groups. However, it is predicated on representatives of local groups being honest and running their groups democratically. Members also say that it helps if representatives can speak some Spanish, so that they can better protect group members from pos-sible exploitation. Occasionally a leader doesn't do her job well. Most groups have found ways to correct this problem by confronting the leader about her deficiencies and electing a new representative if necessary. Fre-quently husbands have gotten involved during conflicts such as these.

Women must carefully weigh the advantages and disadvantages of cooperative work, as these become apparent and as priorities shift. Ad-vantages women report include:

1. The cooperative store is a safe place in San Cristóbal where weavers can speak their native languages—Tzotzil, Tzeltal, Tojolobal, and Chol—and be treated respectfully by Ladinos and Indian women and men from other townships.

2. Young girls learning to weave may join cooperatives and benefit from the guidance of many older women.

3. Weavers receive a fair price; if there is a price dispute between a weaver and others in her cooperative or representa-tives of the cooperative store, she can put her weaving in the store at the price she wants and see if it sells.

4. Weavers have a voice in how the store is run and rela-tive autonomy in their local groups.

5. The all-women environment of hamlet and regional meetings allow women who might be shy with men present to express themselves freely.

6. Weavers do not have to leave home in order to earn money so in the course of a day they can combine weaving with other household work.

7. Weavers can meet frequently with local cooperative members without travelling to other hamlets or cities.

8. Weavers may compete with other weavers for "perqs" such as prizes given out at local competitions or grants to study old designs that are in danger of disappearing.[7]

9. Weavers have the potential to expand their sales beyond San Cristóbal to the state capital, other Mexican states, and foreign nations.

10. Weavers can solicit aid in the form of grants, loans, or materials on credit or at lower prices from state and federal government officials and other nations.

11. Weavers have indirect access to the lucrative fine art market that galleries and museums control and thus the potential to earn more for their work than it commands as native craft.

12. While engaged in collective work weavers feel respected and supported for their ideas about the cosmos and their place in it. Weavers also say they enjoy working with other women who speak their languages and believe as they do.

The disadvantages of cooperatives include:

1. Weavers often have to wait as long a six to eight months to receive pay for their work.

2. Time spent weaving for sale and in numerous meetings competes with other responsibilities.

3. Marital tension can result from women's increased public role and earning power.

4. Representatives take on additional financial risks from transportation. (Bus fare back and forth to the cooperative store in San Cristóbal to deliver weavings or pick up pay often exceeds the percentage of their pay that members contribute.)

5. Relatives and neighbors may be envious of weavers and try to thwart them in their organizational work or in their family life.

6. In cooperatives which work through representatives not all women have direct access to the store, and internal competition for scarce resources and prestige can lead some representatives to take advantage of their position as intermediaries, paying fellow cooperative members less than is their due.

7. In some cooperatives women say they feel left out of the most important administrative decisions (For example, members of Sna Jolobil are concerned that the 100 percent mark-up on their weavings at the cooperative store makes them less competitive in the market. Furthermore, weavers say they want to know where this extra income goes and have a say in how it is used.)

8. While store owners are often Ladinas most cooperative leaders are men; cooperative personnel say that, given the patriarchal structure of Mexican and indigenous society, men make more suitable leaders, although some indigenous women are capable of assuming these duties, as women like Antonia demonstrates from her leadership of her local group.

9. Outsiders working with indigenous women in cooperatives (e.g. church workers, government representatives, and anthropologists like ourselves) often lack expertise in marketing artisan products. Relying solely on the tourist market in San Cristóbal, there are not enough customers for the large number of productive indigenous women. The glut of artisan products in the local market is bringing prices down. Women have their hands full producing their products and surviving; cooperative office workers and others who help the women organize have their hands full, as well. Developing outlets on the national or international level requires much time, marketing knowledge, and contacts that few people have.

New cooperatives are forming continuously in the Highlands. In a recent trip to highland Chiapas in February 1990, Rosenbaum visited a relatively new cooperative in Tenejapa, a Tzeltal community bordering Chamula and Chenalhó. The Catholic Church began this cooperative as a part of a larger program of religious instruction and literacy. Some of the funding for this program comes from a sister parish in Milwaukee, Wisconsin. Working with Catholic sisters, indigenous women from Tenejapa have been able to organize women in some of the most remote hamlets of their townships. As is the case in Chenalhó and Chamula, women in remote hamlets are less likely to join cooperatives than women living in head towns, or in hamlets within a few kilometers of head towns.

Rosenbaum also met with members of *Chi'iltak* (Tzotzil for companions), an organization in San Cristóbal de Las Casas that provides legal assistance to indigenous groups. Working as volunteers with Chi'iltak, Ladinas offer advice and legal assistance to indigenous women in various aspects of their lives, from organizing collectives to dealing with domestic violence. We applaud such efforts between local Ladinas and indigenous women to explore their common differences as women living in two closely related but distinct patriarchal societies. Such exchanges between Ladinas and indigenous women are rare, especially as Ladinas, too, are struggling to support their families and have little time or energy for volunteer work. As we have found from our privileged positions as a Ladina and a white woman in our respective countries, Guatemala and the United States, it is easier to address issues of inequality between classes and between men and women than inequality brought about by institutionalized racism. The lack of dialogue about racism in Mexico is ironic as so much of Mexico's national identity and revenue from tourism come from indigenous traditions and products.

Despite efforts to the contrary, most cooperatives perpetuate paternalistic relationships between Indians and Ladinos and keep indigenous women more or less dependent on their husbands. As many indigenous women live in distant hamlets, do not speak Spanish, and are uncomfortable in Ladino society, they often depend on their husbands to make commercial decisions, deliver their weavings to San Cristóbal, or accompany them to cooperative stores, especially when they have a problem to discuss with cooperative personnel.

Although cooperatives provide women with economic opportunities, they have yet to realize their full potential. In our opinion, the most pressing problems facing cooperatives are their inability to provide weavers with a reliable and stable income, the unfair economic risks weavers shoulder, and the need to give indigenous women greater control over administrative decisions and functions. The failure of most cooperatives to adequately address these issues leaves women economically insecure and still enmeshed in traditional dependent social relations.

EFFECTS OF COOPERATIVES ON SOCIAL RELATIONS

Cooperatives affect indigenous women both positively and negatively. While increasing women's political power and presence, they also cause tension in households and complicate already difficult political and religious situations in hamlets and townships. Cooperatives can further divide women at a time when religious and political differences are dividing households and communities. They also have the opposite effect of creating common cause between women from diverse religious groups and townships.

Marital tension is an inevitable consequence at this time. Men and women are no longer clear about what others expect of them. Women like Antonia are breaking new ground. The changes in her life brought about by collective work require her to carefully balance her new economic independence and broader influence with traditional expectations about women. She may not be so willing to comply with traditional expectations if Domingo resents or challenges her new roles. Rus (1990) reports that in Chamula, where women have been economically independent for a longer time, some couples are making the kinds of adjustments necessary to keep their unions complementary, and therefore more or less traditional. However, when women first became involved in sales to tourists, their husbands accused them of being "women of the street" or destroyed their work (Gómez Pérez 1990). When women kept their money from sales separate, for fear their husbands would buy rum with it, their husbands got angry and beat them. Rus states that couples resolved some of these conflicts as women's financial contributions became more important to family survival and as more women became involved in artisan production. Chamula men now take a more active role by acting as Spanish-speaking go-betweens and security guards for their wives on trips to San Cristóbal, and they carry their wives' products with them to sell when they go looking for work. However, as Nash (this volume) reports for Amatenango del Valle, although men and women worked out similar compromises, as women replaced men in the market men became fearful and resorted to violent repression.

Indigenous women recognize that their relation to their male relatives to a great extent conditions their ability to negotiate with state representatives and outside organizations. However, Antonia's story demonstrates that recognition of women's artisan work by political leaders on township and state levels can legitimate indigenous women's work in the eyes of their husbands as well as legitimating native culture in the eyes of outsiders. But political leaders also use women for their purposes, pulling them out of traditional roles and then plunking them back at whim.

Women like Antonia are attempting to translate the *modus operandi* of their households into the personal style that oils the political machinery in Mexico. On the local level they are often the brunt of rumors. Antonia has borne up well under accusations of envious men and women who have accused her of lying, being self-serving, and looking for illegitimate influence in local affairs. She struggles to stay out of the kind of contests that Nash notes have characterized indigenous men's—and now many women's—involvements in the market economy. Nash (this volume) tells the tragic story of two young women from Amatenango who were murdered because of their leadership roles related to artisan activities.

While conflict in Chamula and Chenalhó takes place in the arena of gender relations, it is especially intense between different religious groups. Conflict in Chamula reached a peak in the early 1970s and resulted in traditional Chamula caciques expelling thousands of Protestant Chamulas from their land. About 10,000 to 15,000 Chamulas have been expelled since 1974. Some founded evangelical communities around San Cristóbal. Others live in squatter settlements.

Religious differences in Chenalhó have grown in importance since the 1950s when Protestant mission work began in earnest. Protestant missionaries encourage their followers to see rum and traditional rituals and healing practices as the source of their poverty, and personal salvation through Jesus Christ and private capital accumulation as ways out of it. Religious tension reached a critical point in the summer of 1989 when the president of Chenalhó, a compesino, forced the issue of *cooperación*. Cooperación is the monetary contribution each household makes to the major fiestas and masses held in hills and caves throughout the township three times a year. For about thirty years Protestants in Chenalhó have not had to contribute. As the numbers of Protestant converts have grown steadily in recent years (some estimate their numbers are well over one-third of the township population), many Traditionalists and members of Catholic Action[8] fear that they can no longer bear the burden of financing fiestas and masses. Seeing these events as focal points of unity and important to cultural survival, the current political and religious authorities are forcing Protestants to cooperate. Protestants do not agree among themselves how to respond. Some are contributing, others are withholding. While at present most cooperatives are composed of women from the three major groups, such religious differences could eventually divide cooperatives.

Class differentiation is increasing in indigenous communities in highland Chiapas; in most communities weavers risk being envied as rich, even if they earn only a little more than their neighbors. While a class of powerful men has developed in Chamula, weavers in Chamula and Chenalhó have not been able to amass the kind of wealth that Nash (this volume) reports for women potters in Amatenango.

Although not an economic class, Protestants set themselves apart by encouraging more individualistic economic goals for their members and by rejecting traditions such as ritual drinking and traditional fiestas. But they often form their own communities and neither need outsiders' acceptance nor fear their envy. Those Protestant cooperative members whose neighbors and fellow cooperative members are Traditionalists or members of Catholic Action are grappling with how to live with and work through differences. Unlike their Traditionalist and Catholic Action sisters, these women's collective actions do not reinforce their religious beliefs. Generally Protestant groups do not value collective social action outside of their groups, nor do they give women a voice in community affairs.

One incident in the fall of 1989 in a hamlet of Chenalhó highlighted the struggle women cooperative members face to live differently but at peace with their neighbors. Scarce resources, such as water, can become friction points when one group of people appears to be benefiting more than others from this resource. Weavers must use many buckets of water to wash one finished weaving, as dyed threads bleed considerably. Envious neighbors see a direct link between using more water and making more money. In-marrying men are also a target when there is stress on local resources. In one hamlet where several cooperative members live, hamlet officials decided that only people born in the hamlet could use the water. The conflict broke up at least one extended family of weavers. The mother was able to stay, but one of her married daughters had to leave with her husband to live in his hamlet, and another now has to walk an extra half hour at least twice a day to a tank located in her husband's hamlet. The husbands of both daughters are leaders in Catholic Action.

CONCLUSION

Indigenous people in highland Chiapas no longer live in homogeneous, closed corporate communities perpetuating age-old democratic traditions, if indeed they ever did. As we have demonstrated they are capable of creating differences and divisions among themselves, in response to both economic domination from outside and competition from within.

Like their sisters in Latin-America and women throughout the Third World, indigenous women in highland Chiapas have not had a voice in the public arena since the Spanish invasion. The cooperative movement of the 1970s, 80s, and 90s has given women a context in which to speak out about domestic concerns such as water, health, shelter, and alcohol abuse. Many indigenous women are speaking out for the first time. Cooperatives and Catholic Action are providing women forums in which to critique their work and community problems such as abusive drinking. However, most women remain unconnected to markets or forums to express their views. Of the approximately 400,000 indigenous people in highland Chiapas, we estimate that about 125,000 are economically productive women. Of this number only a small percentage, perhaps 10 to 15 percent, participate in cooperatives.[9]

In their cooperative work indigenous women are moving out of their confinement in the more private sphere of the household. However, like Latin American women of all classes and races indigenous women in highland Chiapas reject organizing movements that threaten their identities as mothers and wives (Safa 1988). As their cooperatives currently stand, indigenous women seem to have found a way to maintain their families that validates their household-based identities and supports their people's traditions. However, for these cooperatives to function for them and their families women must continually balance household and community, a task complicated by intense religious conflict, increased contact with outsiders, and increasing economic marginalization.

For those of us wanting to support indigenous women in their efforts to perpetuate their traditions and raise healthy, proud children, it is important to consider how our efforts to integrate them into national and international economies relate to their vision of their lives. When speaking about their weaving and collective work, weavers do not talk about personal empowerment through the symbols that they weave nor the solidarity they create. Instead they speak about their weaving, along with their organizing work, as service to the families and communities, at once practical and sacred. Leaders like Antonia say that it's good to work through cooperatives, as long as people respect each other and their gods.

NOTES

1. Christine Eber conducted her research in San Pedro Chenalhó and has been involved with the Sna Jolobil group of which Antonia is the representative. Brenda Rosenbaum conducted her research in San Juan Chamula and has been working with a widow's cooperative in Guatemala and with cooperatives and stores in San Cristóbal de Las Casas. We have been trying to find nonexploitative markets and grant support in the United States, as well as to educate our people about the impact of tourism and consumer patterns on traditional cultures. The Hispanic Women's League in Buffalo has committed itself to providing annual grants for weavers in Sna Jolobil to study old designs that are in danger of disappearing. Antonia applied for and received a grant from Church Women United Intercontinental Grants for her local group of Sna Jolobil, through a grant application Eber provided and assistance from the director of Sna Jolobil, Pedro Mesa.

2. In the traditional bride petition, which is still the predominant practice, a boy picks out a girl that he would like to marry and petitions her parents to marry her. Parents consider their daughters ready for marriage by the time they have reached fourteen or fifteen, at which time they have learned to weave and do household work. Parents do not expect their daughters to be emotionally mature, as they believe they will grow into maturity alongside their husbands while living with them or with their husbands' parents.

3. According to the Chamula account of the coming of order, coldness, femininity, and lowness came before heat, masculinity, and height. By sitting on blocks of wood and going barefoot, women are in close touch with the cold ground. The tiny chairs on which men sit raise them above the ground and the sandals they wear separate them from it and complement their masculine heat (Gossen 1974:37). While Chamulas stress that a man's heat is linked to strength and a woman's coldness to relative powerlessness (Rosenbaum 1987:333), Pedranos say that the cold earth, and by extension women, have the power to give and take away life. They say that heat, like heart size, increases with age and community service, for both sexes.

4. Men stack and reorganize corn in its bins in the house and cut, carry, and stock firewood on a regular basis; when needed they shuck and grind corn, carry babies and care for children, feed chickens and other animals, collect fruit from nearby trees, buy the kerosene for lamps and starting fires or an item of food the family needs, comfort children who wake up from bad dreams and lead them outside in the dark to urinate. Nevertheless, these latter tasks are principally women's work.

5. If a woman has no daughters and sons are interested in learning how to weave or make tortillas, she will teach them. Invalid sons or sons of women who have no husbands may learn these skills whether or not there are daughters. Women do not think sons unmanly if they want to learn these tasks.

6. Weavers are aware that outsiders collect their work as something special, to hang on a wall, lay on a table, or wear on special occasions, and that these people have their own criteria for judging weaving. This is fine with weavers, although they view their weaving first as work, not any more or less important than other tasks they perform. When they critique each other's work they discuss the overall effect of the colors, the finishing

off of edges, the size and placement of particular designs, the number of hours it took to complete a certain part. In contrast to tourists who prefer muted, naturally colored dyes, indigenous women and girls prefer to weave with brightly colored acrylic and cotton threads. They see the naturally dyed colors their grandmothers used as sad.

7. An important part of Sna Jolobil's work is developing an historical collection of weavings from which weavers can draw inspiration. These are displayed in the Bartolomé de Las Casas Museum in San Cristóbal. Study grants enable women to study weavings from Sna Jolobil's collection without having to travel to San Cristóbal. In their homes, integrated into their daily routines, weavers can study pieces from the collection. This program supports women in learning how to make designs that might be forgotten, while respecting women's household based roles.

8. *Acción Católica,* Catholic Action, began in highland Chiapas in the early 1960s under the direction of Vatican II and Bishop Samuel Ruíz García. Today over 7000 Indian men and women lay leaders, assisted by nuns and priests, organize their communities into small groups which identify and study the sources of their economic exploitation and political oppression and develop strategies to confront these.

9. In 1988, only three women out of forty-five Eber interviewed in a household survey of one hamlet belonged to a cooperative.

REFERENCES CITED

Calnek, Edward
    1962   *Highland Chiapas Before the Spanish Conquest.* Ph.D. dissertation, University of Chicago.

Benjamin, Thomas
    1989   *A Rich Land, A Poor People: Politics and Society in Modern Chiapas.* Albuquerque: University of New Mexico Press.

Collier, George A. and Daniel C. Mountjoy
    1988   *Adaptando a la Crisis de los Ochenta: Cambios Socioeconómicos en Apas, Zinacantán. Documento de trabajo.* San Cristóbal de Las Casas: Instituto de Asesoría Antropológica para la Región Maya, A.C.

Eber, Christine E.
   1991   *Before God's Flowering Face: Women and Drinking in a Tzotzil-Maya Township.* Ph.D. dissertation, SUNY Buffalo.

El Tiempo
   1989   Article about tourism. 13 August.

Gómez Pérez, María with Diane Rus and Salvador Guzmán.
   1990   *Bordando Milpas.* San Cristóbal de Las Casas: Instituto de Asesoría Antropológica para la Región Maya, A.C. (Tzotzil-Spanish).

Gossen, Gary H.
   1974   *Chamulas in the World of the Sun: Time and Space in a Maya Oral Tradition.* Cambridge: Harvard University Press.

Leacock, E. and June Nash
   1977   Ideologies of Sex: Archetypes and Stereotypes. In *New York Academy of Sciences Annals.* 285:618–45.

Morris, Walter F.
   n.d.   *Crafts, Crap and Art: The Marketing of Maya Textiles in Highland Chiapas, Mexico.* Ms.

   1988   *Living Maya.* New York: Harry N. Abrams, Inc.

Nash, June
   1978   The Aztecs and the Ideology of Male Dominance. In Signs, 4, no. 21:349–362.

Nash, June and Geraldine Casey
   1987   *Women and Petty Commodity Production in Chiapas, Mexico.* Ms. To be published in Instituto de Asesoría Antropológica para la Región Maya, A.C. INAREMAC, San Cristóbal de Las Casas.

Proskouriakoff, Tatiana
   1961   Portraits of Women in Maya Art. In *Essays in Precolumbian Art and Archaeology,* ed. S. K. Lothrop et al., pp. 81–99. Cambridge: Harvard University.

Rosenbaum, Brenda
1987   *With Our Heads Bowed: Women, Society, and Culture in Chamula.* Ph.D. dissertation, SUNY Albany.

Rus, Diane
1990   *La crisis económica y la mujer indígena: El caso de Chamula, Chiapas.* San Cristóbal de Las Casas: Instituto de Asesoría Antropológica para la Región Maya, A.C.

Rus, Jan
1988   Changes in Employment Patterns Among Chamula Men, 1977–1987. Oral presentation, XIV International Congress of the Latin American Studies Association Conference, New Orleans, March, 1988.

Safa, Helen
1988   Gender and Social Science Concepts in Latin America. Paper prepared for XIV International Congress of the Latin American Studies Association, New Orleans, March, 1988.

Wasserstrom, Robert
1977   *Ingreso y trabajo rural en los Altos de Chiapas.* San Cristóbal de Las Casas, Chiapas: CIES.

1983   *Class and Society in Central Chiapas.* Berkeley: University of California Press.

San Juan Chamula Woman spins Woolen Yarns
Drawing by Christine Eber

8

Belts, Business, and Bloomingdale's: An Alternative Model for Guatemalan Artisan Development

Tracy Bachrach Ehlers

INTRODUCTION

In 1977, Don Manuel Sicajan Perez, mayor of San Antonio Palopó, came to Peace Corps worker Jerry Goldstein to have a talk. He said, "Don Geronimo, I'm worried about my son. He's working with your weaving cooperative and doesn't have time for the milpa. He's not going to have any money or any future going as he is going." Jerry told Don Manuel

This research began as a field story I shared with June Nash when she was Distinguished Visiting Professor in Women's Studies at the University of Colorado in Boulder. June encouraged me to follow up on it with a field trip, and what had been an anecdote in 1987 has turned into a long-term commitment to working in San Antonio Palopó. Earlier versions of this paper were read by Paul Shankman, Duncan Earle, and Michael C. Ehlers. As with all my work in Guatemala, none of this would have been possible without the guidance and advice of Jerry Goldstein. All the names in this article are fictitious except that of Jerry Goldstein.

just one thing: "Be patient." He was right. Ten years later, his son, Julio Sicajan is one of the richest men in San Antonio, and also one of the most respected. He is a textile subcontractor with hundreds of weavers working for him. He owns two diesel-driven mills, has three boats for cargo and passengers, is past president of Acción Católica, head of the National Committee for the Protection of Lake Atitlán, Secretary of Artexco Guatemala. He gives injections and sets up intravenous tubes as part of his duties as a certified health assistant. The Agency for International Development (AID) sent him to Miami for entrepreneurial management training. He installed a shower, a refrigerator, and a color television in his house. Clearly, Julio has made it. Always a natural leader, an alert and charismatic person, it was probably in the cards for him to rise in the esteem of his fellow villagers as well as in his economic fortunes. But the introduction of weaving into San Antonio Palopó provided Julio with an unheralded opportunity to go beyond the traditional parameters of success. His entrepreneurial instincts have had a field day as grassroots development took San Antonio into the world of international trade.

As we shall see, only a handful of men have profited to this extent, and even in that group, Julio is exceptional. The lives of most natives of San Antonio (called Tunecos) have changed in far subtler, less substantial ways. Yet the lives of everyone in San Antonio—weavers and nonweavers alike—have changed because of the introduction of the weaving business.

My first visit to San Antonio Palopó was in 1977 when my good friend, Jerry Goldstein, was the Peace Corps worker there. Jerry had worked as a designer and interior decorator and was, at thirty, older and more experienced than the average volunteer. He was bored in California and, after watching the end of the Vietnam War on television, decided to do something meaningful with his life. The first time around, the Peace Corps rejected him because of his age and because they thought him unqualified to do anything useful in the Third World. He persisted, reapplied, and when they offered him Guatemala, jumped at the chance to work with artisan cooperatives. It was through him that I learned the story of the weaving co-op.

It seems a road was being built from Panajachel, the tourist center of Lake Atitlán, to San Antonio, thirteen kilometers away. The townspeople wanted to take advantage of this commercial link by learning to weave items they could sell to the tourists they imagined flooding into town or now reachable in Panajachel. Things were just beginning then, but I kept in touch with the progress of the road (it took three more years to reach San Antonio) and the development of the cooperative. I went back ten years later and again in 1988 and 1989 to document the impact that the weaving business had had on the village. Jerry is now Guatemalan manager of the American fabric and clothing exporter, here called Hilos del Lago, living in Panajachel and in San Antonio on weekends. I begin my paper with this introduction to Jerry Goldstein because it was largely through his efforts as a Peace Corps volunteer and with Hilos del Lago that San Antonio's weaving business expanded exponentially. Working with local leaders and entrepreneurs, he brought a level of sophistication and business sense to their production that was previously unheard of among village weavers. The success of Hilos del Lago encouraged other firms, so that now weavers have orders from nearly a dozen major buyers. More than half the homes in the village have looms and year-round work producing the belts and placemats that have made them famous over the last decade.

This paper will take you through those ten years. It is at once a history, an ethnographic sketch, and a critique. I say "critique" because San Antonio's accomplishment is not a simple matter of the correct application of lively entrepreneurship to the advancement of artisan trade. On the one hand, yes, this town's success story is emblematic of the potentials for Third World participation in international business and industry. But on the other hand, I must confess that I am still not convinced that San Antonio's achievements are not at too high a cost to them in terms of loss of productive autonomy and external market dependence. Still, one cannot deny the benefits of an income-producing activity that is a popular substitute for picking cotton on coastal plantations.

The study examines the role that textile production is playing in this small Mayan village. It traces the development of commercial weaving over the last ten years as well as the town's relationship to one U.S. clothing company. The considerable success of this firm (over a million dollars grossed in 1987) has been based on the production of textiles in several Guatemalan communities. Like the dozen or so other textile businesses exporting hand-woven goods from Guatemala, the profits of Hilos del Lago are partly due to inexpensive labor costs. The sophisticated designs conceived in New York are expertly executed in San Antonio for between four and six quetzales a day. (In 1989 the value of the quetzal was Q2.70:$1.) The central question posed here is whether this is a partnership made in heaven or merely clever exploitation of cheap Indian labor. In other words, has the hunger for commercial income that motivated them to form their weaving cooperative turned the people of San Antonio into rural proletarians vulnerable to the faddish tastes and volatile markets of the industrialized North? Or, is weaving offering the people of San Antonio the opportunity to rise out of desperate poverty while still maintaining their integrity as Mayan artisans? I think we shall see that there is no easy answer.

HISTORY OF THE COOPERATIVE

San Antonio Palopó is a small (approximately 2650 people) Cakchiquel-speaking town on the eastern shores of Lake Atitlán. For centuries it had only been possible to reach the town by boat or footpath, but since 1980, a dirt road has connected the town with Santa Catarina and then Panajachel on the northern side of the lake. This isolation partly explains the tenacity with which the people have maintained their language (45 percent speak Spanish as a second language), their indigenous costumes, and their Mayan traditions. Protestantism is a recent innovation, one that, along with the introduction of electricity three years ago, creates a nightly din of loudspeaker proselytizing. The town's main commercial crop of onions depends on careful maintenance of *tablones* or small terraces built steeply up from the lake like a Greek amphitheater. Deforestation has made scarce the water needed to irrigate onions, so in the dry season, people tediously haul lake water to their tablones in large, tin watering cans. Water for domestic consumption is piped into town from a spring above. But that water is also in short supply, and it comes only every three days. Only a fourth of the houses have water in their homes; the rest must go to public faucets to fill their jugs. Like the rest of the towns on the lake, San Antonio's water supply is not potable and must be boiled to drink. Houses are made of adobe and thatch, or in a few cases, block and *lamina* (tin roofing sheets). Commonly, seven people live in one fifteen-foot square room with a three-stone cook fire in the corner, although some families may have a separate cooking stall outside. Milpa is cultivated in small fields up the side of the mountain several hours walk away. The average family owns one tablon for onions, and about four scattered *cuerdas* for corn and beans (about a half acre). Only the wealthiest grow enough food for the year, so the production of a cash income from the sale of onions or anise is essential. In addition, for decades the need for supplementary cash has been met by seasonal migration to coastal plantations to pick cotton.

The steepness of the site creates a feeling of tenement living. Plots are so tiny that neighbors live quite close together above, below, and on both sides. Crowding exacerbates the abysmal sanitary conditions: one expert estimates that only 10 percent of the population properly utilizes outhouses. Because boiling water requires burning costly amounts of wood, parasites are endemic among the people, constituting the major cause of death. The only doctor for the 5,000 people in the *municipio* (the town and its outlying villages) is a medical student doing five months practice in the Puesto de Salud. The diet is based on tortillas eaten three times a day, supplemented by small servings of beans, fish, crabs, and occasionally eggs. Only 16 percent of the village is considered literate by the census takers; my own estimation is that the number of people who can actually read is far less. Although there is a six-room school, few families can spare the labor of their children for even the three years needed to be considered literate. Given this rather bleak demographic profile, it is no wonder that in his report, the latest medical student said,

> What we find here is a typical highland population where people and diseases exist side by side; where there are no opportunities or resources to help people to rise above their poverty; where women are given subordinate roles; and where children cannot dream of achieving anything better because they are sick, malnourished, working all the time, and improvizing toys, which like so many other things, they will never have. What I have confronted here is a reality consistent with so many poor communities where life just consists of being born, growing up, having children, and dying. (author's translation)

Ten years ago, a group of Tunecos realized that they could do something about the quality of life by incrementally increasing the income-producing work in their town. Fishing and onion production barely provided the cash necessary to sustain the milpa. Trips to the coast were miserably hot months of fourteen-hour days, poor food, no sanitation, and in their own words, "being treated like mules" for the small remuneration they earned. There had to be an alternative. Their first plan was to learn to weave well enough to produce themselves the *cortes* (traditional skirts) they had always bought in Solola. They brought in a weaver from Salcaja to teach them on a borrowed foot loom, but the quality was poor and they dropped that idea. They tried again. They knew the road was coming, providing them with potential customers and commercial access. They decided to develop a product to sell to tourists. Through his work for Radio Atitlán, Julio Sicajan had visited the successful weaving co-op in Santiago Atitlán. He immediately understood that properly organized, a weaving cooperative in San Antonio could provide its members with a real cash income. Several of his friends agreed. So one week Julio and Santos Perez Cumas took the mail boat to Panajachel to talk to the Peace

Corpsman in charge of the artisan cooperative store, Jerry Goldstein. Although they did not know how to weave, they said they wanted to start a
weaving cooperative. Of course, the women wove on backstrap looms,
but none of them knew how to use the larger, commercial foot looms that
the Catholic Church was willing to donate to the project. Goldstein accepted their proposal and eventually moved from Panajachel to San Antonio to help the weavers evolve into a legal artisan cooperative.

As his first step, Jerry gave classes on the functions and philosophies
of cooperativism, on members' obligations to the cooperative and what
they could expect in turn. One of the most important classes offered fea-
tured the use of a tape measure. Until then, weavers utilized a span or a
hand spread (*cuarto*) equaling about eight inches. Measurements could
thus be one cuarto and two fingers, etc. Clearly, if the cooperative was to
be professional, the need for precise measurements was now critical. Next,
he brought in a weaver from San José Caben, San Marcos, where he had
worked before, to demonstrate traditional warping patterns and techniques. These and other classes were unusual social opportunities for the
cooperative members who became quite close from being together so
much. All the meetings were held at Jerry's house. He donated his Peace
Corps salary ($200 a month) to buy supplies such as carbon paper that
they used and reused so many times they had to paste the pieces together.
Looking back, he has said, "We were all poor then."

The question then arose, now that we know how to weave different
patterns, what products will we make? There were several options.
Women who wove clothing on backstrap looms started making tourist
blouses, napkins, placemats, and purses on their *palitos*. Others took turns
on the foot looms weaving rolls of material. Based on the idea of creating
a product from a traditional design they all knew, Jerry worked to develop
a commercial shirt fabric from the traditional *huipil*. Their carrying cloths
became the next fabric, then came one based on the sleeves they wove for
men's shirts. From day one, the quality was excellent. In fact, it was so
good that Jerry's first markets were the Museo Ixchel gift shop and noted
Guatemalan clothes designer, David Ordoñez.

Two Maryknoll nuns lived in San Antonio, and from the beginning
they were very involved and supportive. They lobbied the priest in Panajachel until he secured Q8000 from the German bishops to build a cooperative building. AID and Oxfam also contributed in the early stages so
that they could purchase materials. Very quickly they had six looms. People learned to pack orders, follow through on business dealings, maintain
quality control. Jerry meanwhile was developing a clothing line making

dresses from American Folkways patterns. The *madres* taught people to sew on donated sewing machines.

The cooperative quickly grew as people recognized its potential. Begun with 18 members, they soon had 48, then 108, 150, and at its peak, 240 members. Initially, cooperative membership was overwhelmingly female palito weavers seeking markets. Eventually, this changed as both men and women learned to weave on foot looms. The first small group was made up of eighteen-year-old men and aged grandmothers. Only in the second group did a mature man join, and he immediately became the cooperative president.

From the start, San Antonio's goods have had the reputation of being highly priced. Perhaps this is because of the process they went through to set prices. Jerry asked them, "How much do you want to earn each day?" The answer was women one quetzal, men two quetzales. Based on these incomes, they figured out how much yardage was possible each day, the cost of the thread, 20 percent for the co-op, etc. Thus the price of the fabric worked out to be Q2.75/yard, at that time an outrageously high price. But because the people had to make their projected salaries, the price had to be maintained. They figured that men could weave two and half to three yards a day, making Q.85 a yard. In comparison, commercial weavers from Totonicapán were making only Q.30 a yard. Also, they only used high quality mercerized cotton because it was easier to get, thus making the cloth even more expensive. But in the end, their high standards paid off. The quality of their product made it more desirable for the European and American home design industries that were placing large orders for placemats and napkins.

To ship their fabrics, every couple of weeks, six or eight men arose at 3 a.m. to carry rolls of material to Guatemala City. Some of what they carried was ordered; some was just brought along to try to sell. They carried the heavy packages on their backs because they were so cash-poor they could not afford the fifty-cent mules. It took an hour and a half to climb the steep path to Godinez where they could catch the bus at dawn. Often it was full and they had to hitch a ride to the coast, then change to the coast road back to Guatemala City. Once in the city, they delivered their goods, then bought supplies and thread, and tried to get more paperwork done toward legalizing the cooperative. As it turned out, they were the very first cooperative legalized by the new umbrella organization, the National Institute of Cooperatives (INACOP).

By 1980, Jerry Goldstein had reached the end of his second Peace Corps stint. He went to work for a government agency advising co-ops all over the country. He was replaced by Robert Strong who worked with the co-op for the next three years. Robert had a business and accounting background which had been Jerry's weakness. When he left, Jerry knew the town had a basis of quality work. They knew how to make a good product, how to sell it, and how to walk away from a sale if they could not get their price.

Enter Hilos del Lago and its American owner Malcolm Rosario. Hilos, based in Panajachel, was producing a line of ceramic jewelry and beads, but Malcolm was eager to develop a line of woven sashes for export to the United States. He started doing business with the cooperative for several reasons: they had gringo advisers, they were sophisticated, had productive capacity, and he liked the idea of cooperativism. The cooperative promised him exclusivity and timely deliveries. What he did not count on, however, was that cooperative officers were embezzling thousands of quetzales of the group's working capital. Two years into Hilos' relationship with the co-op, the improprieties of the director became well known in San Antonio. Julio Sicajan threatened to blow the whistle and was promptly kicked out of the cooperative. Members left in droves to work for the expelled Julio, who was running his business pretty much like the cooperative, loaning money without interest, and reinvesting his 20 percent cut back into the business. (Ironically, in 1986, Julio's 250 weavers deserted him for similar reasons. Six new middlemen picked up the slack. Corruption, then, spread entrepreneurship and fostered local competition.)

Between 1980 and 1981 when military terrorism in the highlands was peaking, it became increasingly uncomfortable for Jerry Goldstein to carry out his national cooperative activities. Government repression of indigenous organizers finally caught up to him in the Polochic Valley where he was establishing a basketry and fabric cooperative. Driving into town, he found the cooperative truck bullet-ridden and burned. Seven of the members had been murdered on their way to telegraph him not to come because it was too dangerous. He quickly left the country. Ironically, those bloody years proved to be a period of growth for the San Antonio cooperative. Tourism was down dramatically in Panajachel. Weavers whose sales were based upon tourists were practically giving their goods away. But because San Antonio's orders were for export, they were untouched by local economic woes.

Jerry Goldstein did not come back to Guatemala until 1985, and when he did it was as production director of Hilos del Lago. What he liked then about Malcolm (who had also left the country) was that he never did anything small: when he ordered a sash, they did it in every color. Hilos' philosophy has been that there would be no export business without the cooperation of the Guatemalan people who work with the company. The company respects its producers and the dignity of their work. Throughout Guatemala, more than 1000 weavers are organized into work groups to produce Hilos products for export. The leaders of the groups, the *patrones,* know that beyond making a decent profit, they will learn what quality is, how to be fair with workers, to focus their product, and to specialize. Most important, Hilos has tried to encourage patrones to pay workers well and treat them honestly. The result is that Hilos weavers make some of the best fabrics and accessories in Guatemala.

Some examples:

1. Huipil sweater. First made in Cerro de Oro, this sweater is based on the San Lucas Tolimán traditional huipil. It was so beautifully made that one catalog wanted 1200 units a month. They only had the workforce to make 150–200 despite the fact that women were making it in San Lucas, Zunil, Nahuala, and Santa Lucia Utatlan. Hilos pays Q18–22 for each sweater, whether made on a palito or a foot loom. A palito woman can only do three a month, but three a week on a foot loom.

2. T-shirts. This product was developed when Hilos' handmade bead business was slow and they wanted to keep their Panajachel women employed. They now have twenty-two women embroidering shirts, plus twenty-three more working at home. Also there are twenty women from the Monja Blanca Co-op in Cantel, a group in Nahuala, and others. The white T-shirts are made for them in Guatemala City; then the design is stenciled on by hand to be embroidered. They pay Q3.50–5.00 for each shirt, higher prices to those who draw the design. Each woman can do about one shirt a day.

3. Sweaters. There is a great story about the Peace Corps volunteer who went to a large town in the Oriente on assignment. Like Jerry, she was older, and more critical of the project given to her, which she considered a waste of time. While she was brooding over her fate, she was knitting. Her neighbor asked if she would teach her to knit and soon more than 100 women were producing sweaters for Hilos del Lago. Jerry provides the patterns and the materials. They pay Q25 for each sweater, which a knitter can do in five days.

4. Miscellaneous. Totonicapán weavers produce fabric and belts. Leather belts come from a work group in Samayac, and

fifty people work in Panajachel making beads. Most of the beadmakers are single mothers who bring their young children to play on the grounds. Many have worked there for over twelve years, and they keep bringing their relatives in to work. Jerry's next project is to work with bag weavers from San Juan Atitán, Huehuetenango to provide them with market access for their products which have always been overshadowed by those made in Todos Santos.

As soon as he returned to Guatemala, Jerry went back to Panajachel to run the business, then off to San Antonio to assure Julio that the town would always have work. By this time, just about every weaver had a loom. There were literally hundreds, sometimes supplied by Hilos to the weaver. Jerry yanked all Hilos business from the corrupt cooperative and gave it all to Julio and his 150 weavers. Since then the weaving business has spread beyond the cooperative and Julio to half a dozen other private subcontractors. The cooperative has been reorganized on sound footing and shares Hilos orders with two or three other groups. Members weave for the cooperative and private bosses both. Orders come in from nearly a dozen European and American companies for table linens, belts, and fabric. Analysis of productive capacity and of the number of houses with looms suggests that there are approximately 700 weavers in San Antonio, or about 40 percent of the population. How has the rapid development of this industry affected the town? In the next section of the paper, I will discuss the impact weaving has had on the Tunecos by focusing on a few members of a large extended family that has dedicated itself to this craft.

IMPACT OF WEAVING ON THE COMMUNITY

Roberto Sicay's success story is about an entrepreneurial, hardworking young man who saw an economic opportunity in the weaving business and went for it. It begins nearly twenty years ago when he went with his brother to Santiago to buy a *trasmaya* (fishing net). It did not take him long to realize that it was foolish to keep buying the nets from the Atitecos when he could learn to make them himself. He learned, taught others, and soon everyone in San Antonio had nets. They fished offshore at midnight, catching so many fish that wholesalers started coming to them to buy. Hungry for more cash income, this fishing group decided to pursue their economic fortunes beyond the lake. They formed the core of the weaving cooperative in search of a market.

Along with the other members, Roberto learned to weave, but he was never satisfied working one month on, two months off the two looms they had in the beginning. So he studied, he wove, he fished, he crabbed, he visited his milpa. But as weaving grew in the town, Roberto found a niche that provided a sizeable source of money. He perfected the preparation of thread for the loom, and got so good at it that the novice weavers hired him to do theirs. He charged Q1.50 for setting up one-color warps, Q2 for plaids and stripes. It took him only an hour or two per loom. He was in such demand that he worked from 6 a.m. to 3 a.m., sleeping only two hours. He was making nearly Q25/day, sometimes for three weeks at a stretch. When he was not setting up other peoples' looms, he wove himself. With this money, and the income he accumulated in the years ahead, he bought twelve cuerdas of land for milpa and coffee and he hired three *mozos* (laborers) to work it for him. Last June he opened a *tienda* (store) from which he sells the town's only bread, brought down from Godinez on the baker's back. Roberto is renown for his crabbing technique, and he still crabs in the dry season when he can make Q20–25 for two hours' work. Most recently, he has become patrón to three weavers, and is looking for work for more. He owns three houses, and although he wants to improve his family's small traditional house, his money will go instead for a refrigerator for the tienda.

It is interesting that some customs have changed with the advent of weaving, and others have not. For example, only Julio has invested his money in absolutely unheard of things like a shower and a color television. Neither Roberto nor his brother Marcos—also a patrón—have significantly changed their diets or improved their one-room houses. Almost all their money goes right back into business ventures.

Marcos Sicay, for example, put together money he made from fishing, honey, and weaving to establish his tienda eight years ago. It provides his most important income, at about Q200/month. Based upon that cash flow, three years ago, Marcos took advantage of the opportunity to begin his own weaving business with the local hotel owner, Don Geraldo. He now has twenty-five weavers and an outstanding reputation with weavers and buyers alike. Concerned with a drop in quality when his weavers get bored, he has arranged with another brother, Antonio Sicay, to provide variety by exchanging orders. And he is lobbying Hilos del Lago for more business. Marcos is not satisfied. His tienda is on land rented from the church. Ahead he sees a two-story tienda on a site he recently purchased. The cost comes in at about Q8000, money he does not want to borrow. So he figures he can save Q2000 a year, and soon he will have enough.

Although his one-room house is small, he sees it lasting for twenty more years, so he figures he can let that slide.

Another common characteristic of the weaving patrones is that they have abandoned the traditional red blouse and woolen skirt worn by 99 percent of the men in the town. Roberto says he abandoned his *traje* because he grew tired of ladinos calling him *mujer* (woman) when he traveled to the coast to sell onions. Other itinerant sellers of vegetables have maintained their Indian dress, so my guess is that Roberto's decision was as much an unconscious attempt at class distinction as a personal choice. Dress is just one traditional Mayan symbol that may soon be gone. Besides showing their status by eschewing Indian clothing, patrones—and weavers who share the new international tastes—find themselves increasingly outside the normal Tuneco worldview. For example, though most of these Young Turks are Catholics, their new business activities have marginalized them from the customary *cofradía* (Mayan civil-religious hierarchy also known as the cargo system) sources of prestige. They are not investing their money in traditional religious offices. Patrones are reinvesting in their businesses by expanding their work force, while their weavers purchase radios or watches. There is one status symbol, however, that quite closely follows conventional cofradía guidelines, but with a sophisticated twist. The biggest holiday of the year takes place during the week surrounding the town's saint's day in June. When I visited in 1977, the two cofradías had a monopoly on the rituals, processions, speeches, and fiestas surrounding the event. Now these older, more traditional men have competition from the weaving entrepreneurs. In 1980, Roberto and his brother Marcos established the Comité de Control Remoto to transmit the *feria* (fair) to other parts of the lake via Radio Nahualá. Every year, an elaborate sound system is set up next to the church to broadcast the Mass and the music and dancing that follows. The fact that Control Remoto's marimba stands right next to the cofradía's marimba is symbolic of the parallelism inherent in this source of prestige. For the system to work, founding members of the committee have to contribute or collect sizeable sums of money. In return for their generosity, donors are allowed to sit behind the marimba, or, as most do, stand near the equipment with a bottle of beer, looking important. Many of the new members cannot afford more than a nominal contribution, but the importance of this new group of non-cofradía members signals a clear change in direction of power and sources of prestige for locals.

Not all the members of the Sicay family are upwardly mobile storeowners and entrepreneurs. Their sister, Julieta Sicay, works as a contract weaver. Julieta lives in her husband's compound in one small room whose major feature is the bulky wooden foot loom taking up two-thirds of the floor space. Julieta, twenty-seven, has six children, all of whom sleep together on one reed mat in the corner. She had her first child at thirteen, the same year she began palito weaving. She has four years of school and can read Spanish although her husband, Felix, a vegetable trader, is illiterate. Julieta was one of the founding members of the cooperative. Basically, her motive was to make some real money. Until then, women wove only cheap, inconsequential items for middlemen who took their time paying. Moreover, the work was irregular. Now she has work every day weaving shirts for the co-op or belts for her brother, Antonio, a subcontractor for Hilos. Assisted by her thirteen-year-old daughter, Julieta can weave every day. When we spoke, Julieta was weaving a new product that Jerry wanted to try, fringed scarves. Antonio was paying her Q1.85 for each. Although she is a fast and accurate weaver, the scarves called for zigzag finishing and tedious knotting of the fringe. Every time I visited them, both she and Felix were tying knots. (I also tied knots and found it annoyingly difficult and predictably dull. The family found that very amusing.) Despite her husband's assistance during the three days needed to prepare her thread and set her loom, it took Julieta ten days to do all forty-five. When the cost of the thread was subtracted, she ended up with about Q4 for a day's work.

Doña Julieta's schedule is typical for women weavers. She gets up at 5 a.m. to go to the mill with her corn and cook a 7 a.m. breakfast. Next she cleans and washes until 9, then can prepare her thread or weave until 10 or 11:30. Lunch takes up her time until 2; she weaves for two or three hours, cooks again, and perhaps has time for more weaving at night. This timetable totals up to six or seven hours a day weaving, an optimistic figure given the children's demands, time set aside for visiting her mother, etc. The best analysis is that for most women, domestic responsibility seriously cuts into time at the loom, making them less desireable workers for subcontractors. While men can weave for long hours, attended by wives who cook and nurture the children, women can rarely find such uninterrupted periods of time. Since weavers get paid by the piece, this means that men average a higher *daily* income, although agricultural or fishing responsibilities allow them to weave only three or four days a week. (Antonio Sicay told me that most men can weave a dozen scarves in a day; his sister managed less than half of that. Nonetheless, my analysis is that over a year, their total incomes are quite similar. While she may have fewer free hours each day, Julieta weaves six or seven days a week while most men do not.) In short, weaving provides the women of San Antonio with their first source of independent income. Never before have women been able to make such a sizeable contribution to the family's productive system. This kind of cottage industry is a satisfying endeavor, in part because it is so compatible with women's domestic tasks. And Julieta's Q4/day makes a considerable difference to her household's economic stability.

Like all weaving families, Julieta and Felix have added an income-producing strategy to their productive system that allows them to make it through the year. Their meager landholdings only produce corn for half the year, *frijol* (beans) for even less. They spend one quetzal a day just on frijol, and they must also buy fish, oil, eggs, corn, etc. When their tablon of onions is harvested, Don Felix figures he usually just covers costs; the cash flow enables him to buy fertilizer for his milpa. Adding weaving income to this subsistence pattern provides a cushion for food, medicine, religious celebrations, and a little bit of savings toward the purchase of consumer goods.

Conclusion

To summarize my findings, I have to ask two things: What did San Antonio do right to set up a locally based industry that has grown and thrived for the last ten years? And, secondly, what does the presence of this industry mean for the people of the town?

First, the development process: My sense is that weaving came to this town due to the coming together of a number of fortuitous circumstances: the road, young entrepreneurial citizens willing to sacrifice and work hard to expand their economic potential, the anomaly of an experienced and smart Peace Corps worker whose commitment to San Antonio has been crucial, and supportive Maryknoll sisters who contributed important resources. Now, ten years later, the nuns are gone, the Peace Corps worker is a businessman, and the entrepreneurs have been doubly paid off for their diligence. The weaving business persists in San Antonio due in part to the quality of the work produced, the reputation the town has developed for sophisticated business deals, and the hard work of its cooperative and private patrones. All of these were original goals set forth by Jerry and the cooperative founders, and they have been achieved.

What remains, then, is the issue of what benefits local weavers have derived from this new industry. Have a U.S.-based business and local wheeler-dealers enriched themselves from the cheap labor of townspeople or has everyone improved the quality of their lives? Well, it is clear that Julio, with his three boats and color television, came out way ahead. And other middlemen certainly did as well. But my assessment of their success is that it is not based on weaving alone. Weaving is only one of the many productive strategies that they used to achieve their economic security. Each of them relies on other business ventures and their agricultural production to make it. Marcos may be able to save Q2000 a year, but he still visits his milpa every week just like everyone else. And that is the key for the rest of the town as well. Similarly, weaving has not been a miracle cure for poverty in San Antonio. Instead, it has become the latest scheme for putting some cash into the productive system. It is an attractive alternative to picking cotton, one that could potentially provide considerably more income as well. But as this brief study suggests, weaving is not a panacea. Basically, there are not enough orders for everyone who weaves to have work all year. Some, like Julieta, work whenever they want to; others are still lined up to become members of the cooperative when extra business comes in. The workers are there, their looms ready. It remains to be seen whether entrepreneurial Tunecos have the skills necessary to hustle the additional business that would mean, at the least, year-round work for everyone who wants it.

Another change is that women are contributing to the family budget by weaving. They were the early organizers, and are still dominant in terms of numbers in the cooperative. Nonetheless, they remain secondary producers because of their domestic responsibilities. More analysis waits to be done on their changing status as well as comparison between their contract weaving and the businesses of independent huipil weavers.

I also want to point out that the dignity of this type of work does not go unnoticed. Local labor contractors bemoan the dramatic drop (from 600 a month to 200) in people willing to migrate to the coast as peons. Weavers are able to stay home, work at their own pace, play with their children, eat decent meals, look at their watches, and listen to their radios. It is clear, however, that besides affording a new and satisfying economic strategy, weaving has also created structural problems. Income distinctions are far greater than ten years before; a small elite group of weaving subcontractors has emerged. It is they who control commercial activity and they who will be setting standards for behavior in the future. For example, ten years ago, the cooperative brought in National Geographic movies about seals to show in the church during the fiesta. This year Roberto showed Rambo II on a rented video in front of his store.

A second concern, more fundamental to the economic fortunes in San Antonio, is the dependence on foreign markets and decision-making. Although they now have more than a dozen buyers from four countries, the link is still tenuous. For example, despite all their humanistic good intentions, Hilos del Lago has considered switching their belts from hand-woven to machine-made. Their bottom line is that it is simply easier and cheaper to buy the product in the United States than to have it imported from Guatemala. Hilos now ships nearly 7,500 yards of San Antonio belting every three weeks. Yanking production will close down weavers at thirty or more looms. Although Jerry Goldstein convinced the owners to replace belts with another product, I am still concerned. For example, what would happen if Hilos fired Jerry or he found another job? Would the next production manager have the commitment to San Antonio to replace belts with bags? Tuneco entrepreneurs know their business well enough to find other smaller buyers in Panajachel to make up for losing Hilos, but will that be enough? Or perhaps, as happens repeatedly, weavers in India or Malaysia or another underdeveloped country will soon be able to produce these same placemats and belts cheaper and faster. The vagaries of international business are beyond the expertise of San Antonio's brightest entrepreneurs; production decisions are out of their control. Is there anything they can do to solidify their business relationships or will they always be left hanging?

Lastly, there is the question of wages. On my way out of town this summer, I ran into Don Manuel, Julio's father. When I asked him what he thought about the impact weaving had had on the town, he became irate. "Hey," he shouted, "They are only paying us Q1.75 each for belts that sell in the States for $7–8 [Actually, they sell for $15–25]. This is a rip-off. So, ok, we've got work, but your back is strained, your body aches, your whole life is spent at that loom. It is better than being a mule on the coast, but it still sucks."

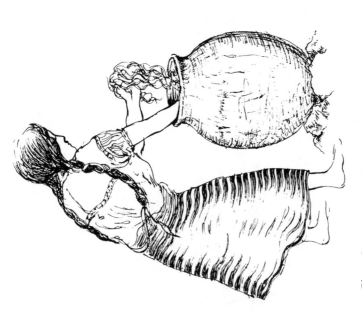

*Chamula woman collecting plants to dye wool (right)
and dyeing wool (left)
Drawing by Christine Eber*

9

Discontinuous Warps: Textile Production and Ethnicity in Contemporary Highland Guatemala*

Robert S. Carlsen

INTRODUCTION

To the casual observer, peasant artisan production can seem to be a delightfully simple and unconstrained activity. In reality, the creation of ceramic vessels, hand-loomed weavings, and so on, represent but single factors in a dynamic complex of variables. Included is an integral relationship of the individual artisan, the local community, and the world beyond. Artisan production can involve inputs from localized traditions with deep historical and sometimes sacred roots. Examples of this abound, including the paper cutouts made for local consumption during Mexico's "Day of the Dead" ceremonies, or in the Buddhist *thangka* paintings produced for export in Tibetan refugee camps. Importantly, however, peasant artisan

*I would like to thank Sheldon Annis, Suzanne Baizerman, Margot Schevill, and Nathaniel Tarn, whose comments greatly helped the final version of this essay. Particular gratitude is extended to Vicente Stanzione.

production often also reflects the vicissitudes of the world economy, including the decisions of foreign entrepreneurs, and the fleeting desires of distant consumers. The "friendship bracelets" braided by the millions in various Guatemalan towns for markets in the United States exemplify this, as did the much celebrated "rain gods" contracted from artisans in New Mexico's Tesuque pueblo for packaging in boxes of candy at the long defunct Guenther Candy Company.

Obviously, when the study of artisan-produced crafts is expanded to include these sorts of considerations, there exists a greater possibility of learning, not only about the crafts themselves, but about the dynamic environments in which they are made. Utilizing this type of approach, the present study attempts to trace the factors which affect the decisions to weave textiles in a highland Maya community, Santiago Atitlán, Guatemala. Particular consideration is given to the role of ethnicity. The study shows that not only does ethnicity affect local textile production, but that this production can itself be used to further the understanding of local ethnicity. In addition, to demonstrate the variability of inputs which can affect the decisions by highland Maya weavers to produce cloth, comparison is made to the Cakchiquel Maya community of San Antonio Aguas Calientes.

The present study proceeds from an ongoing project at the University of Colorado Museum that is researching the occurrence through time of the dyes and fibers used in ethnographic Guatemalan textiles (Carlsen and Wenger 1991). Working with weavings from ten well-documented museum collections of Guatemalan textiles, histories of many of the weaving materials used in highland Maya textile production have been established. This project found that the production of cloth by Guatemala's indigenous weavers is influenced, even dictated, by local, national, and international factors. Examples of this are found in a near total abandonment of the synthetic dye alizarin in the mid-1930s, or in the substitution of rayon for silk brocade yarns soon after. Alizarin, a dye which our research determined to have been the sole dye for red cotton in Guatemalan indigenous textiles during the period of approximately 1875–1930, was primarily imported from Germany. A dramatic shift away from alizarin use occurred between 1930 and 1935 and reflects dye-source disruption due to the growing instability of pre-World War II Europe. Likewise, the drop from a point of the peak use of Asiatic silk in Guatemalan Maya textiles around 1935 to its near total disappearance a mere five years later, reflects source disruption due to the eastern theater of that same war. Importantly, however, this research demonstrates that when confronted by these sorts of disruptions, Guatemala's indigenous weavers have integrated changes into their weaving traditions. By way of example, in numerous highland Guatemalan towns, the precipitous decline in silk use, cited above, was matched by the weavers' adoption of rayon. Or in contemporary Guatemala, economic crisis, spawned in part by the current political violence in that country, has resulted in a shift from cotton to cheaper acrylic yarns.

In this context textiles woven by Mayas demonstrate decisions to retain a distinct culture despite their political and economic vulnerability. Important to this consideration is a contention that textiles provide a record which demonstrates that in spite of vulnerable existences in economic peripheries, many Mayas have made decisions whose intent has been the retention of a distinct cultural sameness. It is evident that the decision by weavers to make changes has allowed the continuity of highland Maya textile production. Clearly, had those weavers not integrated change, were they still bound by labor-intensive methods of yarn production and dyeing, there would no longer be a high percentage of habitual use of native costume. Stated differently, the Mayas have made changes so that they could remain the same. In this, the record of the textiles is consistent with what has been characterized as the Guatemalan Mayas' "fierce resistance" toward acculturation (Carmack 1983:218). Indigenous cloth serves as both a symbol of, and a tool for, this resistance.

This contention touches on an important and somewhat controversial issue. It is explicit that textiles have causal, not epiphenomenal, cultural value. Together with Martin Prechtel, I have argued that textiles and textile production in Santiago Atitlán join in a local system of integrated cultural elements (Prechtel and Carlsen 1988). The components of this system, which include such diverse elements as agricultural production, kinship, and understandings of birth and cosmos, are symbolically informed by specific cultural paradigms. We have also argued that this integrated cultural configuration has allowed defense from nonindigenous intrusions (Carlsen and Prechtel 1991). Specifically, using an essentially cybernetic approach, we explained that as individual elements of this cultural nexus have been challenged from without, the aggregate pressure of the system's other members have, by and large, been successful in normalizing the intrusive element. As a result, changes to the local culture have been gradual, and engineered largely according to indigenous standards.[1]

This capacity, however, is now engaged in a rapid process of change. The confiscation of vast amounts of land from Mayan communities, coupled with exploitative labor practices (McCreery 1976), explosive population growth (Early 1983), and the militarization of Guatemala's rural areas (Smith 1990) have all contributed to overwhelming the traditional adaptive mechanisms of the indigenous communities. As a result, the structure and functions of highland Maya culture are undergoing significant change. The following pages consider how one aspect of that culture, textile production, is being affected. It should be helpful, however, to first give brief consideration of certain idiosyncrasies of "Indian" culture in Guatemala.

BEING "INDIAN" IN GUATEMALA

Discussions of contemporary Guatemalan indigenous culture and acculturation are hampered by the multiplicity of identities that have come to be lumped under the rubric "Indian culture." Even in the best circumstances, discussions of culture, that "difficult to talk about and impossible to agree upon" entity, can be problematic (Boon 1973:1). This is especially true in Guatemala. Added to the inherent difficulties of culture is that in Guatemala even an acceptable definition of the category Indian is elusive.

In Guatemala, most of the population of nearly ten million would be classified as Indian if based on genotype. The fact is that only about half of the population is so identified. As Carol Smith (1990:3) writes, "most of Guatemala's Indians are descendants of the Maya, but, given the very small numbers of Europeans who immigrated to Guatemala . . . , so are most of Guatemala's non-Indians." Most of Guatemala's non-Indian population is classified as *Ladino* (see Early 1974, 1975). Adding meaning to Lowie's (1966) contention that culture must ultimately be explained in terms of itself, in contemporary Guatemala one is "Indian" because of a self-determined identification. Any Guatemalan Mayan can "pass" (become Ladino) at any time: no Guatemalan is forced by reason of genetic heritage to be classified as Indian. Demonstrating the vagaries of this situation, definitions for "Indian" in the Guatemalan context range from the standard "a person who uses native costume and/or a native dialect," to a person who "lives an Indian style of life." However, definitions such as these, formulas which attach specific cultural attributes, are invariably met by significant exceptions. Beal's suggestion (in De la Fuente 1952:95) that an "Indian" in Guatemala is a person who identifies himself or herself as such, seems the only viable definition.

This identification, however, must confront a most important consideration. In Guatemala, the word *indio* (Indian) is considered to be highly derogatory (much like the label *nigger* in the United States). No Guatemalan would refer to himself or herself as indio. Instead, since long before the Conquest, it has been typical that Mayans refer to themselves using the local word for twenty. (Carlsen and Prechtel 1991 discuss the symbolism of this identification). When speaking in Spanish, however the most common generic reference to oneself is *natural,* which literally means "native." In many cases, this term attaches a sense of ancient place, a sentiment which excludes Ladinos. As this essay is concerned with ethnic considerations related to these indigenous sentiments, where appropriate, I shall use native.

Given the ambiguities of ethnicity in Guatemala, the value of cloth as a heuristic device is evident. Clearly, the wearing of native dress (*traje*) signifies a Guatemalan's self-perceived identity as a native. As an exemplar of ethnic identity, cloth need not be limited by either the differing stages of, or the reasons behind, Guatemalan "Indianness." However, at the same time it can provide a context through which to study those very reasons and stages. It should be made clear that this does not assume that the wearing of native costume is a necessary criterion of being native in contemporary Guatemala. In fact, some of the country's most conservative natives no longer use a native style of costume. (For instance, see Tedlock's 1982 study on Momostenango).

TEXTILE PRODUCTION IN SANTIAGO ATITLÁN

Santiago Atitlán is a Tzutujil Maya speaking community located on the south shore of Lake Atitlán. Over 95 percent of Santiago Atitlán's approximately 18,775 inhabitants are natives.[2] Contemporary Atitlán presents a complex mix of the traditional and the modern, a collision of old with new. In part, this represents a confrontation of the until recently "closed" town with the steadily increasing encroachments of the non-Mayan world. ("Closed" is used to indicate the legal and cultural capacity to resist Hispanic intrusion, as defined by Wolf 1957.) This encounter has led to a configuration of local social and economic competition, a situation given daily performance in the arrival to Atitlán of tour boats from across the lake.

With convenient boat service from the popular Lake Atitlán resort of Panajachel, Atitlán is commonly included in the travel itinerary of foreign tourists. A primary draw is Atitlán's reputation for indigenous traditionality, including a high degree of native costume use. The typical tourist stint in the town is brief, with most staying only the hour and fifteen minutes until the boat returns to Panajachel. During the time in which the foreigners are present, Atitlán's shopping district, sometimes called by the locals *Calle Gringo* ("Gringo Street"), is transformed into a money-extraction machine.[3] Although hand-woven textiles are the primary commodity of trade, peanuts, bananas, and locally braided *pulseras* ("friendship bracelets") are for sale everywhere.

As the gringos begin to arrive, indigenous merchants elbow each other for position. Shouts of *compre* (buy) and *regaleme* ("give me") soon fill the air. With the ubiquitous vendors a driving force, the tourists quickly wind their way up Gringo Street. Their harried stroll carries the visitors past the Four Square Gospel mission and past the video theater with its posters depicting "Chook" Norris, Bruce Lee, and Rambo killing faceless terrorists. At the side of the road just before the Assembly of God mission, an aged and serene Tzutujil woman who daily spins cotton using a drop spindle invariably draws the tourists' attention. At last, here is what they came for: a "real Indian." Soon enough, however, the visitors learn that photos even of this category of native do not come cheaply. After a peek into the sixteenth-century Catholic church where they hope to see an Indian doing some kind of ritual—"take-peekch-mister, one dollar"—the tourists typically seek refuge from their rude confrontation with petty capitalism behind a coke in one of the town's grungy restaurants. There they wait anxiously for the boat's departure.

Clearly, Atitlán is no longer a "closed" community supporting a unified indigenous peasantry. However, this very fact makes the town an ideal locale in which to study the dynamics of contemporary indigenous culture change. For one thing, Atitlán continues to support a significant number of traditionalist natives, who in this study are referred to as *costumbristas*. As well, the town has numerous shamans. (For the *costumbrista* aspect of the culture of Santiago Atitlán see Mendelson 1965; O'Brien 1975; Tarn and Prechtel 1986. Carlsen and Prechtel n.d. focus on shamanism in Atitlán.) Atitlán currently supports fourteen *cofradías* (ten public and four private); *cofradías* being costumbrista religious sodalities.[4] At the same time, the Protestant missionization so characteristic of contemporary Guatemala is highly evident. In the town there are eighteen Protestant missions, five *campos blancos* (missions of the missions), and a Mormon mission. Even the Unification Church (the "Moonies"), a group more noted for reactionary politics than for its religious agenda, is represented. That group, which in Atitlán normally goes under the name World Student Services Corps, has constructed a "community center" and sponsors a primary school. In spite of its competition, the Catholics (*Catequistas*) continue as the single largest religious sector, the centuries-old church providing the physical and social center of the town.[5]

In the face of this religious diversity and the competition that it engenders, Atiteco patterns of costume use are surprising. (*Atiteco* is the common name for a person from Santiago Atitlán.) The town is some-

Figure 27. The majority of men and boys in Santiago Atitlán continue to dress in the local style of costume. Nonetheless, the intrusions of nonindigenous dress are apparent. For instance, in this photograph, all but the man at the right foreground are wearing industrially manufactured shirts. (Photograph by Paul Harbaugh, 1987).

Figure 28. Women in Santiago Atitlán invariably wear locally woven attire. The woman in the center of this photograph is dressed in ceremonial costume, while those women on her sides are attired in the daily variety of local dress. Distinguishing the two is the style of blouse, which in Tzutujil is called pot, *and the presence of a ceremonial shawl (*zut*). The head ribbons worn by all of the women, called* xk'ap, *are a type of garment documented to have been used by Mayans since at least the Late Classic period (*A.D. *600–900), and is not ceremonial. (Photograph by Paul Harbaugh, 1987).*

Figure 29. This photograph is of dancers in the Deer-Jaguar dance of the cofradia San Juan. This dance recreates an Atiteco creation myth, and probably dates from before the Conquest. Note the "Stallone" shirt on the deer dancer, as well as his industrially manufactured shoes. (Photograph by Paul Harbaugh, 1988).

what atypical in that unlike most contemporary indigenous Guatemalans, a majority of the men continue to dress in native costume (Figure 29). In a 1988 survey of five hundred Atitecos, I found that just under 75 percent of the men dressed in native costume. This figure includes 71.5 percent of those in the one- to ten-year-old category, 55 percent of the ten- to twenty-five-year olds, and 95 percent of those over twenty-five years of age. Moreover, nearly 100 percent of the indigenous females of all ages wear native costume. It is common for even the town's *Ladinas* to occasionally use the local style of handwoven shawl (*zut*). In addition to wearing native dress, almost all female natives weave, using a backstrap loom. Of particular importance to the present inquiry is that in a town where Protestants accuse Catholics of idolatry and accuse costumbristas of demon worship, where costumbristas do not even consider Protestants to be truly "Atiteco," the salience of ethnic costume use crosses all social lines. So why do such a diverse people continue to wear a mode of dress which identifies them as a single group?

A recent essay on Atiteco textile symbolism (Prechtel and Carlsen 1988:130) argued that the conservative nature of Atiteco costume use can reflect a belief that wearing the proper costume puts one in the form of the ancestors, a factor which in traditional Atiteco belief is of vital importance.[6] Kay Warren (1978:57) cites a similar belief for costumbristas in the nearby Cakchiquel Maya community of San Andrés Semetebaj. But could it be that something so thoroughly emic as this belief could actually be influential in indigenous textile use and production? My answer is a qualified yes. For support, let us turn briefly to another aspect of Atiteco textile production, the hand-spinning of yarn.

The spinning of wool, as well as of natural brown cotton (*G. mexicanum Tod.*), using a drop spindle remains fairly common in some parts of Guatemala. However, for at least the past half century (O'Neale 1945:7), it has been far rarer to encounter the hand-spinning of white cotton (*G. hirsutum L.*). Sperlich and Sperlich (1980:3) claim that only in Todos Santos Cuchumatán is this still regularly practiced. Yet, as reported by Anderson (1978:41), various women in Atitlán continue to spin white cotton by hand. Anderson suggests that tourism—more specifically, payment to the spinner for permission to photograph—is a reason for this continuity. While this interpretation might account for the activities of a very few women, I would argue that it cannot explain why hundreds of Atitecas maintain knowledge of what in almost all other parts of Guatemala is forgotten. It is significant that a single woman, she of Gringo Street, is generally depicted in tourist pamphlets, post cards, and books on

Guatemala, including that by Anderson. To explain the continuation of hand-spinning in Atitlán, one must turn to religious custom.

The persistence of hand-spinning white cotton in Atitlán becomes understandable when a certain local funerary custom is considered. Upon death, and before burial, it is customary for Atiteco costumbristas, and most Catholics alike, to have their groin area bound in a ritual manner using *batzin batz,* handspun white cotton.[7] Hence, many Atiteco households routinely have a couple of balls of handspun white cotton available, this cotton often spun by the women of the household. It should be noted that in addition to funerary custom, and strengthening a case for ideological determinism, religious custom in Atitlán dictates that women's cofradía blouses (*nim pot*) must be woven using handspun white cotton. Far more than tourism, religious belief accounts for the continuity of Atiteco hand-spinning.

Just as ideology explains the persistence of hand-spinning in Atitlán, I would argue that ancestor-based religious belief exercises a conservative function in textile use. However, for reasons to be explained, ideology alone cannot be causal. For one thing, it should be mentioned that even Costumbrista behavior is typically in violation of strict conformity to religious factors for costume use. Specifically, most Atitecos—Costumbristas, Catholics and Protestants alike—no longer wear local-style shirts. It is notable that in July 1988, the deer dancer in a Deer-Jaguar dance, one of the town's most important Costumbrista rituals, even wore a T-shirt emblazoned with "Stallone Rambo"—perhaps a modern Mayan icon (Figure 29). More telling, however, is that the town's Protestants, although rejecting anything which smacks whatsoever of native religiosity, are at least as conservative as the Costumbristas in the wearing of indigenous costume.[8] While religious belief seems to be a factor underlying the choice of some naturales to continue wearing traditional styles of costume, it is evident that other factors must also be in operation.

In his 1987 study *God and Production in a Guatemalan Town,* which focuses on some of these same considerations, Sheldon Annis argues that contemporary trends in the production and use of textiles in San Antonio Aguas Calientes reflect underlying economical, ecological, and social patterns in that Cakchiquel community. Annis structures his arguments around the identification of what he calls *milpa logic,* a minimizing strategy that has acted to transfer local labor into the production of small quantities of a large number of products. He argues that by utilizing "microquantities of resources that the family may have in abundance but have no use for without the transformative suprastructure" (1987:37), this strategy allows the absorption of labor that would otherwise be wasted. Importantly, Annis stresses that by optimizing inputs rather than maximizing outputs and hence working against the accumulation of capital, milpa logic is antithetical to entrepreneurship. It is his contention that historically this system has reinforced the egalitarian nature of the community and has been socially stabilizing. However, Annis contends that all of this is breaking down; a consequence of "anti-milpa" forces.

Central to these forces, according to the author, is a situation in which an increasing number of people are having to support themselves on decreasing amounts of land. Specifically, ecological crisis, made worse by inequitable distribution of land, is affecting social structure. Resulting in part from this unstable situation, there has been a dramatic increase in conversions to Protestantism, a sect whose largely pro-entrepreneurial ethic contributes to "anti-milpa" tension.

Annis bases much of his argument on observed patterns of textile use and production in San Antonio Aguas Calientes. He argues (1987:120–137) that in San Antonio, Catholic weavers continue to produce textiles according to milpa logic. Specifically, weaving primarily for commerce, the (low) wages received supplement various other sources of income, hence stabilizing rather than changing the underlying productive system. On the other hand, Protestants tend to trade in textiles and accumulate capital, thereby altering social homeostasis. It is Annis' contention that in San Antonio, "Protestantism is a process that separates community from self." He suggests that, for this reason, it would be no surprise that only a little more than a third of the Protestant women in that town continue to wear backstrap-woven huipiles. Significantly, Annis argues that regardless of religious identification, economics,—specifically commerce—is the primary reason for continuity of weaving in San Antonio Aguas Calientes.

Annis' theory of the dynamics that influence the evolution of the weaving traditions is intriguing. And his contention of an economical basis to continuities in indigenous weaving is reasonable, even likely. But how well does it explain the Atiteco data?

The selling of textiles in Santiago Atitlán is fairly recent; more so than tourism. Eleanor Lothrop (1948:100) describes the difficulty of finding locally woven textiles to buy in Atitlán in 1928. She states that the Atitecos believed that selling handwoven clothes could expose oneself to "witchcraft."[9] At the same time, Lothrop mentions (1948:81) that, even in the 1920s, tourist boats from Panajachel regularly visited Atitlán—the female tourists "usually in high heels, would stumble along the stony street up to the plaza." The radical transition among Atitecos from actu-

Table 8.   The Religious Identification of the "Gringo Street" Textile
Merchants

Religion	Actual #	Anticipated #	Actual %	Anticipated %
Costumbrista	6	1.25	22.2	4.66
Protestant	5	9.89	18.5	36.66
Catholic	16	13.85	59.3	51.33
None	0	1.97	0	7.33
Total	27	26.96	100	99.98

Note: The anticipated numbers are based on an approximation of the total local populations
of the considered groups. The actual and the anticipated numbers for Costumbristas are
based on recent cofradía membership. If calculated according to participation in cofradía
functions, this figure would be considerably higher. All figures are for heads of households.

ally denying tourists access to locally woven textiles to resorting nearly to
duress in an attempt to force them to buy is what might be expected given
underlying changes in indigenous social structure, as argued by Annis.
Moreover, a similar ecological dynamic to that described by Annis is in
operation: considerably less than half of the Atitecos are able to support
themselves on the available land (Early 1970, 1983; Madigan 1976). And
the mere fact that there is discussion about constructing a bank in town is
indicative of the evolution away from a minimizing subsistence economy.
However, at this point I would argue that the similarities between San
Antonio Aguas Calientes and Santiago Atitlán end. Let us return to
Gringo Street.

As indicated above, this street is the mercantile center of Atitlán. In
1990, I conducted a survey of the twenty-seven outlets which specialize in
the sale of indigenous textiles. All were owned and operated by natives.
My results are included in Table 8. The data indicate that when put into
the context of the total population, both the Catholics and Costumbristas
are over-represented, at the expense of the Protestant and the None categories. Clearly, this situation indicates a marked contrast to San Antonio
Aguas Calientes where the Protestants tend to trade in textiles. (It should
be noted that these data do not include the various merchants who conduct their business outside the community. I do not presently have data on
those *comerciantes de fuera*).

An inventory of the textiles for sale on Gringo Street reveals other
pertinent information. For one thing, although the proprietors of textile
outlets typically claim to have personally woven "by hand" everything in
stock, a substantial percentage is actually "foreign"—textiles created in

other communities. Of those textiles manufactured in Atitlán, the vast majority are used. This is certainly not the type of inventory that one might expect were commerce the driving force behind Atitlán's thousands of weavers. The fact is that relatively few women in Atitlán are professional weavers.[10] Instead, most weave primarily for domestic use. While selling textiles can provide a source of emergency cash, Atiteco weavers often fail even to recover the cost of materials. Hence, Annis' finding for San Antonio (1987:125) that " 'to sell them' is the answer that most women give to queries about reasons for weaving" is not true for Atitlán. Added to this, the significant variation in costume use among the Protestants of the two communities indicates that different dynamics are in operation. As stated, unlike in San Antonio Aguas Calientes, Atiteco Protestants are at least as conservative in native costume use as the local Catholics.[11] Evidently, if we are to fully understand the dynamics which explain weaving in contemporary Atitlán, other explanations must be sought.

It has been argued elsewhere that the breakdown in indigenous traditionality in Atitlán results from ecological imbalance (Early 1983). For instance, loss of religion is partially explained by the decreasing relevance of agricultural symbolism in a society where decreasing numbers of people are able to support themselves by agriculture. (In Atitlán, agricultural endeavors attach decreasing esteem. Consistently fewer adolescent boys look forward to a life spent in subsistence agriculture.) Although this situation ultimately stems from inequitable distribution of land, resulting particularly from the nineteenth-century Liberal "land reforms" (see Cambranes 1985), I believe that this argument has merit. So why then does weaving on a backstrap loom, a traditional activity, continue nearly unabated? I suggest that this continuity derives in part from the very fact of the ecologically-stimulated disruptions in Atiteco society. Specifically, it is an environment of increased poverty, high unemployment, and nearly endemic underemployment that incentives to weave can be found.[12]

Consider that a pair of simple Atiteco hand-loomed pants (*skav*) can be purchased for under ten dollars. On the other hand, "Indian quality" (poorly manufactured: the words belong to an indigenous informant) commercially produced pants cost about fifteen dollars. People must wear clothes, and it is possible to buy the locally made product for less money. (The case for another type of clothing, used throw-aways from the United States, will be made below.) The obvious incentive for choosing the locally made pants is even greater when they are woven by one's wife. Moreover, the fact that the locally made pants are far more durable than the industrially manufactured counterpart raises the tendency toward conservatism in native costume use. An argument for economic incentives is strengthened when one considers the earlier mentioned preference among Atiteco men for industrially produced shirts. "Indian quality" industrially manufactured shirts cost around six dollars, whereas hand-loomed shirts (*k'tuon*) cost around sixteen dollars. Even when one factors in durability—locally made shirts last considerably longer—cost explains the observed patterns away from the use of the k'tuon. Incidentally, there is an even more pragmatic reason for the observed transition away from locally made shirts. Men typically complain that in Atitlán's sub-tropical environment the k'tuon is too hot.

While a case for economic causality in Atiteco patterns of dress is strong, evidence suggests that preference based on aesthetics is also a factor. Those questioned during the research of this study invariably dismissed the suggestion that cost might be the primary reason for the continued use of native costume. Instead, aesthetic preference was most often claimed. Those Atitecos argue, quite simply, that they choose to wear the local costume because they like it more. At this point, however, the value of status becomes evident. It should be noted that thus far the cost analysis of locally made textiles has considered only the low end in quality. While, as mentioned, it is possible to buy Atiteco pants for around ten dollars, depending on the amount and quality of embroidery one can also pay up to one hundred dollars. Likewise, the price range for a traditional woman's blouse (*pot*) is from fifteen to two hundred dollars. The decision to produce and to wear finer garments, those embellished with elaborate and expensive supplementary designs, is best explained by the preference based on aesthetics and status. The influence of these factors on local textile production is most evident in Atitlán prior to the town fiesta in July. It is common at that time for those women who can afford it to be frantically embroidering the final birds and flowers on a prized weaving, a creation to be worn proudly during the festivities.

Finally, it should be noted that the weaving art in Santiago Atitlán is in the midst of a renaissance. Until a few decades ago, nonspecific social controls, such as gossip, dictated conservatism in the use of costume. Today, however, weavers in Atitlán are free to devise new variations of the local costume. These variations integrate novel weaving techniques and design motifs, an expanded use of the color palette, and new weaving materials. There is, however, an evident irony in this. The creativity apparent in the contemporary weaving art is clearly due to the fact that tightly structured patterns of traditional normality no longer dictate Atiteco behavior. The price of this break with tradition, however, is discernible in an anemic capacity to resist the often exploitative intrusions from the outside world. Hence, just as the weaver is now free to experiment with her art,

so is the Atiteco ever more likely to exchange his local costume for a pair
of slacks, a double-knit shirt, and some Nike shoes. Embedded in those
factors which have allowed the renaissance of weaving in Atitlán are the
seeds of the local weaving art's potential demise. In short, the license for
the contemporary weaver's flings with creativity also permits the laying
down of her loom forever.

Discontinuous Warps: Discussion and Conclusion

This study integrates analysis of indigenous Guatemalan textile production and costume use with an investigation of ethnic identity. Particular consideration is given to explaining why in a society in which being
"Indian" places a person in a subordinate position, in which *naturales* are
often targeted for violence, and in a society in which there are increasing
opportunities for acculturation, the decision is made to produce and wear
native costume, hence signifying one's indigenous ethnicity. A variety of
wide-ranging and at times contradictory data suggest it is futile to attempt
to reduce this inquiry to a single cause. Reductionist theoretical biases,
such as those which have "-etics explain -emics," or vice versa, ignore the
complexities of the situation (e.g., Harris, 1980). It has been demonstrated that in actuality, significant regional variation combines with dis-
parate local dynamics and multiple voices. On one level, the importance of
material factors, such as the availability of weaving materials and the related factor of cost, is evident. However, other evidence suggests that
while these types of factors limit options and influence decisions, those
decisions ultimately incorporate inputs derived from religious belief, aesthetic preference, and status orientation.

It has been argued that in Guatemala, ecological factors have contributed to economic crisis. While this situation has resulted in changes of
indigenous culture, it is suggested that in Atitlán this crisis has actually
functioned to promote the continuity of weaving. However, as weaving
on a backstrap loom is ancient, and Guatemala's ecological crisis is fairly
recent, how can this argument be sustained? I suggest that just as Guatemalan indigenous culture is evolving, so are the reasons which explain
Atiteco textile production. Seemingly, the continuity of local textile production and costume use represents an evolving interaction of old and
new factors. For instance, it is possible—even likely—that the ideological
factors which inform the Atiteco textile art are becoming vestiges of times
past, whereas weaving as an adaptation to an environment of increasing
poverty is recent.

Until just a few decades past, the use by Atitecos of traditional costume was a de facto requirement of membership in the community. The local culture functioned to sustain the textile art, with the use of costume in turn serving to reinforce the culture. While elements of this functional relationship remain intact, the emergent role of textile production as an adaptation to increasing poverty exposes a different operation, one which may bode ill for the future of the local weaving enterprise. I am thinking here of a recent and potentially significant turn in the evolution of Atiteco patterns of dress, one which underscores the town's increasing integration with a global economic system over which it can have little control. Atitlán, like the rest of Guatemala, is coming to be inundated with used clothing from the United States. Vendors of this by-product of a distant throw-away culture now even have their own section in the Atitlán market. The obvious key to these vendors' mercantile prowess is that the clothing, which is generally only slightly used and often sports the labels of manufacturers (the symbolism of which is lost on the native consumer), costs only pennies apiece. To the average Atiteco consumer, whose wages have lost nearly 50 percent to inflation in the past year alone, the wisdom of exchanging utilitarian quality local costume for foreign garments of which even a discerning Los Angeleño would be satisfied, is becoming increasingly evident. And as that happens, the frayed warps of ancient traditions have become increasingly apparent.

NOTES

1. It should be noted that various scholars argue that indigenous cultures in Mesoamerica reflect what Waldemar Smith (1975:238) calls "an ecology of colonial repression." Accordingly, some contend that "the quaint . . . distinctive patterns of dress . . . so dear to the hearts of anthropologists, has another side to it" (Harris 1964:29). According to this argument, that "other side" stems from a "forced identity," one in which cultural elements have been employed by the dominant Hispanic sector in order to manipulate the indigenous population toward what Friedlander (1981:139) describes as being "accomplices in their own oppression." However, recent research demonstrates that for the highland Maya, these types of interpretations are problematically simplistic. For instance, Carol Smith (1984) and Carol Smith, et al. (1990) show that throughout most of the post-Conquest period, many highland Mayas have successfully resisted proletariatization and hence have moderated the advances of exploitative interests. This is not to deny indigenous exploitation, but merely to say that there has been a give and take in indigenous-Hispanic

relations, what MacLeod (1973) calls "bartering." In light of this research, it now seems that "fought for" better describes highland Maya culture and identity than does "forced."

2. This population statistic is based on a survey conducted by
Project Concern in 1987. My 1991 figure reflects an adjustment based on
3 percent annual growth. I would like to thank Betsy Alexander for allowing me to use the Project Concern data.

3. During two one-week periods, in March and May 1990, I directed a survey of 150 tourists in Atitlán. In each case, a questionnaire was
filled out by a visitor while waiting on the boat prior to departure. The
average tourist questioned reported spending $7.73 in Atitlán. In a sep-
arate survey, I estimated that an average of sixty-three tourists visit the
town daily. Based on this, it can be roughly estimated that tourism generates around $175,000. However, it need be realized that Sol Tax (1953)
coined the term "penny capitalism" for the Lake Atitlán region. This
brand of capitalism remains alive and well in Santiago Atitlán. The actual
profit margin for goods sold to the tourists is quite low. Incidentally, a
common complaint cited in the questionnaires dealt with the aggressive
nature of the local "penny capitalists."

4. While cofradías were introduced into Mesoamerica by the
Spanish in the sixteenth century, in many cases, the indigenous population
quickly refabricated them into distinctly native institutions. Cofradías
came to be the loci of localized and autonomous semi-secret indigenous
religions. As well, the local native populations used the capital generated
by the cofradías to buy off potentially intrusive Hispanic interests. For
this reason, MacLeod (1973) termed the cofradía a "barter institution."

5. In 1990, I directed a survey of the population of four city blocks
in Atitlán, each block spatially separated from the others. The survey covered approximately 3.8 percent of the town's total population. One of the
topics that this survey dealt with was religious behavior. 51.3 percent of
the sample population reported being Catholic, 36.7 percent being Protestant, 7.3 percent reported having no religion, and 4.7 percent reported
being Costumbrista. While I am comfortable with the ordinal accuracy of
these reports, I believe that only the percentage for Protestants offers a
fairly accurate integral account. For one thing, several of those reporting
no religion confided that they regularly attended cofradías, but that because of hounding from Protestant family members, they now publically

claim religious neutrality. Moreover, the spectrum of "Catholic" ranges from those who reject the cofradía religion to the best of their abilities, to those whose personal religion is heavily weighed with attributes of the Costumbrista religiosity. Included among those attributes are regular attendance of cofradía fiestas and the maintenance in their homes of cofradía gods. I should add that, in fact, even most Atiteco Protestants have failed to rid themselves of significant attributes of Costumbrista religiosity, such as belief in the personality of some days, or that the neighboring volcanoes are endowed with anthropomorphic qualities.

6. Atiteco Costumbrista religion includes the belief that an ancestral life force continues to be recycled in all living things. The process of this recycling is known as *Jaloj-K'exoj*, and is akin to reincarnation. (Carlsen and Prechtel 1991 discuss this process in detail. Mondloch 1980 discusses its application to Quiché Maya naming patterns.)

7. I am grateful to Martin Prechtel who first explained this custom to me.

8. It should be noted that Protestants in Santiago Atitlán never participate directly in the town's cofradía system and therefore do not wear cofradía-specific garb.

9. Fear of "witchcraft" is understandable, given the Atiteco belief that handwoven textiles are alive, with the process of weaving understood as a birthing process (Prechtel and Carlsen 1988).

10. In his book *Beyond the Mexique Bay*, Aldous Huxley refers to Santiago Atitlán, and its neighbor San Pedro, as being the "Manchester and Bradford" of the Highlands, this in reference to those towns' purported textile exporting economies (1934:129). From my experience, I would judge that Huxley, who never visited Atitlán or San Pedro, was incorrect in his assessment.

11. In light of this, an example of anomalous Protestant behavior deserves mention. The Protestant Alfa y Omega grade school's students (1990 enrollment: 418) are given annually a new set of clothes. The girls are given the most traditional style of indigenous costume. The boys, however, receive ladino style clothes: black slacks, a red button-down shirt, and shiny black shoes. This program, financed by Dutch Protestant donors, must be having a long term effect on the patterns of local dress.

12. While not challenging Annis' interpretation of the data, I suggest that underemployment would account for what that author identifies as continued adherence to a "milpa-logic" ethic. Specifically, were a person unable to acquire full employment, he or she might be forced to supplement income with other menial sources—for instance, braiding "friendship bracelets" or spinning cotton for the gringos. While there would be an appearance of similarity to "milpa logic," in fact the actual cause would be substantially different.

References Cited

Anderson, Marilyn
    1978   *Guatemalan Textiles Today.* New York: Watson-Guptill Publications.

Annis, Sheldon
    1987   *God and Production in a Guatemalan Town.* Austin: University of Texas Press.

Boon, James
    1973   Further Operations of "Culture" in Anthropology: A Synthesis of and for Debate. In *The Idea of Culture in the Social Sciences,* Louis Schneider and Charles Bonjean, ed. Cambridge: Cambridge University Press.

Cambranes, J. C.
    1985   *Coffee and Peasants: The Origins of the Modern Plantation Economy in Guatemala,* 1853–1897. South Woodstock, Vermont: CIRMA. Centre de Investigaciones Regionales de Mesoamérica.

Carlsen, Robert S. and Martin Prechtel.
    1991   The Flowering of the Dead: An Interpretation of Highland Maya Culture. *Man (NS)* 26:23–42.

    n.d.   Walking on Two Legs: Shamanism in Santiago Atitlán, Guatemala. In G. Seaman ed., *Ancient Traditions: Culture and Shamanism in Central Asia and the Americas.* University of Colorado Press (*forthcoming*).

Carlsen, Robert S. and David A. Wenger
    1991   The Dyes Used In Guatemalan Textiles: A Diachronic Approach. In *Textile Traditions of Mesoamerica and the Andes: An Anthology,* ed. M. Schevill, J. Berlo, and N. Dwyer. Garland Press.

Carmack, Robert M.
    1983   Spanish-Indian Relations in Highland Guatemala, 1800–1944. In *Spaniards and Indians in Southeastern Mesoamerica,* ed. Murdo J. MacLeod and Robert Wasserstrom. Lincoln: University of Nebraska Press.

De la Fuente, Julio
    1952   Ethnic and Communal Relations. In *Heritage of Conquest: The Ethnology of Middle America,* ed. Sol Tax. New York: Cooper Square.

Early, John
    1970   A Demographic Profile of a Maya Community—The Atitecos of Santiago Atitlán. *Milbank Quarterly* 48: 167–178.

    1974   Revision of Ladino and Maya Census Populations of Guatemala. *Demography* 11:105–117.

    1975   Changing Proportion of Maya Indians and Ladino in the Population of Guatemala, 1945–1969. *American Ethnologist* 2:261–269.

    1983   Some Ethnographic Implications of an Ethnohistorical Perspective on the Civil-Religious Hierarchy Among the Highland Maya. *Ethnohistory* 30:185–202.

Friedlander, Judith
    1981   The Secularization of the Cargo System: An Example from Post-Revolutionary Central Mexico. *Latin American Research Review* 16:132–143.

Harris, Marvin
    1964   *Patterns of Race in the Americas.* New York: W. W. Norton and Company.

1980   Cultural Materialism: The Struggle for a Science of Culture. New York: Vintage Books.

Huxley, Aldous
1934   *Beyond the Mexique Bay*. New York: Harper and Brothers

Lothrop, Eleanor
1948   *Throw Me a Bone: What Happens When You Marry an Archaeologist*. New York: Whittlesey House.

Lowie, Robert H.
1966   *Culture and Ethnology*. New York: Basic Books. *

MacLeod, Murdo
1973   *Spanish Central America: A Socioeconomic History 1520–1720*. Berkeley: University of California Press.

Madigan, Douglas Glenn
1976   *Santiago Atitlán, Guatemala: A Socioeconomic and Demographic History*. Ph.D. dissertation, University of Pittsburgh.

McCreery, David
1976   Coffee and Class: the Structure of Development in Liberal Guatemala. *Hispanic American Historical Review* 56: 438–460.

Mendelson, E. Michael
1965   *Los escandolos de Maximón. Seminario de Integración Social Guatemalteca, Publication no. 19. Guatemala*.

Mondloch, James L.
1980   K'E?S: Quiché Naming. *Journal of Mayan Linguistics* 2:9–25.

O'Brien, Linda
1975   *Songs of the Face of the Earth: Ancestor Songs of the Tzutuhil Maya of Santiago Atitlán, Guatemala*. Ph.D. dissertation, University of California at Los Angeles.

O'Neale, Lila M.
   1945   *Textiles of Highland Guatemala*. Publication 567. Washington, D.C.: Carnegie Institute of Washington.

Prechtel, Martin and Robert S. Carlsen
   1988   Weaving and Cosmos Amongst the Tzutujil Maya. *Res* 15:122–132.

Smith, Carol A.
   1984   Local History in a Global Context: Social and Economic Transitions in Western Guatemala. *Comparative Studies in Society and History* 26:193–228.

   1990   The Militization of Civil Society in Guatemala: Economic Reorganization as Continuation of War. *Latin American Perspectives* 17:8–41.

Smith, Carol A., ed.
   1990   *Guatemalan Indian and the State, 1540–1988*. Austin: University of Texas Press.

Smith, Waldemar Richard
   1975   Beyond the Plural Society: Economics and Ethnicity in Middle American Towns. *Ethnology* 14:225–243.

Sperlich, Norbert and Elizabeth Katz Sperlich
   1980   *Guatemalan Backstrap Weaving*. Norman: University of Oklahoma Press.

Tarn, Nathaniel and Martin Prechtel
   1986   Constant Inconstancy: The Feminine Principle in Atiteco Mythology. In *Symbol and Meaning Beyond the Closed Community: Essays in Mesoamerican Ideas,* ed. Gary Gossen. Studies on Culture and Society Vol. 1. Albany: Institute for Mesoamerican Studies.

Tax, Sol
   1953   Penny Capitalism: A Guatemalan Indian Economy. Smithsonian Institute of Social Anthropology Publication no. 16. Washington, D.C.: Smithsonian Institution.

Tedlock, Barbara
    1982   *Time and the Highland Maya.* Albuquerque: University of
            New Mexico Press.

Warren, Kay B.
    1978   *The Symbolism of Subordination: Indian Identity in a Guate-
            malan Town.* Austin: University of Texas Press.

Wolf, Eric R.
    1957   Closed Corporate Peasant Communities In Mesoamerica
            And Central Java. *Southwestern Journal of Anthropology*
            13:1–18.

Woman from Chenalhó
Drawing by Christine Eber

10

The Guatemalan Refugee Crafts Project: Artisan Production in Times of Crisis

Erica Verrillo and Duncan MacLean Earle

Dedicated to Jahanara Romney

INTRODUCTION

Craft projects, as significant components of community-wide development efforts, have been notoriously difficult to organize and sustain. Even in a relatively stable social environment, and with the support of local and national authorities, self-sustaining, independent, and economically viable artisan projects are not easy to facilitate from beyond the community (Stephen 1990). They require a thorough knowledge of regional economic and sociopolitical dynamics, in-depth appreciation of artisan skills and limitations, an understanding of production logistics, and moreover, insight into the thorny world of marketing. In situations of social and political crisis, where the artisans are traumatized by conditions of dislocation following political violence and by the stresses and strains of constructing novel refugee communities in a foreign country, the obstacles to establishing viable craft production projects are indeed difficult to surmount. Refugees, disoriented and disempowered by the loss of their community and control over their future, are especially vulnerable to paternalistic projects which foment dependency and prevent the transition to renewed community control. Refugee communities are recent, unstable constructs where factionalism and faction-monopolization of project resources are constant dangers, and where representative, popular organizations remain hard to sustain. Not only are these settlements embedded in a foreign, hostile social and political landscape, but their members are hesitant to reorganize themselves anew, burdened with the painful memory of repression of community-based organizations and leaders before the exodus and fearful of the reaction of their new hosts.

Yet refugee communities are among those most in need of the sustainable source of income that artisan projects are often able to provide. And perhaps even more importantly, they are in need of the social tonic of community revitalization that typically emanates from viable community organizations. This discussion of a craft project established in predominantly Maya Guatemalan refugee communities in Chiapas, Mexico, documents an effort at supporting this type of revitalization. It also addresses some of the central problems that such refugee aid efforts confront. From the experience gained in the process of establishing and modifying the project, a series of development issues are raised which we believe relate directly to the success and failure of craft projects. They are discussed here in the interest of sharing this experience with applied social scientists and the aid and community-development promotion community. The subsequent discussion of project problems and the dynamics of interaction between the evolving community-based refugee organization and the craft project represents our contribution to the growing critical discourse addressing grassroots development.

BACKGROUND AND SETTING

The decade of the 1980s was a traumatic one for Guatemala's highland Maya population. Beginning with the regime of Lucas García up through the "scorched-earth" policies of Ríos Montt and Mejía Víctores, the highland Maya population has been repeatedly victimized by counterinsurgency campaigns conducted by military regimes (Carmack 1988; Manz 1988; Falla 1983). Though ostensibly designed to eliminate a small but very vocal guerrilla insurgency in the Western Highlands, these military campaigns more often than not targeted uninvolved civilians and their community organizations (Davis and Hodson 1982). The results were high population losses, up to a third or more in some areas, and massive dislocations. It has been estimated that by 1984, in addition to the many thousands killed, a million people had been displaced from their

Figure 30. A refugee child. (Photograph by Duncan Earle).

homes (Davis 1988:10). Of these, some 150,000 found their way to the border state of Chiapas, Mexico, where they managed to construct a fragile existence in makeshift refugee settlements, often in sight of their homeland (Conde 1983).

An account of group history by members of the Pujiltic refugee camps provides a testimony of the terrible experience of forced relocation suffered by so many in their exodus to Mexico:

> In the early morning of January 6th [1982], our community was razed. They killed several people and burned houses, and we had to flee, warning other communities. This is when we came to Mexico the first time, on January 8th. The Mexican people received us with open arms, but soon the Immigration Service found out and sent us back to Guatemala. Others who were further from the border were concentrated more to the interior of Mexico. In March of the same year there was a coup which overthrew Lucas García and put in Ríos Montt. We were already returning to the border when the new government declared a state of siege and started a scorched-earth policy, razing entire communities. They bombed in the mountains and villages from helicopters, burning crops, houses, and mountains, cutting down fruit trees, killing any animal they found and eating them, breaking into houses and stealing radios, televisions, sewing machines, tape recorders. They brought pack animals to carry all the goods they robbed. Also the government organized entire communities into civil patrols to carry out community sweeps. We were living in our new communities when they returned to invade our new places, abducting three men . . . [their] cadavers were found in the settlement of Jacabal and Pie de La Virgen. This is why we had to abandon our new homes, fleeing step by step until we arrived at Mexico. We passed by Cruz de Soliman and another camp two kilometers from the border, arriving the 11th of August. In those very days the army came to burn our houses which we abandoned when we left Guatemala. (excerpts from "Our History, Experienced Through Our Lives, Suffered in the Flesh", written by "a group of Guatemalan Refugees", in Pujiltic, September 9, 1986, translation ours.)

The sudden influx of tens of thousands of refugees into Mexican territory created a crisis of tremendous proportions, and prompted widespread concern from international aid and relief agencies. None were officially permitted to work in Mexico, at least initially. Instead the Mexican Ministry of the Interior set up an organization called the Mexican Commission for Aid to Refugees (COMAR) to handle all funds coming in through the United Nations High Commission on Refugees and to monopolize aid efforts. COMAR was the only group to receive federal approval to work directly with the refugees, guaranteeing governmental control of recognized aid delivery. Unofficially, other groups were sporadically tolerated. The Catholic diocese of San Cristóbal set up a special committee whose function was to provide relief to the refugee population. Other independent aid ventures were also allowed to exist simply because they were not large or wide-reaching enough to pose a real threat to COMAR's control over refugee aid. Due to the difficulty of reaching the refugees, most of whom were located in isolated settlements scattered throughout virtually inaccessible jungle, only the Church, of all the independent groups, had sufficient resources to reach a significant percentage of the refugee population.

The main difficulties faced by the refugees were lack of food, medicine, shelter, and some sustainable means by which to gain and maintain self-support. A survey of both jungle and Comalapa-region camps revealed that most people were eating half their minimum requirement.[1] Malnutrition, whose primary victims are small children, was endemic in the refugee population; many had fled to Mexico after spending weeks and sometimes months foraging in the wilds nearby their homes before finally being driven from their hiding places. The companion diseases of war, typhoid and dysentery, were rampant and the new problems presented by the jungle environment, malaria and dengue fever, took their toll. In addition, refugees who arrived during the rainy season found themselves drenched by torrential downpours on a daily basis, adding respiratory problems to their already considerable woes.

Primary aid efforts were, of course, focused on providing food and basic shelter for the near-starving refugee population. Each aid group spent a substantial part of its budget on food programs which involved shipping tons of corn, beans, and basic foodstuffs into refugee camps. The problems encountered in shipping enough food to feed over a hundred thousand people in remote communities were all but insurmountable. Some food could be shipped in by truck, but many of the jungle communities were not located near roads, and so food supplies had to be trekked in or shipped via small boats. During the rainy season (approximately six months a year), rivers become swollen and unnavigable, and the refugees had to walk days through the jungle to drop-off points to receive meager and inadequate supplies. When overland travel was possible, primitive roads became clogged with heavy trucks that quickly made them impassable. Food shipments were at best irregular, and insufficient to meet the demands of the refugee communities even when they did get through. Many of the foods supplied were either substandard or inappropriate, including such items as very old corn and beans, or unfamiliar foods like oil, soybeans, and milk products. The provision of inappropriate foodstuffs as "aid" to a starving population was cruel indeed for the refugees were largely incapable of digesting milk or soy products, and oil was not only culturally alien, but useless in the absence of anything to fry. Such foods, when eaten, often caused digestion problems such as diarrhea, an unwelcome additional illness for an already beleaguered population.

Had the refugee population been given money—or the means to earn it—culturally appropriate, nutritious food could have been purchased locally, and many of the problems that arose in the context of food assistance could have been avoided. Nearly all the refugee camps were established in areas adjacent to rural Mexican communities who produced such foods, and which dedicated considerable time and expense to getting them to distant markets. A local purchasing arrangement would have solidified positive, mutually beneficial relationships between these Mexican hosts and their new neighbors, and would have ended the dependency upon uncertain shipments from groups entertaining various alien agendas.[2]

Such arrangements, based either upon providing income or some productive activities that would generate it, were not part of official Mexican refugee policy. Officials at every level were worried that empowering refugees might exacerbate a fragile political situation at home in Mexico, a situation involving economic crisis, widespread disenchantment with the official party, rural labor strife, and land invasions, as well as demands for political rights by the Mexican highland Maya population. Some in the Mexican Right portrayed refugees as freeloading guerrillas spreading revolution from Central America. As a result of these unfounded fears, the official Mexican aid organization tended to treat refugees as political undesirables and sought every means possible to hinder or prevent local self-help efforts, or aid which would have decreased dependence on outside sources.[3]

Far more surprising to us than official paternalism was a similar attitude among nongovernmental aid groups. The Church and many other "progressive" organizations prioritized their political agenda of opposition to the Partido Revolucionario Institucional over aid policies that might promote self-empowerment. Other groups sought control on a more territorial basis, hoping to demonstrate the superior virtues of their agency or approach. Everyone wanted to control "their" refugees, whether it was to promote a political cause, aggrandize their organization, or test out some new "theory" of refugee aid. It seemed clear to us that while many people saw personal or organizational reasons for extending assistance to the refugees, few sought to operate in the best interest of the recipients. As one international observer remarked, ironically, "The refugees have helped many people."

THE GUATEMALAN REFUGEE CRAFTS PROJECT

This is perhaps a good time to talk about how the idea of starting a crafts project originated. To begin with, we really had no intention of founding what was to become a nine-year ongoing program involving several hundred people in four communities and stimulating a number of aid efforts amounting to more money than we had cumulatively earned in our lifetimes. That idea would have seemed preposterous at the time. Conditions for starting and maintaining refugee aid projects were so poor that in spite of our best hopes it seemed that our project would be small, brief, and limited. The refugee camps were hard to reach and officially "off limits." Independent aid workers were harassed by the official aid organ, COMAR, in collaboration with *migración*, (Mexican immigration) and aid efforts were constantly undermined by an atmosphere in which unofficial aid organizations competed with one another, much to the detriment of all. In addition the refugee communities themselves were highly impermanent. They could be moved at any time by the Mexican authorities and were under constant danger of attack from the Guatemalan military which had made frequent incursions into Mexican territory. The refugees were demoralized, frightened, traumatized, and dispirited. And helping them would entail risks for everyone. These were hardly the best circumstances in which to begin an aid effort.

The idea of doing "something" persisted, however, as it had for a number of other individuals who had visited or were living in the area. Perhaps it was the presence of so much human tragedy at such close range that prompted foreigners and local Mexicans to step out of their lives for a time and extend themselves beyond the daily concerns which normally engross us. We shared that general feeling of urgency which so many had felt after visiting the refugee camps and witnessing the sorrow and suffering of innumerable refugee families. There was no letting down those sad silent faces, which is perhaps why so many aid workers forgot to ask the refugees what it was they needed. It all seemed so obvious. They are dying of hunger, so give them food. They are sick, so give them medicine.

And in spite of the endless difficulties encountered with shipping food and medicine across rugged terrain and past hostile officials, the aid orientation usually centered on getting the goods through.

We were struck by the idea that it would be much easier to simply give cash, which was easier to transport, and let the refugees do their own buying locally. For some reason this idea, when we suggested it to some of the aid groups, was met with scorn. There were numerous reasons given for not giving money, such as "It would be stolen" (although the aid goods were continually raided) or "They don't know how to spend it" (even though refugees had earned and spent money at home). We were not satisfied with those explanations and so with the nagging idea that there must be a better way to get aid through we asked a local and impeccable source for the best way to solve this problem—the refugees.

The inhabitants of the different refugee communities we spoke with all agreed that what they needed was work. That way they could earn money to buy themselves food. As it happens this idea was also not well received by most of the aid community in Mexico. So between the persistent feeling of urgency to do "something" and the nagging suspicion that the "something" was as the refugees suggested, we sought and gained support for a proposed aid program to provide income through crafts production (which was the only type of work we could provide given the restricted access to land) from Seva Foundation. (One of Seva's board members, who was by happy coincidence visiting with our landlord next door, remarked after hearing about the refugees that she had some "friends" who might be willing to help.)

We were determined not to fall into the errors of other aid groups and to offer the best, most genuinely helpful type of assistance that we could. The proposal submitted to Seva Foundation in 1984 stated that we would provide "constructive and unharmful aid" to Guatemalan refugees. We specified some guiding principles which would orient us in this endeavor. These were to serve both as reminders to ourselves of how to help without causing damage to an already traumatized population, and as a future model for constructive aid. In short these principles were centered on the following ideas:

> 1. Noninterference in community life. In too many cases we had seen that aid was used as a tool to further the social or political agenda of the aid-givers. In the case of the Pujiltic refugee communities, the Catholic Church had tried to use a withdrawal of aid to force the conversion of one of the non-Catholic communities. Aid was denied to all of the three com-

munities in the area until the third "offending" community would give up its "pagan" ways. They wouldn't and so none received aid. We were determined not to act as social mediators in camp problems, either. Nor would we promote our own ideas as concerned group organization or membership.

2. Accountability. Theft was a real and continuous threat to any type of activity in which goods were exchanged for cash. The first camp we worked with, Santa Rosa, had recently shipped off several hundred dollars worth of crafts to San Cristóbal for sale. The crafts were mysteriously "lost" and the refugees never received a peso for all they had spent on thread plus their labor. We decided that all goods would be purchased "up front" and that nothing would be accepted on consignment. This would also facilitate the accounting process, and would provide the weavers income when they needed it.

3. Self-management. Even though at the beginning the logistics of having refugees run the entire project were somewhat difficult due to the fact that the refugees were not allowed out of the camps, we strove toward that goal. Prices were determined by the weavers based on minimum wage for labor plus materials rather than on our judgment. This was a payment system of their own devising based on their need to keep all wage earners on an even par (so as not to create a "weaving elite"). After a while the refugees were able to make their own thread purchases as well which diminished dependency and increased community self-control, and they soon learned to manage their own accounts.

4. Familiarity. The refugee population had already experienced a great deal of physical and psychological upheaval. We realized that introducing innovations in weaving styles or patterns would simply compound the deep disorientation felt by the refugee community. Therefore refugees wove what they were already familiar with both in terms of overall design and patterns. At later points we suggested some changes regarding dimension, but the weaving designs which were part of their local regional culture were left intact. We also decided to focus on some of the smaller items in an effort to decrease both the time it would take to make each item and the risks entailed in marketing larger "speciality items." Smaller items would be easier to sell both locally and to the popular commercial market in the United States.

Figure 31. Guatemalan refugees have abandoned the use of their own traditional costumes although the art of making them survives. (Photograph by Armando Alfonzo).

5. Community support. Since this was a central theme to the project, the idea of supporting the cohesiveness of the community as a whole found voice in every aspect of the work we did. Rather than favor individual talents, we tried to incorporate all weavers, even children, so that the weaving traditions could be passed down and shared in a manner consistent with Mayan culture. Our emphasis on noninterference at the social level was to enable them to re-establish their own community decision-making processes. By not choosing representatives for them (or giving salaries to individuals for the purpose of "running" the project), we hoped to avoid the divisiveness and favoritism which had hindered other aid efforts. And lastly by insisting on an "open-books" policy of accounting in which every expenditure was known we hoped to minimize both the reality and accusations of theft which were endemic in refugee aid programs and which had splintered refugee communities in the past.

These were our hopes and goals as we set out to begin what we saw as a service rather than an aid project. Needless to say, our program was highly ambitious, very idealistic, and, some thought, impossible to enact given the track record of previous crafts projects. We were determined, however, and so with our goals and ideals intact we set out to work with one of the most problematic of all refugee communities—Pujiltic.

PUJILTIC AND PRODECO

The sugar-cane producing region of Pujiltic in Chiapas had not experienced the same dramatic influx of refugees as much of the rest of the border region. This was because Pujiltic was not particularly close to the border, and is extensively cultivated. Several hundred refugees had come to this region with their families however to act as sugar-cane cutters for local Mexican *ejidos* (national land grant collectives). When we started working with the Pujiltic communities (there were three) they had been there for several years already living as "permanent migrant laborers" and had lost their status as acknowledged refugees. Living conditions were abominable. Housing was minimal, the water supply was contaminated, diseases such as malaria and typhoid were rife, and all the children were malnourished.

A number of other groups, such as Save the Children and the Catholic Church, had already tried to work with the Pujiltic communities but had run into difficulties. To begin with the local host ejido members were hostile to aid efforts on behalf of their refugee laborers. For half the year during the annual sugar-cane harvest, or *zafra,* refugees worked at very low wages for the ejido. As it was not to the advantage of the Mexican ejido members to raise the standard of living among the refugees (and thereby perhaps lose them as a source of cheap labor) ejido members tried to discourage outside aid efforts by planting false rumors about aid givers and in some cases stealing goods supplied to the refugees. At the same time many of the aid efforts, when not sabotaged by the ejido themselves failed because of the promotion of self-interested agendas, such as the Church's efforts at forced conversion. By the time we met them, the refugees had developed a cautious attitude toward newcomers.

By good fortune we were working with a very low-key and politic Mexican who established a limited relationship with these three communities while in the context of working on crafts production with five other communities in a farther-removed area of Chiapas. Over time, however, the relationship with the initial crafts-producing communities diminished and our involvement with the Pujiltic communities gradually expanded until we found they were our sole partners. As our role with the communities became more formalized we encountered many of the same difficulties as other groups had before us. After the loss of our first low-key contact, we began to work with a previously unknown and much more involved intermediary. Salaries became an issue for the first time. Almost immediately accusations of theft began circulating among the refugees. Divisions began to appear within the communities and it looked as though the project would fold.

After much drama and some highly charged confrontations between intermediary and refugees, the refugee communities decided (with our full support and heart-felt relief) that from now on they would manage themselves without help from an intermediary. They opened up their own bank account, got a post office box, and formed an organization of their own to manage all incoming aid, either actual or future. They called their organization PRODECO (Program for Community Development). The year was 1988. After four years it looked like the goal of independence for the refugee project was about to be realized.

This was a first, both for us and for them. They had never had the opportunity to manage their own aid directly and we had not heard of any previous cases of refugees controlling outside efforts. We were thrilled. Within a very short time new lines of direct communication were opened with the refugee crafts committees, and project expenditures were quickly doubled.

All was not smooth sailing however. It was clear from the beginning that our production goals would be difficult to realize. Traditional items found a very limited market in the United States and so new items had to be introduced. We began with one new item a year, usually with a strong resemblance to traditional items. Bags were made smaller and "passport style" with the addition of a button. The traditional *servilleta* became a placemat. They learned to cut up unsalable broad belts to make change purses and wallets. Large bags were transformed into pillow covers. And of course the children began producing thousands of macrame *pulseras*, the wristbands which have been the rage for half a decade. These new items, while not immediately familiar as a textile form, retained many established weaving patterns and colors. In spite of attempting to remain within the bounds of familiar motifs, color combinations, and methods of manufacture, it was clear that these items were in a different conceptual category for the weavers. Crafts were now an export into the world market, not an integrated activity within the prior cultural tradition of making textiles for home use, and it took getting used to.

The principal problem was how to maintain quality of weaving. Expert *huipil* weavers were capable of producing very poorly woven wall hangings, purses, and bags once their identification with the finished product was no longer important. The huipil was a statement of the weaver's skill which she wore on her back for all to see. It also served as a social statement of cultural identity and aesthetics. A wall hanging did not have the same status as it was not recognized as a useful item, and in any case it was going to be shipped off to a far-distant and strange place where showing one's weaving skill and cultural self-identity were no longer important. It took many long meetings in which we both had to demonstrate our knowledge of and appreciation for good weaving to convince the weavers to maintain their normal quality of weaving for a foreign destination.

Once that hurdle was crossed we met the problems of quantity and color. When an item seemed easy to make and lucrative, we would receive hundreds and at times thousands of them at the expense of all other items. Lime green and bright orange placemats were popular among weavers one year. Once convinced that this must be what we had in mind when we suggested "cheerful" colors it was difficult to change their minds. If we were gringos then what we meant by "nice" couldn't mean what they meant by the term. This type of problem was perhaps predictable because the weavers had never woven for commercial purposes before—having come from an area of Guatemala fairly undiscovered by tourists. Communication was not always easy as we did not speak Mam and many of the weavers did not speak Spanish. Production misunderstandings were inevitable.

After two years most of the production problems were worked out and a steady, pleasant rapport had been established. The weavers were producing high-quality work in traditional motifs and were earning enough to support their families for half the year. It seemed as though success was near. The last obstacle to security however had nothing to do with the refugees. The American market became soft. Commercial *típica*, made popular by the colorfulness of the cloth and the "Maya mystique," fueled imports of a huge volume of cheap textiles that the less discriminating buyers grabbed up. The flood of cheaply made goods from Guatemala seriously undercut our ability to sell the high-quality crafts which the refugees were producing at the prices we needed to maintain in order to provide fair wages. The American public did not usually distinguish backstrap weaving from commercial weaving or traditional motifs from tourist motifs. The drop in value for handmade items seriously affected the quantity and type of items we could market and created a source of contention among the refugees. Thread prices in Mexico were climbing steadily with the devaluation of the peso and the weavers were demanding higher prices for their labor even as the market value of the finished product here in the United States was plummeting. We began to depend more on the "sympathy market" for sales, such as churches and alternative trading organizations, and our goal of selling to a larger popular market had to be abandoned.

One of the authors has in a spirit of irony called the crafts project "the longest running aid failure in Chiapas," since it was never able to become independent of our marketing support. However, after nine years it is in fact the oldest surviving crafts project among Chiapas refugees. Their continued need for craft income and our persistence at serving that need perhaps explains its longevity as much as the project methods and goals we originally set out. Certainly not all of those goals were met. The project cannot manage itself to the point of initiating its own sales in the United States—in spite of many efforts to set up direct relationships with buyers in the States—and so depends on us for nearly its entire income. Items are not sold on the popular market but instead depend on the compassion and sympathy of the buyer. And lastly some of the items produced have been unsalable. For all that, the project has continued producing a steady and fair income for eighty families and has allowed us to remind those who purchase the crafts that those who made them are still, after twelve years, refugees. Equally important, it has served to provide some sense of continuity and stability in a very precarious social and political landscape.

EPILOQUE

In the summer of 1990, we made our annual visit to the Pujiltic weavers and crafts committee representatives, unaware that it would likely be our last. The meetings had been very positive. We had discussed issues such as quality of weaving, new ideas, and prices. People seemed more relaxed and secure than we had ever seen them. The Seva Foundation program of education, health, and breakfasts for children, coordinated with PRODECO, had served to provide greater security and hope for the future in the three camps. PRODECO had learned to do its own accounting, was managing large sums of money, and had made itself responsible to the whole community with monthly meetings for everyone. It had avoided the pitfalls of *personalismo* by rotating service among different committees. Weavers were insisting on having the principal voice about production and prices. We left with the feeling that things were going well. Little did we know that in less than a month everything would change.

Just days after we left in July, most of the men and four boys from the camp of Agua Bendita, while working together on a drainage problem at the edge of the camp, were mistaken for land-invaders of an opposition political organization by the state police, and were all taken away to prison.[4] There, in the jail of the state capital, the men remained for nearly two months, ill-fed, forced to sign confessions they could not read, and at one point, nearly deported to Guatemala. Word got out to the national press, and their unjust detention quickly became an international scandal.[5] No one admitted to any mistakes. Their conditional release was contingent upon acceptance of immediate relocation to a new refugee camp in Campeche, with the understanding that COMAR would assist the other two camps in also being moved out of Pujiltic. This plan would prove difficult, for many refugees felt reluctant to move and did not understand the political impact of being associated with a cause célèbre that the word Pujiltic now evoked in the political circles of the state and the nation. The Agua Bendita camp's remaining members, mostly women and children, left and joined the released men in November, men who had never been allowed to again see Pujiltic. Together again after four harrowing months, they went off to a new life in Campeche. The remaining Pujiltic refugees, after first signing an agreement with COMAR to move (some say only out of fear), and informing Seva of their relocation needs, began to question whether they wanted to move. One camp voted to reject the idea, and replaced any camp representatives who favored the move. The other camp became divided on the issue. People's reasons for wanting to stay are complex, and have to do with both old and new circumstances, but while they remain in the region, aid projects are impossible to manage for a couple of reasons.[6]

First of all, the project functioned well largely due to the efforts of PRODECO, which spanned the three Pujiltic camps. With the most traditionalist camp gone, the community organization lost its anchor, and now each camp was organizationally on its own. There had always been a problem of certain strong personalities conflicting and disrupting the solidarity between the representatives of the three camps in PRODECO, especially from those members who had become most involved in the "outside" world either before leaving Guatemala or more recently. Some had even obtained Mexican papers, which put them on a different legal footing from most other camp members and made them more able to blend into the Mexican community. While these diverse views had helped enliven the PRODECO meetings in the past, the more traditional members had insisted upon a more collectivist and consensus-oriented position which kept the loud voices of the few in check. With the most traditional group, Agua Bendita, now shipped out to Campeche by COMAR, old divisions and self-serving positions again gained sway over one of the camps and divided the other, making PRODECO basically inoperative. Without a community organization, the project could not continue to operate equitably, even if the state authorities had allowed the project to continue.

This led to the second problem. As long as outside authorities remained unaware that there were three camps in Pujiltic, it was quite easy for refugees to move about, mail packages, and manage bank accounts. But since October of 1990, there has been a renewed effort by the Mexican authorities to check papers, as part of a new policy of refugee control brought on in part by the embarrassment of the Pujiltic false-arrest incident, and also as a reaction to renewed Guatemalan military incursions along the Chiapas border. Stationary and mobile checkpoints have been set up all over eastern Chiapas. Most Pujiltic refugees have had no papers since the authorities took them away over four years earlier, and now they need them even to go visit their border relations. Every camp member is known by name to immigration officials, because the refugees drew up a census of the camps as a part of their initial departure agreement with COMAR. Until the refugees decide either to move to Campeche (where COMAR promises to give them new papers as well as land) or disperse back toward the border, where some of them have relatives, it becomes next to impossible to even evaluate the prospects for continuing the project.

Those who have relocated to Campeche now find themselves a small group among 400 new refugee Maya neighbors in a community that gives each family rights to over two hectares of land. Other employment opportunities exist in the area. It is uncertain whether they will wish to continue to weave beyond personal use, and whether the small group could operate as before without involving many new weavers and forming what would be a whole new and greatly expanded project. We await news from them, but without expectations for a continued support relationship.

Those who still remain in Pujiltic will most likely disperse, return to Guatemala voluntarily, or—at worst—be returned by force. Very recent news from the *Comisiones Permanentes,* the political umbrella group that represents Mexico-based Guatemalan refugees, suggests there are active negotiations with Guatemala to effect a large-scale return (as of late February, 1991). Many Pujiltic refugees may remain where they are, to see what becomes of this new repatriation effort, unwilling to be moved to Campeche only to move again within months or even weeks. But they cannot safely remain there indefinitely, and once the cane-cutting is over, if the return plan stalls in negotiations, they will be back to where they were when they first fled Guatemala: powerless, unemployed, and a political target.

When we first conceived of this project, we knew its structure had to be capable of adapting to outside political changes, and that our effort might be just temporary emergency relief until voluntary return or integration into the Mexican population eliminated the need for such a project as ours. For those who have left it, we can hope that the organizational experience, the years of earned income based on culturally familiar tasks, and the sense of control over one area of their lives will count as contributions to all who participated, and that the skills that developed as a result of that control and involvement will continue to serve them as they once again reconstruct their community

NOTES

1. Camps surveyed include Boca Chajul, Río Azul, Santa Elena, Ojo de Agua, Pacayal, Tziscao, Cuahtémoc (Yalambojoch II), Las Cascadas, Santa Rosa, Cruz Quemada, Paso Hondo, and Nuevo Delicias. In addition, we interviewed people who had visited and surveyed dozens of other camps. We also interviewed personnel in the Comitán Hospital, and all data suggested the refugees were receiving less than half what their typical diet was before fleeing Guatemala.

2. The control and manipulation of refugees by outside organizations was and remains a generalized practice. As we note later, there are clear reasons why the Mexican government would want to have this control, even though their chief concern, that refugees are guerrilla supporters or leftist trouble-makers, finds no basis in factual evidence. What is equally troubling is the efforts at similar forms of manipulative control by the Church and private voluntary organizations, even those without any evident political agendas and with, ostensibly, the refugees' interests at heart. It is a sad commentary on the ethnocentric nature of aid and development practice, and the theory that informs it, to find that efforts at material aid must inflict such social damage. It was this realization that helped motivate us to do something ourselves.

3. This hostility towards the Guatemalans becomes more intelligible in the context of Central American politics of the recent decade. In 1979 the Somoza regime in Nicaragua was overthrown, and the policies of surrounding countries became more hard-line in response. Guatemala launched its brutal counter-insurgency campaign in full at that time, and the other Central American countries, some with guerrilla movements of their own which took strength from the success of Nicaragua's revolution, also became more militarized. Borders were "strengthened" as a result and the easy flow of Central Americans between the republics was curtailed as the different Central American countries sought to halt the spread of potential revolutions, no doubt strongly pressured to do so by the U. S. State Department. In this context, it is easy to see how Guatemalan refugees in Chiapas could become personae non gratae. Moreover, Chiapas was suffering from its own political problems stemming from conflicts between local large land owners and a peasant population which had never received the benefits of the land reform promised in the revolution. Chiapas is the poorest state in Mexico, receiving the smallest amount of federal assistance, and yet it produces more in energy and coffee than any other single state. With these potentially explosive local dynamics it becomes more clear how refugees could be equated with political undesirables and potential spreaders of revolution, although there is no good evidence that this has ever been the case. Relief work in this particular atmosphere, exacerbated further by Church denouncements of official abuses of refugees, was difficult to carry out because the aid workers were also, by association, seen as potential political troublemakers.

4. The Mexican Constitution stipulates maximum land holdings which many properties in Chiapas exceed. Opposition political parties "il-

legally" organize seizures of over-sized properties in order to seek enforcement of the Constitution.

5. The initial discovery of the detentions was made with the help of a Belgian priest, who informed the Human Rights Commission of the diocese in San Cristóbal de Las Casas. He was later deported. Mexico's UN High Commission on Refugees representative asked to speak with the governor, but was said to have been poorly received. Artists and writers from Mexico City wrote in protest, a Mexican Indian village expressed solidarity with the refugees, even the King of Spain was rumored to have called the governor to attempt to effect their release. These activities brought the once-ignored Pujiltic refugees into the center of the political arena, and may have helped facilitate the release from prison of the sixteen men. However, the publicity meant that the Pujiltic region was no longer "available" for refugee settlement, since the refugees were now widely known and believed by some to be criminals.

6. To understand the reluctance of the refugees to relocate to another state of Mexico where they have been promised land and papers, one must take a number of things into consideration. First is the refugee history of bad relations with COMAR, and the terrible experience many refugees had with the 1984 official decision to relocate many Chiapas camps to Campeche and Quintana Roo. Those who had relations in the mega-camps of Puerto Rico and Ixcan recounted to the others how COMAR had forced the refugees on their own "trail of tears," watching their heroically hand-built camps burn and being trucked off to a warehouse near Palenque to wait and suffer for months for their new camps to be ready. Unknown numbers died, and some in Campeche never recovered. Knowing this makes it hard for the Pujiltic refugees to trust COMAR. Some do not believe that COMAR is telling the truth about the need for them to move, and the local Mexican ejido hosts are telling them they can and should stay, and that there will be no problem (although they say they will not defend them if the police or immigration comes around looking for refugees). Relatives from camps closer to the border said they should stay, and that COMAR had told other refugees that could stay in Chiapas, in new "secure" mega-camps, and that what COMAR had said about all refugees having to leave Chiapas was not true. In addition to all these reasons why they don't feel motivated to get on the COMAR trucks for Campeche remains the very ancient Maya reason of not wanting to sever relations with the place where one has become accustomed to living (something refugees know a lot about), compounded by the memory of

the trauma of the past moves, in which many people—mostly children—died. Refugee women said to us, "The last time when we moved from the border to here, many babies died. Their hearts did not become used to this place, to this climate. Surely the same will happen again." This is hard to argue with, even when the political realities make it essential that they move. How does one justify asking refugees who have already been forcibly dislocated three times to relocate again?

References Cited

Carmack, Robert M., ed.
    1988   *Harvest of Violence.* Norman: University of Oklahoma Press.

Conde, Daniel
    1983   Guatemalan Refugees in Mexico. In *Cultural Survival Quarterly,* Winter.

Davis, Shelton H.
    1988   Introduction: Sowing the Seeds of Violence. In *Harvest of Violence,* ed. R. Carmack, pp. 3–38. Norman: University of Oklahoma Press.

Davis, Shelton and Julie Hodson
    1982   *Witnesses to Political Violence in Guatemala; The Suppression of a Rural Development Movement.* Boston: Oxfam America.

Falla, Ricardo
    1983   *Voices of the Survivors: The Massacre at Finca San Francisco, Guatemala.* Cambridge, Mass.: Cultural Survival and Anthropology Resource Center.

Guatemalan refugees
    1986   Our History, Experienced through Our Lives, Suffered in the Flesh. Pujiltic, Mexico.

Manz, Beatriz
    1988   *Refugees of a Hidden War.* Albany: SUNY Press.

Stephen, Lynn
    1990   The Politics of Ritual: The Mexican State and Zapotec Autonomy, 1926–1989. In *Class, Politics, and Popular Religion in Mexico and Central America,* ed. Lynn Stephan and James Dow. Washington, DC: American Anthropological Association.

Contributors

ROBERT S. CARLSEN is currently research associate at the Mesoamerican Archives in the University of Colorado where he received his M.A. and is now finishing his Ph.D. thesis, "Continuity and Culture Change in Santiago Atitlán." He has published several articles on weaving and cosmology, notably one with David A. Wenger, "The Dyes Used in Guatemalan Textiles: A Diachronic Approach," in press. He is collecting evidence on human rights abuses in Guatemala, especially related to the massacre of December 2, 1990 and will publish an article with David Loucky in *Cultural Survival* as well as for the Official Report of the Guatemala News and Information Bureau.

SCOTT COOK is Professor of Anthropology and Director of the Center for Latin American Studies at the University of Connecticut, Storrs. He received his Ph.D. degree at the University of Pittsburgh with a doctoral dissertation on stoneworkers in the valley of Oaxaca. He has written *Zapotec Stoneworkers: the Dynamics of Rural Simple Commodity Production in Modern Mexican Capitalism* (University Press of America 1982), *Peasant Capitalist Industry, Piecework and Enterprise in Southern Mexican Brickyards* (University Press of America 1984), and *Obliging Need: Rural Petty Industry in Mexican Capitalism* with L. Binford (University of Texas Press 1990).

DUNCAN MACLEAN EARLE received his Ph.D. in anthropology from the State University of New York at Albany and is now a member of the Department of Anthropology at Texas A and M. He has been involved in craft production promotion among Guatemalan Maya since 1977, as well

as working in and consulting for a variety of rural community development projects and agencies in both Guatemala and Chiapas, Mexico.

CHRISTINE EBER received her Ph.D. in anthropology from the State University of New York at Buffalo in 1991. Her dissertation research, funded
by the National Institute of Health, treats women's experience with their
own and others' drinking in a Tzotzil-Maya township in highland Chiapas, Mexico. Since fieldwork, she has been involved in expanding markets
for a weavers' cooperative and in speaking to classes and community
groups about Tzotzil-speaking Maya women's lives.

TRACY BACHRACH EHLERS is Assistant Professor of Anthropology at the
University of Denver. Since 1976 she has been to Guatemala many times
to study the impact of development on highland Maya, and in particular
on women. Her work in San Pedro Sacatepequez, San Marcos, resulted in
the 1990 publication of *Silent Looms: Women and Production in a Guatemalan Town*. In 1988 Ehlers undertook a major sociodemographic study
with her students in San Antonio Palopó. She is currently consultant to
Grenada Television's *Disappearing World* series in the production of a doc-
umentary on San Antonio.

FLORA S. KAPLAN is Associate Professor and Director of the Museum
Studies Program, Graduate School of Arts and Science at New York Uni-
versity. She received her doctorate in anthropology from the Graduate
Center of the City University of New York. She has done fieldwork in
Mexico, Nigeria, and the United States. She has published on art and cog-
nitive systems, graffiti, pottery, and museums, including *Una Tradición
Alferería; Conocimiento y Estilo; Un analisis basado en una tradición de al-
ferería mexicana* (Instituto Nacional Indígena 1980, Editorial Libros de
Mexico). This book will soon be published in English under the title, *Ur-
ban Potters of La Lua; Cognition and Style in a Mexican Folk Tradition* by
Southern Illinois University Press.

JUNE C. NASH is Distinguished Professor of Anthropology at the City
College and Graduate Center of the City University of New York. She
wrote her Ph.D. thesis in anthropology for the University of Chicago on
Amatenango del Valle, published by CIDOC as *Social Structure and Behavior in Amatenango del Valle; An Activity Analysis*. She returned in the
1960s to do several stints of fieldwork that resulted in the book, *In the
Eyes of the Ancestors; Belief and Behavior in a Maya Community*. She has re-

turned after many years working in Bolivia and the United States to renew her friendships with people in the town of Amatenango from which this article resulted.

BRENDA ROSENBAUM received her Ph.D. thesis from the State University of New York at Albany, where she now teaches in the Anthropology Department. Her fieldwork among the Maya of Guatemala and Chiapas emphasizing gender studies and symbolic systems is the basis for articles published in the *National Women's Studies Association Journal* and *Jewish Folklore and Ethnology Review*. Her thesis, *With Our Heads Bowed; Women, Society and Culture in Chamula, Mexico* will be published in Spanish.

LYNN STEPHEN received her Ph.D. from Brandeis University in 1987. She is currently assistant professor of anthropology at Northeastern University. She has published two books, *Class, Politics, and Religion in Mexico and Central America* co-edited with James Dow (American Anthropological Association, 1990), and *Zapotec Women* (University of Texas Press 1991). She has also written several articles on gender, class, and ethnic women's participation in grassroots peasant movements in Mexico, Chile, Paraguay, and Brazil, and in a human rights organization in El Salvador. She is working on two books, *Finding the Disappeared: The Story of Maria Teresa Tula of COMADRES,* and *Gender and Rural Democracy: Women Activists in Latin America.*

GOBI STROMBERG-PELLIZZI received her Ph.D. in anthropology from the University of California, Berkeley, in 1976. Her thesis on the Taxco silverworkers was published by the Fondo de Cultura Economica under the title *El Juego del Coyote: Platería y Arte en Taxco* in 1983. She has taught at the Escuela Nacional de Antropología e Historia and worked in the formative period of the Museo Nacional de Culturas Populares and in other museum projects of the Instituto Nacional de Antropología e Historia (INAH) and the Instituto Nacional Indigenista (INI). She is collaborating with various museums and cultural institutions in New York on exhibits and conferences, particularly the Mexican Cultural Institute of New York. She also has a private practice in psychotherapy.

ERICA VERILLO received her degree in linguistics from Syracuse University and is enrolled in the doctoral program in the College of Communications at the University of Texas at Austin. She has served as director of the Guatemalan Refugee Crafts Project since its inception in 1984 in consultation with the Pueblo to People and the Seva Foundation.

Index